Adventures in
Minecraft®
Second Edition

Adventures in Minecraft®
Second Edition

Martin O'Hanlon and David Whale

WILEY

Adventures in Minecraft®, Second Edition

Published by
John Wiley & Sons, Inc.
10475 Crosspoint Boulevard
Indianapolis, IN 46256
www.wiley.com

Published simultaneously in Canada

ISBN: 978-1-119-43958 -5

ISBN: 978-1-119-43957-8 (ebk)

ISBN: 978-1-119-43955-4 (ebk)

Manufactured in the United States of America

10 9 8 7 6 5 4 3 2 1

For general information on our other products and services please contact our Customer Care Department within the United States at (877) 762-2974, outside the United States at (317) 572-3993 or fax (317) 572-4002.

Wiley publishes in a variety of print and electronic formats and by print-on-demand. Some material included with standard print versions of this book may not be included in e-books or in print-on-demand. If this book refers to media such as a CD or DVD that is not included in the version you purchased, you may download this material at http://booksupport.wiley.com. For more information about Wiley products, visit www.wiley.com.

Library of Congress Control Number: 2017954526

For my wife Leonie, without you, this would never have been.

– Martin

For my parents Jan and Alf, who taught me the value of learning.

– David

Publisher's Acknowledgements

Some of the people who helped bring this book to market include the following:

Project Editor
Charlotte Kughen

Production Editor
Barath Kumar Rajasekaran

Copy Editor
Charlotte Kughen

Technical Editor
Cliff O'Reilly

Production Manager
Katie Wisor

Manager of Content Development and Assembly
Mary Beth Wakefield

Marketing Manager
Christie Hilbrich

Executive Editor
Jody Lefevere

Project Coordinator, Cover
Brent Savage

Proofreader
Nancy Bell

Indexer
Estalita M. Slivoskey

Cover Designer
Wiley

Illustrator
Sarah Wright

Cover Image
Courtesy of Martin O'Hanlon

About the Authors

MARTIN O'HANLON has been designing and programming computer systems for all of his adult life. His passion for programming and helping others to learn led him to create the blog (www.stuffaboutcode.com) where he shares his experiences, skills and ideas. Martin regularly delivers presentations and workshops on programming Minecraft to coders, teachers and young people with the aim of inspiring them to try something new and making programming fun.

DAVID WHALE has spent most of his life writing computer programs for devices you wouldn't imagine have computers inside them. He was bitten by the computer programming bug aged 11 when he was at school, and he still thoroughly enjoys writing software and helping others to learn programming. He works with the Micro:bit Educational Foundation on a shared mission to make computer programming accessible to all, and he also regularly volunteers for The Institution of Engineering and Technology (The IET) helping in schools, running weekend computing clubs, judging schools competitions and running programming workshops for young people at community events all around the UK. You can follow his adventures from his Twitter page: www.twitter.com/whaleygeek.

Acknowledgements

Many people are involved in producing a book, too many to mention in this small space. We would both like to give our special thanks to the following people:

- The staff at Mojang for designing such a great game and also for their genius and insight in making the game programmable. Without this insight, this book would not have been possible.

- The Raspberry Pi Foundation and the open-source community, without which there wouldn't be a Raspberry Pi or a free Minecraft server, both of which are vital platforms that enabled this book to be written for a wide audience.

- Our testers and young Minecraft experts, Zachary Igielman, Sam Whale, Ben Foden, Ria Parish, Ashley Cheema and Lauren Trussler who tried our programs and provided really useful feedback, without which we would never have known if we were pitching the book correctly to the target age group.

- Sarah Wright, for the truly amazing illustrations throughout this book. They are beautiful pieces of visual artwork, and cleverly and perfectly capture the concepts being presented in each adventure.

- Ben Ramachandra, the young lad at the Christmas 2013 Fire Tech Camp event at Imperial College, London: You were so determined to follow the Python course entirely in Minecraft, which was the moment that caused the idea for this book to spark into existence!

- Last, but not least, we would like to thank Carrie-Anne Philbin, for having the vision and determination to write her first book *Adventures in Raspberry Pi*, without which the Adventures series of books would not exist—now, see what you've started, Carrie-Anne?!

Contents

Adventure 3
Building Anything Automatically 65

Adventure 4
Interacting with Blocks 95

Adventure 5
Using Data Files 121

Adventure 6
Building 2D and 3D Structures 159

Adventure 9
The Big Adventure: Crafty Crossing 239

Appendix A
Where to Go from Here 273

Foreword

I am a teacher, and my main interest is student learning and engagement. When I teach coding by using Minecraft (my main use has been at Raspberry Jam events and in the classroom to help teach coding in Python), my students are more engaged than they are with other techniques I use. When the lesson plan instead takes us into the areas of theory or other coding tasks, the students regularly say, 'When can we code with Minecraft again, sir?' Simply put, Minecraft lodges itself in the kids' brains, and the coding techniques take deeper root.

Minecraft has the power to engage students in ways that I have not seen before. The simplicity of Minecraft has a universal appeal to all children, much in the same way that building bricks do. When children are exposed to new skills with Minecraft as the vehicle for teaching—in the classroom, library or makerspace environment—the appeal still remains. Because students stay engaged and interested in learning new skills, using Minecraft in the classroom is very rewarding, both for the instructor and the students.

I believe one reason Minecraft is effective as a teaching tool is because there is immediate visual feedback, whether it's in the form of a house, 3D turtle shapes, an entire town or an ISS tracker. After all, Minecraft is a sandbox, which means there are no limitations to what you can achieve with Minecraft—even on the cut-down free version on the Raspberry Pi.

The memories of what the students produce in Minecraft serve as excellent reference material—this helps to signpost conceptual learning and becomes a great revision aid for them. For example, I regularly make reference to 2D arrays by reminding students of one lesson where we created 32 x 32 random block walls.

In my school in North Warwickshire, UK we have 10 copies of *Adventures in Minecraft*, and we use it to help students independently work on projects after introducing them to simple worksheet-type activities. For example, we may complete a task, such as dropping a rainbow when the player walks, and then the students may move on to use the book independently to create a house or make a mini game. The beauty of the book is that the adventures in the book can be picked up in segments or consumed all the way through. You can remix them and take them in different directions. I have found that most of the resources that I create myself start off with initial ideas or code that stems from either David or Martin. This book inspires people of all ages to engage with computer coding. In essence, it provides a platform from which teachers, parents and, most importantly, children can build.

It would be naive to think that learning is confined to the classroom. Activities such as CodeClub, Coderdojo and Raspberry Jams are engaging communities across the world in coding with Minecraft. Families at home or individual students working alone are also learning to code. This book is relevant in each of these scenarios.

I once heard Martin describe this book as 'learning by stealth'. I think that it is the crux of it; you make cool stuff with code and along the way learn how to iterate, use file handling, use conditionals and do much more. Students and children have fun and are constantly challenged and engaged in solving problems while also learning to code.

In this new version of the book, Martin and David have added the BBC micro:bit adventure, which brings in more physical computing. In the last couple of years, the BBC micro:bit has helped bring computing to the hands of children across the world. By adding the BBC micro:bit chapter, Martin and David have again helped to lower the barriers for children, teachers and parents to let their imaginations take over.

I wish you the best of luck with your adventures in Minecraft!

–Chris Penn, IT/CS teacher, Nicholas Chamberlaine School, Warwickshire, UK

These other readers have great things to say about *Adventures in Minecraft*:

'An absolute life saver! I use it daily, and David and Martin are amazing resources!'

–Bob, educator, United States

'We use chapters from the book in our Year 8 Computer Science curriculum as well as using it regularly at the Hull Raspberry Jam.'

–Jon, educator and Raspberry Jam organiser, Hull, UK

'It's an AWESOME book full of exciting ways to introduce the principles of Python and 3D CAD.'

–Frank, UK Raspberry Jam organiser, London, UK

'I recommend it to parents at every event I go to, even in China. It's where my coding journey began!'

–Gemma, participatory artist, Manchester UK

'Has been great for individual and paired challenges at Leeds Raspberry Jam, including family activities. Inspired with signposts to more projects.'

–Claire, educator and Raspberry Jam organiser, Leeds, UK

'Invaluable resource. The kids at Blackpool Raspberry Jam love it!'

–Les, educational trainer and Raspberry Jam organiser, Blackpool, UK

Introduction

ARE YOU AN adventurer? Do you like to try new things and learn new skills? Are you a huge fan of Minecraft? And would you like to push the boundaries of what you can do in Minecraft by learning how to write computer programs (mods) that interact with your game, and amaze your friends with your creativity and magic? If the answer is a resounding "Yes!" then this is the book for you.

What Is Minecraft?

Minecraft is a sandbox indie game, where you build structures, collect items, mine minerals and fight monsters in order to survive. It appears to you as a 3D virtual world made of different types of blocks, each block having its own place inside the grid layout of the 3D virtual world. Figure 1 shows an example of the Minecraft world.

The Virtual World

In a sandbox game, you are a player inside a virtual world (a sandbox with very distant edges, like a playpen filled with sand). Instead of being offered levels in a preset order, you roam around the virtual world and make your own choices about what goals you want to achieve and how to set about them. Because you are making your own choices right from the start, sandbox games have limitless possibilities. You make up your own

FIGURE 1 The Minecraft world

stories and move through the 3D world, learning new skills and features by discovering them by chance and experimentation.

In Minecraft, your player, or avatar, is called Steve. You direct Steve through the sandbox virtual world to achieve whatever mission you decide. If you are successful in surviving your first night against the monsters, you can follow your own enthralling missions to interact with other participants of the game and build huge structures limited only by your imagination.

A sandbox game allows you, the player, to make your own decisions about playing the game, rather than being forced down a specific route by the game designers. You can read more about this type of game design at `http://en.wikipedia.org/wiki/Open_world`. There is a little bit of mystery about why the player is called Steve, but you can read more about it at `http://minecraft.gamepedia.com/The_Player`.

How Did Minecraft Come About?

Indie games are 'independent video games', created by individuals or small teams. They are often developed without any funding or support from a games publisher. As a result of their independent nature, indie games are often more innovative than other, more mainstream games. According to Wikipedia, Minecraft was created by the Swedish computer programmer Markus Persson, who is known by the gamer tag 'Notch'. He first demonstrated Minecraft as an early version in 2009, and the first official release of the game took place in 2011. Notch founded a Swedish company called Mojang AB, which continues to develop the Minecraft game on many computer platforms, including PC, Mac, Raspberry Pi, Linux, iOS, Android, Xbox 360, Playstation and Wii.

You can find out more about the fascinating Minecraft story in a documentary film called *Minecraft: The Story of Mojang* (`http://en.wikipedia.org/wiki/Minecraft:_The_Story_of_Mojang`).

What Is Minecraft Programming?

This is a book about computer programming—it uses Minecraft as a way to teach you about computer programming. If you are looking for some helpful tips on how to build structures and fight combat, there are some other great books on the market listed in Appendix A that will help.

By programming Minecraft, you make your gaming experiences even more exciting, creative, and individual. As you play the normal game, you follow the basic rules of the Minecraft game as set out by the game designers. By writing programs that interact with the Minecraft game world, you can make complex and repetitive tasks—like building huge streets of houses and large structures—automatically. You can make the game and the objects inside it behave in new ways, and you can invent new things that even the original creators of the game didn't think of. But most of all, you will learn a general skill—how to program using the Python programming language. You are then able to apply this to all sorts of other things aside from Minecraft. Figure 2 shows a huge street of houses that was built automatically by a short Python program.

FIGURE 2 A huge street of houses, built by a 20-line Python program

In a video about why all children should learn programming (www.youtube.com/watch?v=nKIu9yen5nc), Will.i.am is quoted as saying 'great coders are today's rock stars'. The new skills you learn while following the adventures in this book will make your Minecraft experiences more personal, more creative, more ambitious. Your new wizardry with programming will amaze your friends and fellow gamers and inspire them to ask you what magic you used to achieve such amazing feats. The answer, of course, is the magic of computer programming.

Who Should Read This Book?

Adventures in Minecraft is for any young person who loves playing Minecraft and would like to learn to program and do more with it. The Adventures series of books is aimed at readers in the age range 11–15, but some of the more challenging later adventures might be appropriate for older readers too. The earlier chapters have also been tested with readers as young as 8.

You might already be an expert in playing the game but find yourself getting frustrated by the length of time it takes to build new structures. Or you might want to find ways to extend the game by adding some additional intelligence and automation to the world. Whatever your reasons, this book will be your guide for a journey through Minecraft programming; and as every adventurer knows, your guidebook is the most important item in your backpack. Your trek will take you from simple beginnings, such as posting messages to the Minecraft chat, through learning the basics of programming Minecraft using the Python programming language, to discovering how to use your new computer programming skills to program your own exciting game inside Minecraft. By the end of your adventures you will have learned the skills you need to become a pioneer in Minecraft programming!

What You Will Learn

You will learn about many aspects of the Minecraft game and how to interact with Minecraft features through the Python programming language. You will discover how blocks are addressed in the 3D world using coordinates, how to sense the position of your player, how to create and delete blocks in the Minecraft world, and how to sense that a block has been hit by the player.

You will learn how to write programs in the Python programming language, from the very beginnings of a Hello Minecraft World program to the creation of and interaction with huge 3D objects that, thanks to your new Python programming skills, you can stamp with your own personality. If you are using a PC or a Mac, you will also learn how to set up and run your own local Minecraft server.

Using the free MinecraftStuff module of Python helper code, you will be able to enhance your ability to create both 2D and 3D objects out of blocks, lines, polygons and text.

Your adventures will not be limited to the virtual world of Minecraft though! We will introduce you to ways to connect Minecraft to other devices, such as the BBC micro:bit, which makes it possible for your Minecraft world to be able to sense and control objects in the real world. Thus, we give you a valuable secret: how to break out of the boundaries of the virtual sandbox world!

 DAVID SAYS: Minecraft has two main modes of working: Survival mode and Creative mode. You will be using Creative mode throughout this book. We won't be covering Survival mode (mainly because it's extremely frustrating when a creeper kills you just as you are watching your program running). There are many good books already on the market that explain how to survive the night in Minecraft, and we give links to those and other resources in Appendix A at the back of this book. However, any programs you create in Creative mode also work in Survival mode.

What We Assume You Already Know

Because this is a book about programming with Minecraft and we want to focus on learning the programming aspects of Minecraft, we have to assume a few things about you the reader and what you already know:

1. You have a computer (a Raspberry Pi running Raspbian, a PC running Microsoft Windows, or an Apple Mac running macOS X), which meets the minimum requirements for running Minecraft and is already set up and working.

2. You have a basic understanding of how to use your computer, such as using a keyboard and a mouse, using the menu system to start programs, and using application menus like File ⇨ New ⇨ Save.

3. You have a connection to the Internet, and you know how to use a web browser to download files.

4. If you are using a PC or a Mac, you already have a Minecraft user ID and a working copy of Minecraft installed.

5. You know how to play the Minecraft game, such as how to start it, how to move around, how to choose items from the inventory, and how to create and delete blocks in the world.

Because this is a book about programming Minecraft, we don't assume you have any prior knowledge about how to program. As you progress through your adventures, we will lead you through the steps needed to learn programming.

What You Need for the Projects

We have written this book to work on three commonly available computers: a Raspberry Pi running Raspbian, a PC running Microsoft Windows, and an Apple Mac running macOS X. Minecraft is supported on other platforms too, such as a PC running various flavours of Linux, but we don't cover the set-up of those platforms in this book.

To make the set-up of the various parts simpler, we have prepared three starter kits, one for each of the supported computer platforms. You can download the correct starter kit for your computer, and in your first adventure we provide step-by-step instructions about how to download and install these and get everything working. These starter kits include everything you need, except Minecraft itself. You'll be up and running in no time!

You need an Internet connection on your computer to download the starter kits. Almost everything you need for the adventures is included in the starter kits. A few of the adventures have special requirements and we note these at the start of the adventure so you can get everything prepared before you start.

In Adventures 8 and 9, we show you how to link the Minecraft virtual world to the real world. For this you need to buy a BBC micro:bit, which is a small, hand-held, programmable computer with a range of inputs and outputs that you can use with your Minecraft games. We provide some links to where you can buy a BBC micro:bit in Appendix A.

The most important things you need on this journey are your own excitement and enthusiasm for Minecraft, and some curiosity and willingness to experiment with your own ideas and push the boundaries of what you already know!

A Note for Parents and Teachers

We have split this book into separate self-contained adventures that you can treat as individual standalone projects, each of which focuses on one specific feature of Minecraft programming. The Python language is introduced gradually and progressively throughout each adventure; the early adventures are aimed chiefly at beginners, with the later adventures becoming more challenging and introducing more Python, stretching the reader a bit more.

Each adventure presents a practical project with step-by-step instructions (that readers can tick off as they complete them), delivered in a descriptive style, very much like a well-commented program listing. Detailed explanations appear in Digging into the Code sidebars that students can read later, meaning that they are not distracted from the progress of typing in and trying the programs.

Each adventure will probably take more than one session to complete, but they are all split into sections, with subheadings at logical points that could be used to provide a goal for an individual lesson, or an activity to be stretched over a number of sessions.

The Python language uses indents on the left side of the program to represent code structure, and it is a case-sensitive language. Extra guidance from an adult may be useful sometimes with very young readers, to make sure they are being careful to use case and indents correctly, thus avoiding the possibility of them introducing errors into their programs. All of the programs are downloadable from the companion website, so if you have problems with indentation you can check our versions of the programs to see where you might have gone wrong.

Changes Made to the Second Edition

This second edition follows the same highly successful style and content as the first edition, with some minor improvements, bug fixes, and one replacement adventure:

- The downloadable starter kits have been slightly simplified. All coordinates on PC, Mac, and Raspberry Pi are now consistently reported to the Python program as absolute coordinates—that is, real coordinates inside Minecraft (rather than them being relative to the spawn point, as was previously the case). This makes the maths associated with locating objects in Minecraft much easier for children to comprehend, at the expense of it sometimes reporting some large numbers. Coordinates reported on screen now match coordinates reported by the Python programs you write.

- To bring the book up to date and in-line with what is commonly used in schools, all programs are now written in the latest version of Python 3, and we recommend in Adventure 1 that this is what readers download. The only difference you might spot in our programs is the use of `input()` rather than `raw_input()` (Python 3 works slightly differently to Python 2 in this respect).

- The Adventure 5 from the previous edition has been replaced with an entirely new adventure where readers use a BBC micro:bit as a programmable Minecraft game controller. The new adventure has been moved later into the book (to Adventure 8) to allow the addition of some larger projects using the BBC micro:bit with Minecraft. The BBC micro:bit is available mostly worldwide from many resellers including some retail outlets that sell them directly off the shelf. It offers a very affordable entry into the world of physical computing that can be used alongside Minecraft; it is also a completely programmable computer in its own right, and we hope that you will also explore the many features that it offers as a standalone computing platform.

- Martin's free `MinecraftStuff` module has been updated to simplify some features, and this has cut down the amount of typing required to enter the programs in Adventures 6, 7 and 9, as well as making it possible to include a new feature: the Minecraft Turtle! This is a fully controllable block within Minecraft that can move in three dimensions and enables readers to draw complex shapes very quickly. It is also well aligned with teaching curriculums, which regularly introduce programming concepts using a programmable turtle.

How This Book Is Organised

Every chapter of the book is a separate adventure, teaching you new skills and concepts as you program and test the projects. The book is organised so that each adventure is a standalone project, but you might find it easier to work through them in order, as we build up your understanding of the programming concepts gradually throughout the book.

It is vital that you do Adventure 1 before doing anything else. This is because it shows you how to download and install everything you need, and to check that it all works properly. We introduce some basic steps in this adventure that you need to know how to do in all the other adventures, but will give you some reminders in the earlier adventures as you get started.

The first three adventures are written for beginners who have little or no programming knowledge, and we explain all the jargon and concepts as you work through them. In Adventures 2, 3 and 4, you cover the key parts of any good Minecraft game. These include *sensing* things that happen in the Minecraft world, doing some *calculations* with some simple maths, and making your programs *behave* differently, for example by displaying a message on the chat or automatically creating blocks in the world. You will use these three concepts of *sensing*, *calculating*, and *behaving* throughout the book to build bigger and more exciting Minecraft programs!

Adventures 5 and 6 build on what you learned in the earlier adventures by introducing slightly bigger programs that are developed and tested in stages. Adventure 5 looks at ways you can bring in large amounts of data from data files to save and duplicate large structures with a 3D 'duplicating machine'.

Adventures 6 and 7 introduce the free `MinecraftStuff` module, which makes it possible to use blocks to build lines, circles and other 2D shapes, and also some fantastic 3D spheres and pyramids. These can form the beginnings of huge structures that would be very hard to build by hand. Adventure 7 shows how you can add personalities to moving objects to give them their own intelligence. With these techniques, you can write some exciting 'games inside a game' that will amaze your friends.

Adventure 8 introduces the exciting topic of physical computing, and if you want to do this optional adventure you will need to purchase a BBC micro:bit (links to resellers are provided in Appendix A). By connecting a BBC micro:bit to your computer you can use a range of input and output devices on the micro:bit to control and interact with your Minecraft games; the BBC micro:bit becomes a programmable game controller for Minecraft.

Adventure 9 draws on all the programming concepts and skills from the earlier adventures to create one final big project—an awesome game with scoring, and moving objects that you have to avoid or carry around with you. In this adventure, you also have the option to experiment again with the BBC micro:bit, allowing you to do things in the game by pressing buttons in the real world.

Appendix A suggests a whole range of resources that you can use to extend and enhance your adventures, learn more about programming in Python and create even more awesome Minecraft programs based on what you have learnt throughout this book.

In Appendix B we have included a comprehensive reference guide to the programming features used throughout the book, along with a reference to the programming statements that are specific to Minecraft, and a table of block types that you can build with. You'll find this is an invaluable reference section to help with all your own projects and inventions as well!

The glossary provides a handy quick reference to all the jargon and terminology we have introduced throughout the book, and is a collection of all definitions from each adventure.

The Companion Website

Throughout this book you'll find references to the Adventures in Minecraft companion website at `www.wiley.com/go/adventuresinminecraft2e`. The website is where you'll find the starter kits you will need to start programming in Minecraft, together with a collection of video tutorials we have put together to help you if you get stuck. You can find code files for some of the bigger projects on the website.

Appendix B contains a handy reference. Keep it by your side as you work through these Minecraft adventures. You can also use it in any programming projects you embark on in the future.

Other Sources of Help

Computers are complex devices, and operating systems and software are changing all the time. We have tried to protect you and your adventures from future changes as much as possible by providing a downloadable starter kit in Adventure 1 that should give you most of what you need. However, if you run into problems or need specific help, here are some useful places to go:

Sign up for a user ID and downloading and installing Minecraft: `http://minecraft.net`

Play the Minecraft game: `http://minecraft.gamepedia.com/Minecraft_Wiki`

Raspberry Pi: `www.raspberrypi.org`

Microsoft Windows: `http://support.microsoft.com`

Apple Mac and macOS X: `www.apple.com/support`

The Python language: `www.python.org`

The IDLE programming IDE: `https://docs.python.org/3/library/idle.html`

Minecraft Pi edition: `http://pi.minecraft.net`

Minecraft server: `www.spigotmc.org/`

RaspberryJuice bukkit plug-in: `http://dev.bukkit.org/bukkit-plugins/raspberryjuice`

Conventions

You'll notice that there are special boxes throughout this book, to guide and support you. Here is what they look like:

 These boxes explain concepts or terms you might not be familiar with.

 These boxes give you hints to make your computer-programming life easier.

 These boxes contain important warnings to keep you and your computer safe when completing a step or a project.

 These boxes feature quick quizzes for you to test your understanding or make you think more about a topic.

These boxes allow us to explain things or give you extra information we think you'll find useful.

These boxes point you to videos on the companion website that will take you through the tasks, step by step.

You will also find two sets of sidebars in the book. Challenge sidebars give you extra tasks you can accept if you want to take the project a bit further, perhaps by making changes or adding new features. Digging into the Code sidebars explains in a bit more detail some concept or feature of the program, to give you a better understanding of the programming language Python. These sidebars mean you can focus on getting the programs working first, and then read in more detail about how they work and ways you can extend them further once they are working.

When you are following our steps or instructions using code, you should type the code in exactly as we have described it in the instructions. Python is a language where the amount of space at the start of the line (the indent) is important to the meaning of the program, so take extra special care to make sure you put enough spaces at the left of each line. We have coloured the code listing boxes for you so that it makes it easier to see how much each line needs to be indented. Don't worry too much about it—we explain indenting in the early adventures when you first need to use it.

Sometimes you need to type a very long line of code, longer than will fit on a single line in this book. If you see ↵ at the end of a line of code, it means that line and the following line are part of a single line of code, so you should type them as one line, not separate lines. For example, the following code should be typed on one line, not two:

```
print("Welcome to Adventures in Minecraft by ↵
    Martin O'Hanlon and David Whale")
```

If you are viewing this book on an e-reader, to make sure that the programs you type in are correctly laid out, please reduce your e-reader font size. This is so that the program listings are not unnecessarily wrapped around the page margins, and to prevent errors being introduced into your programs.

Most adventures include a Quick Reference Table at the end to sum up the main programming statements or concepts. You can refer to these guides when you need a refresher. There is also a reference section in Appendix B, which shows you the most important programming statements for Minecraft and Python. We hope you will find this handy to refer to as you progress through your adventures.

Whenever you complete an adventure, you unlock an achievement and collect a new badge. You can collect the badges to represent these achievements from the Adventures in Minecraft companion website (`www.wiley.com/go/adventuresin minecraft2e`).

Reaching Out

In Appendix A you will find ways to take your Minecraft programming knowledge further, with lists of websites, organisations, videos and other resources. Many of these resources include forums where you can ask questions or get in touch with other Minecraft programmers.

You can also contact the authors and get help from other readers on the *Adventures in Minecraft* forum at `www.stuffaboutcode.com/p/adventures-in-minecraft.html`.

Time to start your adventures!

Adventure 1
Hello Minecraft World

THIS BOOK IS going to help you learn how to write programs or mods that interact with your Minecraft world, allowing you to do some very exciting things. You use a programming language called **Python** to do it. This way of controlling the Minecraft world from a Python program was first created for Minecraft: Pi Edition on the Raspberry Pi. If you don't have a Raspberry Pi but have Minecraft for Windows or Apple Mac instead, that's okay; you just need to do some extra work on the setup before you get started, which this adventure shows you how to do.

Python is the programming language used in this book.

This book is full of adventures that teach you how to write programs for the Minecraft game. It's packed with all sorts of things you can do with Minecraft to entertain your friends and make the game even more fun to play. You will discover some pretty flashy ways to move your player around, and before long you'll be finding it easy to build whole cities and Minecraft creations that have never been seen before.

The Python programming language comes with a code editor called IDLE, which you will use to create, edit and run the programs you create in these adventures.

MARTIN SAYS:

The Python programming language is used throughout the world in business and education. It is extremely powerful but also easy to learn. You can find out more about Python at www.python.org/.

When computer programmers learn a new programming language or a new way of doing something, they always start by writing a "hello world" program. This is a really simple program that displays "hello world" on the screen, to make sure everything is installed and working properly.

In this first adventure, you set up your computer to allow you to write a program that displays the text "Hello Minecraft World" on the Minecraft chat (see Figure 1-1).

FIGURE 1-1 Hello Minecraft World

To do the Minecraft programming in this book, you need one of these three types of computer: a PC running Microsoft Windows; an Apple Mac running macOS X; or a Raspberry Pi running Raspbian with Pixel. The way you set up your computer depends on which sort of computer you have but, once you have set it up, you program

Minecraft in exactly the same way on all of them. To make it easier for you to set up your computer, you can download a starter kit from `https://adventures inminecraft.github.io`. The starter kits have been tested to make sure all the adventures in this book work properly.

You'll see that your starter kit contains a README file, which you should have a look at. It describes what the kit contains and how it was created; you could use this information to set up your own computer from scratch, although this is not recommended. You'll get a lot more out of it by following the instructions in this book.

Make sure you follow the instructions for your type of computer, either "Setting Up Your Raspberry Pi for Programming Minecraft" or "Setting Up Your PC or Apple Mac for Programming Minecraft".

It's essential that you to set up your computer correctly; otherwise you could get yourself into quite a muddle. So please make sure that you follow the instructions very carefully!

Setting Up Your Raspberry Pi to Program Minecraft

If you are using a Raspberry Pi, Minecraft is installed already; you just need to download the Raspberry Pi starter kit. Everything you need to complete *Adventures in Minecraft* is in a folder called MyAdventures. You also will save your Minecraft programs in this folder.

To see a video of how to set up your Raspberry Pi, visit the companion website at `http://www.wiley.com/go/adventuresinminecraft2e`.

The Raspberry Pi's graphical user interface (GUI), known as Pixel, is used throughout *Adventures in Minecraft*. The GUI is installed on Raspbian, but depending on how you have set up your Raspberry Pi, it may not load the GUI when it boots up. You may instead start with a login and command prompt.

If your Raspberry Pi is set up to start at a command prompt, you need to log in, type **startx** and then press Enter to load the GUI when the command prompt appears.

Start *Adventures in Minecraft* with a new installation of Raspbian so you can be sure that your Raspberry Pi is set up correctly. Visit `www.raspberrypi.org/ help/` for information on setting up your Raspberry Pi and installing Raspbian.

Downloading the Starter Kit

Once your Raspberry Pi has booted up and the GUI has started, you can download the starter kit for Raspberry Pi by following these steps:

1. Open a terminal, click Menu (the Raspberry Pi icon in the top left)⇨ Accessories ⇨ Terminal.

2. Change the directory to the Desktop by typing the following command (see Figure 1-2) and pressing Enter:

   ```
   cd ~
   cd Desktop
   ```

3. Download the starter kit entering the following command and pressing Enter:

   ```
   git clone https://github.com/AdventuresInMinecraft/ ↵
     AdventuresInMinecraft-Pi
   ```

```
pi@raspberrypi: ~/Desktop                            _  □  ×
File  Edit  Tabs  Help
pi@raspberrypi:~ $ cd ~
pi@raspberrypi:~ $ cd Desktop
pi@raspberrypi:~/Desktop $ git clone https://github.com/AdventuresInMinecraft/Ad
venturesInMinecraft-Pi
Cloning into 'AdventuresInMinecraft-Pi'...
remote: Counting objects: 18, done.
remote: Compressing objects: 100% (16/16), done.
remote: Total 18 (delta 0), reused 18 (delta 0), pack-reused 0
Unpacking objects: 100% (18/18), done.
Checking connectivity... done.
pi@raspberrypi:~/Desktop $ ▮
```

FIGURE 1-2 Download the Raspberry Pi starter kit.

Visit `https://adventuresinminecraft.github.io` as there may be future updates and help available.

Starting Minecraft on Your Raspberry Pi

After you have downloaded the starter kit, you can run the game and have a go before moving on to creating your first program.

In future adventures, the instructions tell you to start Minecraft. If you ever need a reminder of how to start Minecraft on the Raspberry Pi, just refer to this section.

To start Minecraft, follow these steps:

1. Select Menu ⇨ Games ⇨ Minecraft Pi.

2. Start a new world by selecting Start Game ⇨ Create New.

3. That's it! Now you can start playing Minecraft.

The main menu has two options: Start Game to build a new or enter an existing Minecraft world and Join Game to join another player's world. (See Figure 1-3.)

FIGURE 1-3 Start Minecraft and create a new world.

Once your Raspberry Pi is set up and you have Minecraft running, you can skip the next section (unless you want to set up Minecraft on a PC or Mac as well as on your Raspberry Pi) and go straight to the "Creating a Program" section later in this adventure.

Setting Up Your PC or Apple Mac to Program Minecraft

Whether you are using a Windows PC or a Mac, you need to make sure Minecraft is installed and working on your computer. If you don't have a copy of Minecraft and a user ID to play it, visit www.minecraft.net to purchase the game. If you encounter any problems installing, running or playing Minecraft, help is on hand; just visit https://help.mojang.com.

To program the full version of Minecraft on the PC and Apple Mac, you need to use a Minecraft server and the RaspberryJuice plugin, which is included in the Starter Kit you download later in this section

RaspberryJuice is a Minecraft server plugin that allows you to write programs to change Minecraft in the same way as you can on the Raspberry Pi. A **plugin** is a program that runs inside the Minecraft server and lets you modify (mod) Minecraft.

You need to download the Python programming language and install it on your computer. Throughout *Adventures in Minecraft* you use Python version 3. The programs within *Adventures in Minecraft* have all been tested to work with Python version 3.6.1. Although it is not essential that you use this version, it is recommended and you must use Python 3.something.

If you want to find out more about Python, visit www.python.org. You can download Python from www.python.org/downloads, and the Python Wiki, wiki.python.org, contains lots of information, tutorials and links to Python community websites.

Setting up your Windows PC or Apple Mac to create your first Minecraft program requires three steps:

1. Download and extract the PC or Apple Mac starter kit, which contains a preconfigured Minecraft server with the RaspberryJuice plugin and a folder called `MyAdventures` where you will save your Minecraft programs.

2. Download and install the Python programming language.

3. Configure Minecraft and connect it to the server.

To see a video of how to set up your Windows PC or Apple Mac, visit the companion website at `www.wiley.com/go/adventuresinminecraft2e`.

Installing the Starter Kit and Python on Your Windows PC

If you are using a Windows PC, the next part in setting up your computer involves two steps:

1. Downloading the starter kit for Windows PC and extracting it to your desktop

2. Downloading the Python programming language and installing it on your Windows PC

Downloading and Extracting the Starter Kit

Follow these steps to download the Windows PC starter kit and copy the contents to your desktop. Placing them on your desktop will make it easy for you to find them whenever you need them:

1. Open your PC's web browser (such as Internet Explorer or Chrome), go to `adventuresinminecraft.github.io` and download the starter kit for your Windows PC.

2. When the starter kit zip file has finished downloading, open it. You can do this either by choosing the Open File option or by opening the download folder and double-clicking the `AIMStarterKitPC.zip` file.

3. The zip file contains only one folder, called `AdventuresInMinecraft-PC`. Copy this folder to the desktop by clicking the folder, holding down the mouse button and dragging the folder to the desktop (see Figure 1-4).

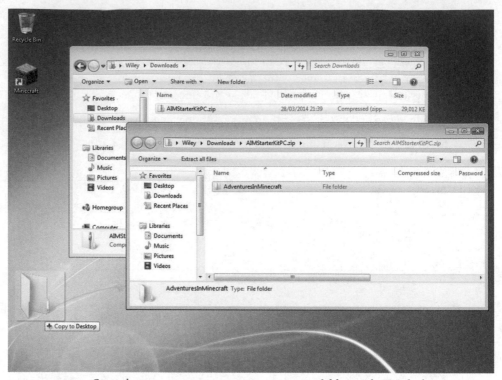

FIGURE 1-4 Copy the `AdventuresInMinecraft-PC` folder to the PC desktop where you will always be able to find it.

Downloading and Installing Python

Because you will be coding using Python, you have to install the Python programming language and the code editor IDLE by following these steps:

If you don't have an administrator account for your computer, you need someone with an administrator account to enter their password before you can install Python.

1. Open your PC's web browser (such as Internet Explorer or Chrome). Go to `www.python.org/downloads/release/python-361/` to download and install Python 3.6.1.

2. Scroll down the page and click the Windows x86 Executable Installer link in the list of files to download the Python installer.

3. When the file `python-3.6.1.exe` has finished downloading, run it either by clicking the Open ⇨ Run menu option or by opening the download folder and double-clicking the file.

4. You may be presented with a security warning box (asking "Do you want to run this file?"). Click Run.

5. Click Install Now to start the installation.

6. User Account Control may ask for your permission to run the setup program. If so, click Yes.

7. Wait for the setup program to complete the installation and click Close.

Installing the Starter Kit and Python on Your Apple Mac

If you are using an Apple Mac, the next part in setting up your computer involves two steps:

1. Downloading the starter kit for Apple Mac and extracting it to your desktop.

2. Downloading the Python programming language and installing it on your Apple Mac.

Downloading and Extracting the Starter Kit

Follow these steps to download the Apple Mac starter kit and copy the contents to the desktop (by placing them on your desktop it will make it easy for you to find them whenever you need them):

1. Open your Apple Mac's web browser (such as Safari, Chrome), go to `https://adventuresinminecraft.github.io` and download the starter kit for your Apple Mac.

2. When the starter kit zip file has finished downloading, go to your downloads.

3. The zip file contains only one folder, called `AdventuresInMinecraft-Mac`. Copy this folder to the desktop by clicking the folder, holding down the mouse button and dragging the folder to the desktop (see Figure 1-5).

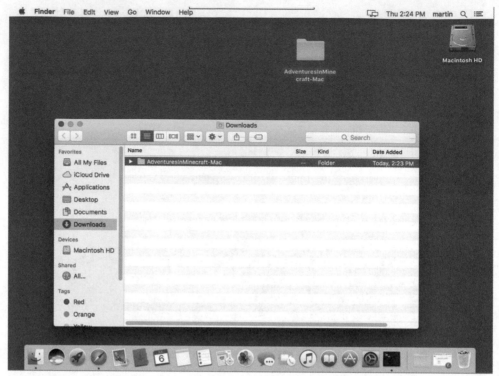

FIGURE 1-5 Copy the `AdventuresInMinecraft-Mac` folder to the Mac desktop.

Downloading and Installing Python

Because you will be doing your coding by using Python, you have to install the Python programming language and the code editor IDLE by following these steps:

Depending on your computer setup, you may need to enter your Apple password or get someone with an administrator account to enter their password before you can install Python.

1. Open your Apple Mac's web browser. Go to `www.python.org/downloads/release/python-361/` to download and install Python 3.6.1.

2. Scroll down the page and click the macOS X 64-bit/32-bit Installer link in the list of files to download the Python installer.

3. When the file `python-3.6.1-macosx10.6.pkg` has finished downloading, open the file by clicking it or opening the download folder in Finder and double-clicking it.

4. The Introduction screen displays information about the Python installer. Click Continue.

5. The Read Me screen displays important information about Python. Click Continue.

6. The License screen displays the Software License Agreement. Click Continue and then click Agree.

7. The Installation Type screen displays how much disk space will be used; click Install. You also have the opportunity to change the install location if you'd like.

8. Enter your Apple password and click Install Software; the installation starts, showing you progress. Wait for Python to finish installing.

9. Click Close when the installation program says the installation was successful.

Starting Minecraft on Your Windows PC or Apple Mac

In future adventures, the instructions tell you to start Minecraft. Refer to this section if you need a reminder of how to start Minecraft and the server and connect to it on your PC or Apple Mac.

You've now installed all the software you need on your Windows PC or Apple Mac. But you're not quite ready yet; first, you need to start up the server and connect Minecraft to it by following these steps:

1. Open the `AdventuresInMinecraft` folder you placed on the desktop by double-clicking it.

2. Run the StartServer program by double-clicking it. The server command window opens.

Your computer may ask your permission to run the Minecraft server or tell you that it can't be opened the first time because it is from an unidentified developer or source.

On Windows you may have to select **More info** and **Run anyway**.

On macOS you may have to run the StartServer program by right-clicking it and choosing Open with Terminal.

3. Press any key to start the Minecraft server. As the server is loading, you see messages on the screen that keep you updated on the server's progress.

The first time the server is run, your computer may display a message asking you to install or upgrade Java or to allow the server access to the network. If this happens, follow the instructions to download and install Java or click agree to give permission/access.

If you are experiencing problems refer to the help section on `https://adventuresinminecraft.github.io`.

4. When the server has finished loading, you see a Done message (see Figure 1-6).

```
"Adventures In Minecraft"
" Minecraft Server Version is 1.12"
  Note - make sure Minecraft is using version 1.12"
"By continuing you are indicating your agreement to our EULA https://account.mojang.com/documents/minecraft_eula."
Press any key to continue . . .
Loading libraries, please wait...
[20:49:31 INFO]: Starting minecraft server version 1.12
[20:49:31 INFO]: Loading properties
[20:49:31 INFO]: Default game type: CREATIVE
[20:49:31 INFO]: Generating keypair
[20:49:31 INFO]: Starting Minecraft server on *:25565
[20:49:31 INFO]: Using default channel type
[20:49:31 INFO]: This server is running CraftBukkit version git-Bukkit-ed8c725 (MC: 1.12) (Implementing API version 1.12
-R0.1-SNAPSHOT)
[20:49:32 INFO]: [RaspberryJuice] Loading RaspberryJuice v1.9
[20:49:32 WARN]: **** SERVER IS RUNNING IN OFFLINE/INSECURE MODE!
[20:49:32 WARN]: The server will make no attempt to authenticate usernames. Beware.
[20:49:32 WARN]: While this makes the game possible to play without internet access, it also opens up the ability for ha
ckers to connect with any username they choose.
[20:49:32 WARN]: To change this, set "online-mode" to "true" in the server.properties file.
[20:49:32 INFO]: Preparing level "world"
[20:49:32 INFO]: Preparing start region for level 0 (Seed: -1769754566252273568)
[20:49:33 INFO]: Preparing spawn area: 30%
[20:49:34 INFO]: Preparing start region for level 1 (Seed: -1769754566252273568)
[20:49:34 INFO]: Preparing start region for level 2 (Seed: -1769754566252273568)
[20:49:35 INFO]: [RaspberryJuice] Enabling RaspberryJuice v1.9
[20:49:35 INFO]: [RaspberryJuice] Using port 4711
[20:49:35 INFO]: [RaspberryJuice] Using RELATIVE locations
[20:49:35 INFO]: [RaspberryJuice] ThreadListener Started
[20:49:35 INFO]: Server permissions file permissions.yml is empty, ignoring it
[20:49:35 INFO]: Done (3.038s)! For help, type "help" or "?"
>
```

FIGURE 1-6 The Minecraft server command window displays "Done" when the server is loaded and ready to use.

The version of Minecraft used in the starter kit is version 1.12. That means you need to create a profile in the Minecraft launcher to run version 1.12 of the game. By using this version of the game, rather than the latest version, the code and programs included in this book are guaranteed to work. You only need to do this once because you will be able to keep using this profile to launch Minecraft.

If you want to use a later version of Minecraft, the `README` file within the starter kit describes how to create your own starter kit; you should only attempt this if you are an advanced user who has a good understanding of how to configure your computer, have experience with editing configuration files and have experience with running Java programs. New starter kits may also be released on the Adventures in Minecraft github page (`https://adventuresinminecraft.github.io`), so be sure to check.

To configure your Minecraft launcher to use version 1.12, follow these steps:

1. Start Minecraft and log in if required.

2. When the Minecraft Launcher window is displayed, click the burger menu (three horizontal lines) in the top right of the screen under your username and select Launch Options.

3. Click Add New, name your configuration `Adventures In Minecraft` and select version 1.12, as shown in Figure 1-7.

FIGURE 1-7 Choose which version of Minecraft to use.

4. Click Save.

5. Click the Minecraft logo to return to the Launcher.

Now connect Minecraft to the server:

1. Select the Adventures in Minecraft profile by clicking the up arrow next to Play.

2. Click Play to start Minecraft.

3. From the Minecraft menu, click Multiplayer.

If you are using a Windows PC, a Windows Security Alert message may pop up asking you to allow Minecraft to access the network. Click Allow Access.

4. From the Play Multiplayer menu, click Direct Connect.

5. Enter `localhost` in the Server Address and click Join Server (see Figure 1-8). That's it! You should now enter the Minecraft world that has been created on your server. You've arrived!

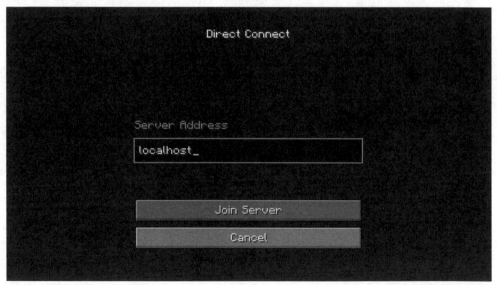

FIGURE 1-8 Connect Minecraft to the server.

Stopping the Minecraft Server

When you have finished your adventures for the day, you need to disconnect from the Minecraft server. Do this by pressing the Escape key to go back to the menu and then clicking Disconnect.

You should also shut down the server safely by typing `stop` in the server command window and pressing Enter.

On the screen, you see a series of updates, telling you what is happening as things shut down.

You can type into the server command window to control many aspects of the Minecraft game, such as the time of day or the weather. For example, if it gets dark in your Minecraft world and you're not ready for night to fall just yet, type `time set 1` in the command window to reset the time back to morning. If it starts to rain, clear the skies by typing `weather clear`. You can find a complete list of commands by typing `help`.

Creating a Program

Congratulations! You've set up your computer and Minecraft is up and running on it. You may have found the setup process a little tedious, but it's done now, and you will only have to do it again if you want to use a different computer. Now it's time for the interesting stuff—creating your first program, "Hello Minecraft World".

In future adventures, the instructions tell you to start IDLE. You can refer to this section if you ever need a reminder of how to start IDLE on your computer.

First, you need to start Python and open IDLE by doing the following:

- On a Raspberry Pi: Select Menu ➪ Programming ➪ Python 3 (IDLE).

- On a PC: Click the Start button and select Python 3.6 ➪ IDLE.

- On a Mac: Click Go on the Finder menu bar and then select Applications ➪ Python 3.6. Double-click IDLE.

The Python Shell window opens.

Once the Python Shell window has loaded, you can create a new program in IDLE. The program you are going to create here won't do anything fancy. Just as computer programmers always start by writing a "hello world" program, you're now going to create a Hello Minecraft World program to check that everything is properly installed on your computer. Here's how:

Future adventures tell you to create a new program and save the program to MyAdventures. You can refer to this section if you ever need a reminder of how to create a new program.

1. Create a new file by selecting File ⇨ New File on the IDLE menu.

2. Save the file to the MyAdventures folder by selecting File ⇨ Save on the IDLE editor menu.

3. Select the MyAdventures folder:

   • On a Raspberry Pi: Select /home/pi in the Directory drop-down list, double-click Desktop, AdventuresInMinecraft-Pi and MyAdventures in the folder browser.

   • On a PC: Click Desktop on the navigation pane on the left, double-click AdventuresInMinecraft-PC and MyAdventures in the folder explorer.

   • On a Mac: Open the folder browser (using the down arrow next to Save), select Desktop, AdventuresInMinecraft-Mac and then MyAdventures.

4. Give your new file a name. Type the filename `HelloMinecraftWorld.py` and click Save. The `.py` added to the end of the file tells your computer that the file is a Python program.

It's important that you save the program in the `MyAdventures` folder. This is where you will save all your *Adventures in Minecraft* programs because it contains everything you need to get your programs running.

5. Now it's time to start programming! Type the following code into the IDLE editor window to start the Hello Minecraft World program. Make sure you get the upper- and lowercase letters correct, as Python is case-sensitive:

```
import mcpi.minecraft as minecraft
mc = minecraft.Minecraft.create()
mc.postToChat("Hello Minecraft World")
```

Python is a **case-sensitive** programming language, which means that you must enter characters in upper- or lowercase correctly. For example, Python treats Minecraft (uppercase M) differently to minecraft (lowercase m). If you enter them incorrectly it results in errors, and you have to retrace your steps to see where you went wrong.

You learn more about what this code means and does in the next adventure. For now, you're keeping it simple and just getting the words "Hello Minecraft World" on the screen to prove that everything works.

6. Save your program by selecting File ⇨ Save from the IDLE editor menu.

Running a Program

You have now created a program! Now it's time to test it. To do this, you need to tell IDLE to run the program by following these steps:

1. Before it can run the Hello Minecraft World program, Minecraft needs to be open and in a game. If it isn't, start up Minecraft using the steps from earlier in this adventure.

2. Move the Minecraft window so you can see both the Minecraft and IDLE windows. (If you are using a PC or Mac and Minecraft is shown on a full screen, press F11 to exit full screen mode so you can see Minecraft in a window.) You should have the following windows open:

   • On a Pi: You should have three windows open: Python Shell; IDLE code editor with your `HelloMinecraftWorld.py` program; and Minecraft (see Figure 1-9).

FIGURE 1-9 Raspberry Pi is ready to run your program.

- On a PC: You should have four windows open: Python Shell; IDLE code editor with your `HelloMinecraftWorld.py` program; server command window; and Minecraft (see Figure 1-10).

FIGURE 1-10 Windows PC is ready to run your program.

- On a Mac: You should have four windows open: Python Shell; IDLE code editor with your `HelloMinecraftWorld.py` program; server command window; and Minecraft (see Figure 1-11).

3. Press Esc to open the Minecraft Game menu. Use your mouse pointer to select the IDLE code editor.

4. Run the `HelloMinecraftWorld.py` program by clicking Run ⇨ Run Module on the IDLE menu, or pressing F5.

Python shell   IDLE code editor   Minecraft   Server command window

FIGURE 1-11 Apple Mac is ready to run your program.

5. IDLE automatically switches to the Python Shell window and runs the program. If there are any errors, you see them displayed here in red. If there are any errors, carefully check the code you typed earlier by switching back to the IDLE code editor and comparing it to the code I provided to see where you went wrong.

6. Bring the window with the Minecraft game to the front. Notice anything? All your hard work has produced results and "Hello Minecraft World" is now displayed in the chat (refer to Figure 1-1).

MARTIN SAYS:

If you have set everything up correctly, "Hello Minecraft World" is displayed in Minecraft chat (as in Figure 1-1); but if it isn't, or errors are displayed in the Python Shell, go back over the instructions in this adventure. It's really important that you get your initial setup right; if you don't, the programs you create in future adventures won't work.

Stopping a Program

The Hello Minecraft World program runs, displays the message on the screen and then stops. It is however important to know how to force a program to stop running, because, in future adventures, the programs you create will not stop until you tell them to stop! To stop a program, select the Python Shell window and then click Shell ⇨ Restart Shell from the menu, or hold down Ctrl and press C.

Achievement Unlocked: **The hard part is over! You have Minecraft up and running, and you've also written your first program and the world says "Hello".**

In the Next Adventure. . .

In Adventure 2, you learn some simple programming skills with Minecraft and Python that allow you to track the position of your player. You learn about the "game within a game" concept, and you write some simple games that change the way they behave depending on where your player is inside the Minecraft world.

Adventure 2
Tracking Your Players as They Move

WHEN YOU PLAY Minecraft, you are playing a game that other people have designed for you. The Minecraft world is fun, but it's even more fun if you can make it do the things that you want it to do. When writing Minecraft programs in Python, you now have a complete programming environment at your fingertips, and you can invent and program anything you can possibly imagine. This adventure introduces you to some of the fun things you can create using Minecraft and the programming language Python.

A really fun thing to do when programming Minecraft is to create a game within a game. Minecraft is the "world", and your **program** makes this world behave in new ways. You will find that most Minecraft programs have three things that make them fun and exciting: *sensing* something about the world, such as the player position; *calculating* something new, such as a score; and *behaving* in some way, such as moving your player to a new location.

This adventure shows you how to sense your player's position and make different things happen in the game as your player moves. In the welcome home game you build a magic doormat that greets you when you walk on it. We introduce a technique called *geo-fencing* using a real Minecraft fence, and your game will challenge you and your friends to compete to collect objects in the fastest time possible. Finally you learn how to move your player by making your game catapult your player into the sky if you don't get out of that field quick enough!

A **program** is a series of instructions or statements that you type in a particular programming language, which the computer then follows automatically. You must use the correct type of instructions for the programming language you are using. In this book, you are using the Python programming language.

A **statement** is a general computing term that usually means one complete instruction that you give to the computer—in other words, one line of a computer program such as `print("Hello Steve")`. Some people also use the word *command*, but that is more relevant when you are talking about commands that you type at a command prompt to a computer.

Python has its own very precise explanation of what a statement is, but for the purposes of this book I use *statement* to mean one individual instruction or line in the Python program. If you want to read more about the Python language, you can read the online documentation here: `https://docs.python.org/3/`.

Sensing Your Player's Position

Before you can sense your player's position, you need to understand a bit about how the Minecraft world is organised. Everything in Minecraft is exactly one block in size, and a block represents a one-metre cube. As your player, Steve, moves around the Minecraft world, the Minecraft game remembers where he is by a set of **coordinates**. The world is constructed of empty blocks that are filled by materials that are usually one-metre cube in volume. There are a number of exceptions to this, for example carpets and liquids such as water and lava that can take up less volume when viewed but cannot be combined with other materials to fill less space than a one-metre cube.

By sensing your player's position in the Minecraft world, you can make your game intelligently react as you move around the world, such as by displaying messages at specific locations, automatically building structures as you move around, and changing your player's position when you walk to specific locations. You find out how to do all of these things in this book, and many of them you learn right here in this adventure!

A **coordinate** is a set of numbers that uniquely represents a position. In Minecraft, 3D coordinates are used to represent the exact position within the three-dimensional Minecraft world, and each coordinate consists of three numbers. See also `http://en.wikipedia.org/wiki/Coordinate_system` for information about coordinates and `http://minecraft.gamepedia.com/Coordinates` for information about how Minecraft uses coordinates in the Minecraft world.

These coordinates are called x, y and z. You have to be careful when you talk about coordinates in Minecraft; if you use words such as "left" and "right", whether something is left or right depends on which way you are facing in the Minecraft world. It's better to think of Minecraft coordinates as relating to the directions on a compass. Figure 2-1 shows how changes in x, y and z coordinates relate to movement in the Minecraft world.

TIPS & TRICKS

It's easier to understand how coordinates change as you move your player in Minecraft by experimenting inside the game. On the Raspberry Pi, the x, y and z coordinates are displayed in the top-left corner of the screen as you move your player around in the world. On the PC/Mac you can display the coordinates by pressing the F3 key. You can learn about all the advanced controls of Minecraft at `http://minecraft.gamepedia.com/Controls`.

The best way to understand x, y and z coordinates is to think of them in relation to a compass:

- x gets bigger as your player heads east, and smaller as you head west.

- y gets bigger up in the sky, and smaller down into the ground.

- z gets bigger as your player heads south, and smaller as you head north.

Getting Started

Now that you've completed the Hello Minecraft World program in Adventure 1, it's time for you to write your own program to link up with Minecraft!

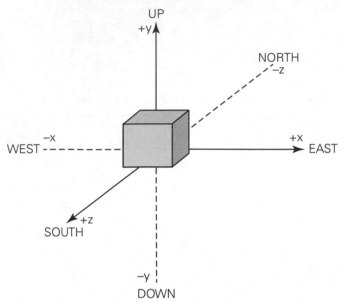

FIGURE 2-1 The x, y and z coordinates in Minecraft relate to headings on a compass like this.

Adventure 1 explains in detail how you get everything running, and you perfect those steps as you work your way through your adventures. All of the steps you need to know to start everything up and begin typing programs are described in Adventure 1, but Martin and I give you some reminders in the first few adventures while you're still learning how to do it:

1. Start up Minecraft, IDLE, and if you are working on a PC or a Mac, start up the server, too. You should have had a bit of practice with starting everything up by now, but refer to Adventure 1 if you need any reminders.

2. Open IDLE, the Python Integrated Development Environment (IDE), just as you did in Adventure 1. This is your window into the Python programming language, and it's where you type and run all your Python programs.

VIDEO

For a reminder on how to get Minecraft running properly on your particular computer, visit the companion website at www.wiley.com/go/adventures inminecraft2e and select the Adventure 1 video.

Showing Your Player's Position

The best way to understand how coordinates work is to write a little experimental program, so that's what you're going to do now. This program shows the 3D coordinates of your player, and you can see the coordinates changing as your player moves.

1. From the Python Shell, create a new program by choosing File ⇨ New File. A new untitled window opens, which is where you type your new program.

2. Before you start to type a program, it is good practice to save the file first, so that if you have to rush away from your computer you don't have to think of a name for the program under pressure. You just have to choose to save it. Professional programmers do this all the time to make sure they don't lose their work. From the new untitled window menu, choose File ⇨ Save As, and type the name whereAmI.py. Make sure that you save your program inside the MyAdventures folder.

3. Your program communicates directly with the Minecraft game through the Minecraft API. To gain access to this API you import the minecraft module, which gives your Python program access to all the facilities of the Minecraft game. Use the following to import the module:

```
import mcpi.minecraft as minecraft
```

4. To communicate with a running Minecraft game, you need a connection to that game. Type the following to connect to the Minecraft game:

```
mc = minecraft.Minecraft.create()
```

Be aware that Python is a case-sensitive language—so be careful how you capitalise words! It's important that you type uppercase and lowercase letters correctly. The second Minecraft in the statement you just typed in must start with a capital letter for it to work properly.

5. Ask the Minecraft game for the position of your player by using getTilePos():

```
pos = mc.player.getTilePos()
```

6. Tell the Minecraft game to display the coordinates of the player's position. print() displays these coordinates on the Python Shell when your program runs:

```
print(pos.x)
print(pos.y)
print(pos.z)
```

7. Save this file by choosing File ⇨ Save from the Editor menu.

8. Run the program by choosing Run ⇨ Run Module from the Editor menu.

You should now see the coordinates of the player's location displayed on the Python Shell (see Figure 2-2). Later in this adventure, you use these coordinates to sense where your player is standing and build a magic doormat that welcomes your player home when he stands on it!

```
● ● ●                    Python 3.6.1 Shell
Python 3.6.1 (v3.6.1:69c0db5050, Mar 21 2017, 01:21:04)
[GCC 4.2.1 (Apple Inc. build 5666) (dot 3)] on darwin
Type "copyright", "credits" or "license()" for more information.
>>>
========= RESTART: /Users/davidw/Documents/MyAdventures/whereAmI.py =========
1
4
7
>>>
                                                            Ln: 9  Col: 4
```

FIGURE 2-2 Use `getTilePos` to show the player position on the Python Shell.

API stands for *application programming interface*. An API gives you a way to safely access parts of an application program from within your programs. It is the Minecraft API that gives you access to the Minecraft game from within your Python programs. The Minecraft game must be running before you can connect your Python programs to it via this API. The mcpi in the line `import mcpi.minecraft as minecraft` stands for *Minecraft Pi*, because the very first version of the API only ran on the Raspberry Pi.

An **interface** is a set of rules that explain how, as a programmer, you can access some other part of a computer system. The API is a set of rules explaining how you can communicate with a running program—in this case, the Minecraft game. All your Minecraft programs access the running Minecraft game through the Minecraft API.

All of the Python programs you create need to access the Minecraft API. For this to work properly, your programs must be able to access the `mcpi.minecraft` module, which is stored in the `mcpi` folder of your `MyAdventures` folder. The easiest way to make sure that this works every time is always to create your Python programs inside your `MyAdventures` folder.

DIGGING INTO THE CODE

Congratulations—you have just used a variable in your program! `pos.x` is a variable, and so are `pos.y` and `pos.z`.

A **variable** is just a name for a location in the computer's memory. Whenever you put a variable name to the left of an equals sign, it stores a value in that variable, for example:

```
a = 10
```

Whenever you use a variable inside a `print` **statement**, the program displays the value of that variable on the Python Shell. So, if `a = 10`, the following

```
print(a)
```

prints `10`, the value of the variable a.

The pos variable that you use from `pos = mc.player.getTilePos()` is a special type of variable. Just think of it as a box with three subcompartments labelled x, y and z:

```
print(pos.x)
```

Try moving your player to a new location and running the program again. Check the coordinates displayed on the Python Shell: these should now have changed to reflect your player's new position. You can use this little program at any time if you want to confirm the coordinates of a position in the Minecraft world.

A **variable** is a name for a location in the computer's memory. You can store new values in variables at any time in your program, and you can read back the values and display them or use them in calculations. Think of a variable as being a bit like the memory button on a calculator.

Tidying Up Your Position Display

Before you move on and do more with your Minecraft programs, you can improve the output of your player position to make it easier to understand. Having three separate lines of output every time you display the position takes up a lot of space; it would be nice to have all three parts of the player position on a single line, like this:

```
x=10 y=2 z=20
```

To do that, follow these steps:

1. Modify your `whereAmI.py` program by removing the three `print()` statements and replacing them with this single line:

   ```
   print("x="+str(pos.x) +" y="+str(pos.y) +" z="+str(pos.z))
   ```

2. Save your program again by selecting File ⇨ Save from the Editor menu, and then run it by clicking Run ⇨ Run Module. See how the output has improved —now it is all on one line!

DIGGING INTO THE CODE

In your new version of the `whereAmI.py` program, a little bit of extra magic took place, which I need to explain.

In Python, `print()` displays anything you put in the brackets, and the output is displayed on the Python Shell. You have already used different ways of displaying information with `print()`. Now you can examine them a little further. Look at this example:

```
print("hello")
```

Just like in your Hello Minecraft World adventure, `print()` displays the word *hello*. The quotes around the word tell Python that you want to display the word *hello* exactly as it is given. If you put spaces between the quotes, those spaces are displayed too. The text between the quotes is called a **string**.

Here is another type of `print()`:

```
print(pos.x)
```

`print()` displays the value inside the `pos.x` variable. This is a number, but the number might change every time you use the `print()` statement depending on what value is stored in that variable.

Finally, you need to understand what `str()` does in your `print()` statement. Python `print()` gives you many different ways to mix numbers and strings together. When you mix numbers and strings inside Python, as in the following code, you have to tell Python to convert the numbers to strings so that they can be tacked on to the rest of the characters in the string that is being displayed. `str()` is built in to Python and it converts whatever variable or value is between its brackets into a string. The plus symbol (+) tells Python to join "x= " and whatever is stored in the `pos.x` variable to make one big string, which is then printed onto the Python Shell window.

```
print("x= "+str(pos.x))
```

Why don't you try this line without the `str()` to see what happens:

```
print("x= "+ pos.x)
```

Using postToChat to Change Where Your Position Displays

It's unusual, but in the whereAmI.py program, you play the game in the Minecraft window but your position appears on the Python Shell window. You can easily fix that by using a technique you have used already, in Adventure 1: postToChat! Here's how:

1. Change the print() statement to mc.postToChat(), like this:

    ```
    mc.postToChat("x="+str(pos.x) +" y="+str(pos.y) ↩
      +" z="+str(pos.z))
    ```

2. Click File ⇨ Save to save your program, and run it again by choosing Run ⇨ Run Module from the Editor menu.

Well done! Your player position should now be displayed on the Minecraft chat, which is much more convenient for you as you play the game.

Introducing a Game Loop

Having to run your whereAmI.py program every time you want to find out the player position is not very helpful. Luckily, you can get round this by modifying your program to add a game loop. Almost every other program you write in this book needs a game loop to make sure that the program continues to run and interact with your Minecraft gaming. Most games you play continue to run forever until you close them down, and this is a useful technique to learn. In computing, this is called an **infinite loop** because it loops forever.

You can add the game loop by modifying your existing program; the new program is very similar, so you save a bit of time this way. Be sure to save the new file under a different file name so you don't lose your first program.

1. Start by saving your program as a new file by choosing File ⇨ Save As from the Editor menu and calling it `whereAmI2.py`. Make sure you save it in your `MyAdventures` folder; otherwise it won't work.

2. Now you need to import a new module that allows you to insert time delays. You do this because if you don't slow down the loop, you will be bombarded with a flood of messages on the chat and won't be able to see what you are doing. Add the following **bold** line to your existing program:

```
import mcpi.minecraft as minecraft
import time
```

3. Modify the main part of your program by adding the lines that are marked in **bold** in the following code, noting that you have to indent the lines beneath `while  True` to tell Python which instructions it needs to repeat. You can quickly insert indents by pressing the Tab key on your keyboard. See the Digging into the Code section to understand why this indent is needed:

```
while True:
  time.sleep(1)
  pos = mc.player.getTilePos()
  mc.postToChat("x="+str(pos.x) +" y="+str(pos.y) +" ↵
    z="+str(pos.z))
```

4. Choose File ⇨ Save from the Editor menu to save your changes.

5. Now you can run your program by choosing Run ⇨ Run Module from the Editor menu. Have a walk around the Minecraft world and notice that, once every second, you see the coordinates of your player posted to the chat.

DIGGING INTO THE CODE

Indentation is extremely important in all programming languages, as it shows how the program is structured and which groups of statements belong with other statements. Indentation is especially important in the Python programming language because it is used by Python to understand the meaning of your program (unlike other languages such as C that use { } braces to group statements together). Indentation is important when you use `while` loops and other statements, as it shows which of these belong to the loop and will therefore be repeated over and over again. In your game loop, all the program statements underneath `while  True:` are indented because they belong to the loop and are repeated each time round the loop.

In this example, you can see that the "hello" is printed once but the word "tick" is then printed once every second. `time.sleep()` and `print()` belong to the loop because they are indented:

```python
print("hello")
while True: # this is the start of the loop
  time.sleep(1)
  print("tick")
```

Indentation is the space at the left edge of each line of a program. Indents are used to show the structure of the program and to group program statements under loops and other statements. In Python, the indents are important as they also change the meaning of the program.

It is important that you get the indentation right. Python can work with both spaces and tabs when you indent code, but if you mix tabs and spaces inside the same program, Python can easily get confused about what you mean. Therefore it is best always to use a consistent method for indenting your programs. Most people like to press the Tab key for each level of indent, as it is quicker than typing in lots of spaces, but if you start using Tab you should always use it and not mix it with spaces.

Now that your program is running in an infinite game loop, it will never stop! Before you run your next program, stop this program from running by choosing Shell ➪ Restart Shell from the Python Shell menu, or pressing CTRL+C on the keyboard.

Building the Welcome Home Game

It's time for you to put your game loop into practice and develop a simple application. The Welcome Home game uses sensing (tracking your player's position) to follow your player as he moves around the Minecraft world. You also learn how to do more complex sensing with the `if` statement in Python. You will build a magic doormat, which makes the message "welcome home" pop up on the Minecraft chat when you stand on the mat.

VIDEO

To see a tutorial about how to write and play the Welcome Home game, visit the companion website at www.wiley.com/go/adventuresinminecraft2e and choose the Adventure 2 video.

Using if Statements to Make a Magic Doormat

To work out whether your player is standing on the doormat, you use an `if` statement to compare your player's position against the position of the doormat. When the two match, your player has arrived home.

First, look at how the `if` statement works; trying it out yourself on the Python Shell will help you to understand it:

1. Click the Python Shell. Make sure you click just to the right of the `>>>` prompt to make sure that what you type goes in at the right place.

2. Type the following line into the Python Shell. Python runs it as soon as you press the Enter key. It doesn't display anything yet, as all this is doing is storing the number 20 inside the variable called `a`:

```
a = 20
```

3. Check that the variable `a` has the correct value in it by typing the following into the Python Shell:

```
print(a)
```

The number 20 should display on the screen.

4. Try out an `if` statement to see if the value stored in variable `a` is bigger than 10. Note that you have to put the colon at the end of the `if` statement. When you press Enter at the end of the first line, Python automatically indents the next line for you:

```
if a>10:
   print("big")
```

5. Now press Enter again to tell the Python Shell that you have finished typing the `if` statement. You should see the word "big" appear on the Python Shell. To see what this looks like, see Figure 2-3.

```
● ● ●                      Python 3.6.1 Shell
Python 3.6.1 (v3.6.1:69c0db5050, Mar 21 2017, 01:21:04)
[GCC 4.2.1 (Apple Inc. build 5666) (dot 3)] on darwin
Type "copyright", "credits" or "license()" for more information.
>>> a = 20
>>> print(a)
20
>>> if a>10:
        print("big")


big
>>> |
                                             Ln: 12  Col: 4
```

FIGURE 2-3 Using an `if` statement interactively in the Python Shell

The `if` statement only ever has two possible outcomes—for example, in the preceding code `if a>10` is either `True` (a is greater than 10) or it is `False` (a is not greater than 10). You meet the values `True` and `False` again a little later in this adventure.

DAVID SAYS...

Checking if Your Player Is at a Particular Location

For your program to be able to work out whether your player is standing on your magic doormat, it has to check at least two parts of the coordinate. If you check that the x and z coordinates of the doormat are the same as your player's position, this acts as a reasonable method to detect that your player is standing on the mat. You can check this by using the keyword `and` inside the `if` statement to check one condition *and* another condition. The y coordinate is less important here, and because you don't check the y coordinate in the program, as your player hovers over the doormat you still see the welcome home message.

Try this out interactively in the Python Shell first to make sure it works:

1. At the Python Shell >>> prompt, type the following to set a variable:

```
a = 8
```

2. Type an `if` statement that also uses an `and`. This statement checks whether the a variable is between two numbers. The first time you type this you see the word "between" appear on the Python Shell, because 8 is greater than 5 and less than 10. Remember to press Enter a second time to finish the indented region of the `if`:

```
if a>5 and a<10:
  print("between")
```

3. Now change a to be smaller than 5, and see what happens (see Figure 2-4):

```
a = 3
if a>5 and a<10:
  print("between")
```

```
● ● ●                    Python 3.6.1 Shell
Python 3.6.1 (v3.6.1:69c0db5050, Mar 21 2017, 01:21:04)
[GCC 4.2.1 (Apple Inc. build 5666) (dot 3)] on darwin
Type "copyright", "credits" or "license()" for more information.
>>> a = 8
>>> if a>5 and a<10:
        print("between")


between
>>> a = 3
>>> if a>5 and a<10:
        print("between")


>>> |
                                              Ln: 15  Col: 4
```

FIGURE 2-4 You use an `if` statement with `and` to check two or more conditions.

When you are testing programs, it is very useful to test them with lots of different numbers. One way that you can reduce a possibly infinite amount of testing to something that is manageable is to look at the conditions of the `if` statements and only test around those numbers. In the previous example, I would test 4, 5, 6 and 9, 10, 11, and if those numbers work it would be safe to assume that all other possible numbers work in the program too.

Building a Magic Doormat

Before you can write your game, you first need to build something in the Minecraft world so that your program has something to interact with. All you really need is a doormat. But first, open Minecraft and load the world you've already been using.

1. To place a doormat on the floor, choose an item from the inventory and right-click to place it on the floor in front of you. Wool is probably a good choice for a doormat.

2. To find out the coordinates of your doormat in the Minecraft world, run your `whereAmI.py` program again, and then stand on the doormat. Write down the x, y and z coordinates somewhere, because you need them when you write your new program so that you can locate the doormat in the Minecraft world.

You're probably already impatient to start building huge structures! In Adventure 3, you learn how to do that automatically by writing Python programs but, for now, just build something simple, focusing on getting the program to work properly. You might like to build a simple house around your doormat, making sure that the doormat is in the open doorway of your house.

Writing the Welcome Home Game

Now that you understand how `if` statements work, you can write the Welcome Home Game by following these steps:

1. Choose File ⇨ New File from the Python Shell menu to create a new program.

2. Choose File ⇨ Save As from the editor menu to save your program, and call it `welcomeHome.py`. Remember that you need to save your program in your `My Adventures` folder for it to work properly.

3. Import the modules you need for this program by typing

```
import mcpi.minecraft as minecraft
import time
```

4. Connect to the Minecraft game, remembering to check the capitalisation of the word `Minecraft`:

```
mc = minecraft.Minecraft.create()
```

5. Put in the main game loop that senses your player's position, with a delay so it doesn't run too quickly:

```
while True:
    time.sleep(1)
    pos = mc.player.getTilePos()
```

6. Add the `if` statement that checks whether your player is standing on the mat. This uses the `if` statement with an `and` to check two conditions. Both the x and z parts of the coordinate for your doormat must match the player's position for the program to say the player is standing on the doormat. Still have the x and z coordinates for the doormat that you wrote down earlier? Enter them here, so that the program knows exactly where your doormat is:

```
if pos.x == 10 and pos.z == 12:
    mc.postToChat("welcome home")
```

Time to see if your program works! By choosing Run ⇨ Run Module from the Editor menu, you can move around the Minecraft world. When your player stands on the doormat, the program should say "welcome home", as in Figure 2-5. Cool!

FIGURE 2-5 Walking on the doormat displays a "welcome home" message.

Notice how you used the == (double equals) symbol in the if statement? A common mistake here is to use an = symbol (single equals). Try that and see what happens; you should see an error when you run your program. Python uses a single equals sign (=) to mean "store the value on the right side of the statement into the variable on the left side of the statement" (like a = 3). Python uses == (double equals) to mean "compare the value on the right side against the value on the left side" (like if a == 3:).

Make sure you get the indentation correct when you code your Welcome Home Game. The code that is part of the while True loop is indented by one level. The mc.postToChat() that belongs to the if statement is indented by two levels. If you get the indentation wrong, your program does the wrong thing.

Believe it or not, you have just learned all the basics you use in your other adventures. Every Minecraft program has to import modules, connect to the game, loop in a game loop, sense that something has happened and behave differently as a result. From these simple beginnings you will find that many great things will grow!

CHALLENGE

Do you think that checking the y coordinate (the up and down direction) improves the detection of whether your player is standing on the doormat? Have a go. Modify your program to test all three coordinates of the doormat and see if the application works any better.

DIGGING INTO THE CODE

Chances are you will have typed something wrong at some point, in which case you will probably have seen a red error message on the Python Shell. It's a good idea to have a look at the type of errors you can make, so you don't take fright when you see them from time to time.

You might see a **syntax** error if you type the wrong symbols or get things in the wrong order. If you miss out a symbol or type in a variable name when it is not expected, you get a syntax error.

For example, if you type the following line into the Python Shell, you see the syntax error shown in Figure 2-6 because the equals sign is not expected to appear on its own; it is usually used together with variables and other values:

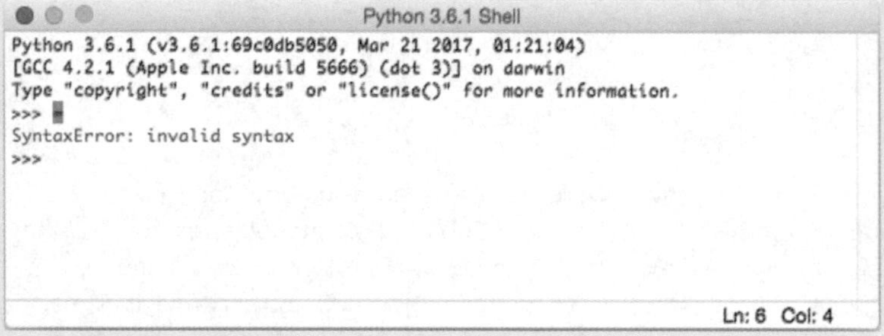

FIGURE 2-6 Python shows that your code contains a syntax error.

Now type this into the Python Shell:

```
print(zz)
```

Python tells you this is a name error (as shown in Figure 2-7) because you have not yet stored a value in the variable name zz, so Python doesn't yet know about a variable called zz.

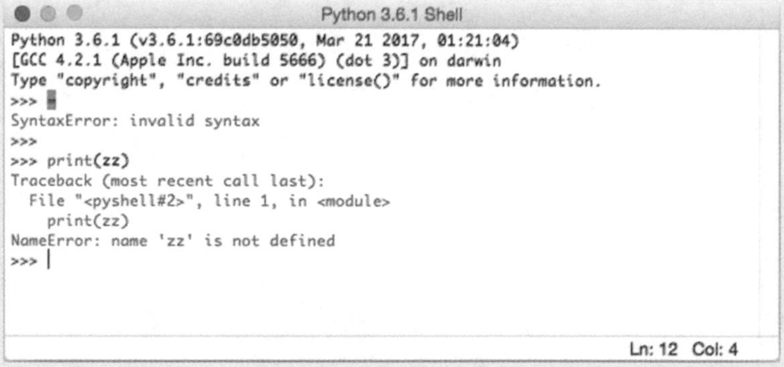

FIGURE 2-7 Python tells you about a name error.

Try typing a `while` loop, but skip that all-important colon (`:`) at the end:

```
while True
```

Again, you get a syntax error, because Python was expecting the colon but you did not use it.

Don't be alarmed when you see an error message coming back from your program. Look carefully at the line it is talking about and see if you can work out what you have typed incorrectly. Sometimes you might get a syntax error because of an error in an earlier line in the program, so check all around the error message to see if you can figure out what the problem is. If all else fails, ask a friend to look over your program for you. It is often easier to spot errors in other programs from other people than your own! When errors are reported on the Python Shell they also include the line number of the error. You can look at the bottom right of the IDLE window to see what line number your cursor is at, or you can use Edit ⇨ GoTo Line from the IDLE menu.

Syntax refers to the rules of a language (in this case, the Python language), and is mainly related to the order in which you type things.

Using Geo-Fencing to Charge Rent

Now you are going to write a new game, called `rent.py`. This game consists of a field with a fence around it. Your program detects when your player is standing in this field and charges rent all the while the player is in the field. Your player's challenge is to remove any objects in this field in the fastest time possible so that rent is as low as possible.

Your `welcomeHome.py` program used an `if` statement to check whether the coordinates of your player were the same as the coordinates of your doormat. For this to work, your player has to be standing exactly on the doormat. You can improve on this a bit by using a technique called **geo-fencing**, which you use in this new game. The detection of your player's position is improved because it checks to see if your player is standing in an area of the Minecraft world, not just at a specific coordinate. This allows you to detect when your player is standing anywhere in a larger region of the world, and you don't have to be quite so precise when standing on blocks.

DEFINITIONS

Geo-fencing is a general technique that builds a virtual fence around coordinates on any map. When something enters this virtual fenced region, something happens as a result. "Something" could mean a player in the Minecraft world, a person in the real world, or a device like a lawnmower or even an animal in the real world.

In many cases, geo-fencing is used to alert the user when something—such as cattle, for example, or a vehicle—moves outside of a predetermined region. You can find out more about real-world uses of geo-fencing at `http://en.wikipedia.org/wiki/Geo-fence` and also find out how geo-fencing is being used in real life to track elephants in the wild `www.cbsnews.com/news/kenya-uses-text-messages-to-track-elephant/`.

For geo-fencing to work, you need two things: an object or region to track and the allowed coordinates of the "fence" around that object. You're now going to find out how to do this by building a field with a real Minecraft fence around it and taking note of the coordinates of the corners of the field.

DAVID SAYS...

You don't have to build the fence for this program to work. The game is a bit more interesting to play if you do, though, because you have to jump over the fence or run a long way round to get to the gap in the fence to get in and out of the field. Adding obstacles to games makes them more challenging and exciting. This Minecraft fence lines up with the coordinates of your virtual geo-fence, and it gives your program a simple way to answer the question "Is the player in the field or not?"

When you have built your field and fence, it should look something like Figure 2-8.

Working Out the Corner Coordinates of the Field

In order to geo-fence the field with your program, you need to have an accurate record of the coordinates of the corners of the field so that you can enter these numbers into your Python program.

The easiest way to do this is to run your `whereAmI.py` program from earlier and then have your player run to each corner of the field to get the x, y and z coordinates of each corner. On a piece of paper, make a sketch of what you're building and write the coordinates on the sketch. You need them when you write your program. Remember that the z coordinate gets bigger as your player moves south and smaller as your player moves north, as you saw in Figure 2-1.

FIGURE 2-8 A field with a fence around it. The field is 10 blocks by 10 blocks in size.

In Figure 2-9, you can see the coordinates of the field that I built when writing this book. I have written down the coordinates for all four corners, as I need them to work out the smallest and biggest numbers in both the x and z directions. Note how the smallest coordinates are at the top-left corner of my field, but this might be different in your field if you have built it with your player facing the other way round.

FIGURE 2-9 Now that you have the coordinates of the corners of the field, it is ready for geo-fencing.

You need four numbers for your geo-fence program. First, you need to know the smallest and biggest x coordinates, so work these out from your diagram. In the previous example, the smallest x is 10 and the biggest x is 20. I have called the smallest x coordinate X1 and the biggest x coordinate X2.

Depending on where your player is standing in the Minecraft world, some of the coordinates might be negative (such as x=-5, y=0, z=-2), which can make these calculations a little tricky. You might find it easier to move to a place in the Minecraft world where all three parts of the coordinate are positive (for example, x=5, y=2, z=4) first. The coordinates may also be quite large numbers such as x=2000, y=65, z=1000, but this is normal. You can check the coordinates where your player is standing by looking at the top-left corner of the Minecraft screen on the Raspberry Pi or pressing F3 on the PC/Mac.

Next you need to work out the smallest and biggest z coordinates. In the example, the smallest z is 10 and the biggest z is 20. I have called the smallest z coordinate Z1 and the biggest z coordinate Z2:

```
X1 = 10
Z1 = 10
X2 = 20
Z2 = 20
```

Number your biggest and smallest coordinates in the same way because you need them in the next step—writing the program.

Writing the Geo-Fence Program

The final step is to write the program that makes the geo-fencing work and charges rent whenever the player is standing in the field. This program is similar in structure to the whereAmI.py program.

You are going to use constants in this new game to make it easier to move your field around later. That way you won't have to hunt through your programs to find the coordinate values you need to change if you move your field.

A **constant** is a name for a part of the computer's memory (just like a variable) where you can store values that normally don't change while the program is running.

The Python language doesn't really have a special way of handling constants, unlike other programming languages. Python programmers usually use a programming convention (which simply means a standard way of working) where constants are always typed using uppercase letters. This makes it more obvious when you're programming something that it is a constant, and you should not change it after you have set an initial value. Other programming languages have their own way of using constants, and in these languages an error is raised if you try to change their value. Python does not have this feature.

To write the program, follow these steps:

1. Start by opening a new window in IDLE by choosing File ⇨ New File from the menu.

2. Choose File ⇨ Save As from the menu, and name the file `rent.py`.

3. Import the modules needed for this program:

```
import mcpi.minecraft as minecraft
import time
```

4. Connect to the Minecraft game:

```
mc = minecraft.Minecraft.create()
```

5. Define some constants for the four coordinates of the geo-fence. Make sure you use the coordinates that you worked out earlier. I've used the coordinates that I used in my program, but yours might be different:

```
X1 = 10
Z1 = 10
X2 = 20
Z2 = 20
```

6. Create a variable that keeps a running tally of how much rent the player has been charged. When the game starts you haven't charged any rent, so create a new variable called `rent` and set it to zero:

```
rent = 0
```

7. Create the main game loop with a `while` statement. Your program ticks round once every second, so use a `sleep` statement to make it delay 1 second each

time round the loop. Delaying a short time each time around the loop slows the program down a little, and also it gives you a convenient method of timing how long your player is in the field. Later you will add 1 to the rent variable each time round the game loop, and as you have added the one-second delay at the top of this loop, this means that the rent will increase by 1 for every second. Make sure you get the indents right at this point:

```
while True:
    time.sleep(1)
```

8. To check whether your player is in the geo-fenced region, you need to know their position. Just like in your earlier programs, do this with `player.getTilePos()`:

```
pos = mc.player.getTilePos()
```

9. You've now arrived at the most important part of the program. This is where you direct the program to use the four coordinates you worked out earlier to decide whether the player is standing in the field and, if he is, to charge him rent and inform him of this by posting a message to the chat. To do this, type

```
if pos.x>X1 and pos.x<X2 and pos.z>Z1 and pos.z<Z2:
    rent = rent+1
    mc.postToChat("You owe rent:"+str(rent))
```

At this point in the program, you have to be very careful to get the indentation correct. Python uses indentation to work out which program statements belong together. You can see that all of the statements under `while  True:` are indented by one level, so Python knows that all of these statements belong to the `while` loop. But look carefully at the `if` statement: The next two lines in the program are indented another level. This means that these two statements are part of the `if` statement and will run only if your player is standing inside the field.

Save the program again, and run it by choosing Run ⇨ Run Module from the menu.

Have some fun making the player run in and out of the field. When he is inside the field, a message should appear on the chat every second, saying how much rent he has been charged. When he runs out of the field he won't be charged rent. Your program also remembers how much rent you have been charged, so when you run back into the field again, it doesn't forget how much you already owe.

To make this game more fun, your player needs something to do while he's in the field. Create a few random blocks in different locations inside the field and then start your program running again. The challenge is to collect all the blocks while paying as little rent as possible. Just hitting the block to remove it could be considered collecting the block. The program won't know this has happened, but it makes your game more interesting. You can come up with all sorts of objects to scatter throughout the field and challenge your friends to collect them, with the winner being the person who collects all the objects while paying the least rent!

Moving Your Player

There is a way to make your game more challenging and exciting, involving another feature of the Minecraft API that you'll find useful in your game creations—moving the player to a different position in the Minecraft world! To do this, you modify your existing rent.py program so that if the player is in the field for more than three seconds, he gets catapulted into the sky and out of the field and has to get back into the field again.

You first need to find a position just outside the field where you want the player to land when he has been in the field for too long. The simplest way to do this might be to look at the biggest of the x and z coordinates for your field, and add 2 to each of them to get some new coordinates. For the dramatic effect you are going to create, choose a y coordinate that is up in the sky. The actual number you choose depends how far up in the Minecraft world you have built your field, but if your field is built at $y = 0$ then you could choose a value for y that is round about 10. This catapults your player into the sky, and gravity makes him fall to the ground again.

You are now going to modify your rent.py program so that if the player is in the field for more than three seconds he gets thrown out of the field. Use the following steps:

1. Set three new constants at the top of your program that remember a home position. This home position is just outside of the field, and when your player gets catapulted out of the field they are moved to these coordinates. The new lines to add are marked in bold:

```
X1 = 10
Z1 = 10
X2 = 20
Z2 = 20

HOME_X = X2 + 2
HOME_Y = 10
HOME_Z = Z2 + 2
```

2. Now you are going to time how long your player is in the field. To do this you need another variable, which you can call `inField`. It stores the number of seconds that the player has been in the field, and it will be used to decide when your player has been in the field for too long! Again, you only need to add the parts shown in bold:

```
rent = 0
inField = 0
```

3. Add a line of code that adds 1 to the `inField` variable if the player is in the field. To do this, add the code shown in bold:

```
if pos.x>X1 and pos.x<X2 and pos.z>Z1 and pos.z<Z2:
    rent = rent+1
    mc.postToChat("You owe rent:"+str(rent))
    inField = inField+1
```

4. Now you're going to add an `else` statement so that the program resets the timer to zero if the player is not in the field. Make sure you get the indentation correct on the `else` statement so that Python knows exactly what you mean. You learn about the `else` statement in a moment as well as what the # symbol is used for but, for now, just type in the code shown in bold:

```
    mc.postToChat("You owe rent:"+str(rent))
    inField = inField+1
else: # not inside the field
    inField = 0
```

5. Add some additional lines of code at the end of the program to catapult the player into the sky and out of the field if he is in the field for more than three seconds. Gravity makes him fall to the ground and he has to run back into the field again. This code goes right at the end of your program. The `if` must be indented one level because it is part of the `while  True` loop, and the statements that belong to the `if` must be indented two levels from the far left of the program. Type the following:

```
if inField>3:
    mc.postToChat("Too slow!")
    mc.player.setPos(HOME_X, pos.y + HOME_Y, HOME_Z)
```

6. Save your program and run it using Run ⇨ Run Module from the editor menu.

You should be having a lot of fun with the game now because you have to plan your strategy carefully, running in and out of the field to avoid getting catapulted into the sky! (See Figure 2-10.) Now, as you did before, choose a variety of objects and scatter them randomly around the field. Challenge yourself and your friends to "collect" (that is, destroy) as many blocks as you can, while clocking up the smallest possible rent bill.

FIGURE 2-10 Your player is catapulted up into the sky when he has been in the field for too long.

DIGGING INTO THE CODE

You have now used two new parts of the Python language, and these need to be explained further.

First, you used an `else` statement. `else` is an optional part of an `if` statement. It should always be at the same indent level as the `if` that you pair it with, and the statements that you want to run as part of the `else` should also be indented. Here is an example:

```
if a>3:
  print("big")
else:
  print("small")
```

If the `a` variable holds a value greater than 3, Python prints "big" on the Python Shell, *else* (meaning, if it is not greater than 3) it prints "small" on the Python Shell. Or put another way, if `a>3` is `True`, it prints big, else if `a>3` is `False`, it prints small.

An `if` statement doesn't have to have an `else` (it is optional), but sometimes in your programs you want to handle the part that is true in a different way than the part that is false.

continued

continued

The other thing you used here was a comment. You will find comments a useful way of leaving little reminders in your program for yourself or anyone else who reads it.

A comment starts with a hash symbol, like this:

```
# this is a comment
```

You can put a comment anywhere on a line. Wherever you put a hash symbol, everything to the end of that line is ignored by the Python language.

Further Adventures in Tracking Your Player

In this adventure, you have learned and put into practice the basics of a game loop, using sensing and geo-fencing, to create a fun game. When you make games, it's a great idea to get your friends and family to play them and tell you what they like or don't like about them. It's a good way of getting feedback to help you improve the game.

- The Welcome Home Game has a problem: If your player stands on the doormat, it repeatedly says "welcome home" and fills up the chat. Can you think of a way to modify this program so that it only says "welcome home" one time when you come into your house?

- A good way to come up with ideas for exciting games is to play other games and see how they keep the player gripped. Play lots of other computer games and make a list of as many different things as possible that a game could do, in terms of the player's position changing.

- Search the Internet for geo-fencing and see if you can find some of the ways it is used to good effect in industry. If any of these ideas grab your interest, have a go at writing a Minecraft program that uses some aspect of them by writing your own simple game based on what you have learned in this adventure.

Quick Reference Table

Command	Description
`import mcpi.minecraft as minecraft`	Importing the Minecraft API
`mc = minecraft.Minecraft.create()`	Creating a connection to Minecraft

`pos = mc.player.getTilePos()`
 	
`x = pos.x`
 	
`y = pos.y`
 	
`z = pos.z`
	Getting the player's tile position

`mc.postToChat("Hello Minecraft")`	Posting a message to the Minecraft chat

`x = 5`
 	
`y = 3`
 	
`z = 7`
 	
`mc.player.setTilePos(x, y, z)`
	Setting the player's tile position

Achievement Unlocked: **Creator of an exciting game that changes as your player moves around in Minecraft.**

In the Next Adventure. . .

In Adventure 3, you learn how to automate the building of large structures such as houses, using Minecraft blocks and Python loops. With a Python program you can build huge structures much faster than you could build them by hand. You can construct a whole Minecraft town in Python in less time than it takes your friends to build it manually.

Adventure 3

Building Anything Automatically

BUILDING THINGS IN Minecraft is great fun. You can build almost anything you can dream up, limited only by the size of the Minecraft world and your imagination. You can build houses, castles, underground waterways, multi-storey hotels with swimming pools, and even whole towns and cities! But it can take a lot of time and hard work to build complex objects with many different types of blocks, especially if there is a lot of repetition. What if you could automate some of your building tasks? Wouldn't that look like magic to your friends?

A programming language like Python is ideal for automating complex tasks. In this adventure, you learn some magic that allows you to automatically build large numbers of blocks inside the Minecraft world and then loop through those instructions to build huge repeating structures, such as a whole street of houses (see Figure 3-1). Your friends will be amazed at your huge creations as they walk through rows and rows of houses and wonder how you built such complex structures! You also learn how to read numbers from the keyboard when your program first runs, which enables you to write programs that your users can vary without changing your program code!

FIGURE 3-1 A house built from Minecraft blocks

Creating Blocks

Each type of block in the Minecraft world has its own block number. If you are a regular Minecraft gamer, you probably already know a lot of block types by their numbers. However, the Minecraft programming interface allows you to refer to block types by name rather than number, which makes things much easier. The name is just a constant (you met constants in Adventure 2) that holds the number of the block type. There is a list of the most common block types and their names and numbers in the reference section in Appendix B.

The Minecraft world is divided into invisible cubes (each with its own unique coordinate), and the computer remembers the number of the type of block that's in that invisible cube at any one time, even if it's just a block of type AIR. As a Minecraft programmer, you can ask the Minecraft programming interface for the block type at any particular coordinate, and you can change the block type of the block at any coordinate. This changes the block that is displayed there. You can, for example, build bridges by changing the block type from AIR to STONE, and you do this in Adventure 4.

You are now going to start by writing a simple program that demonstrates this, by automatically placing a single block immediately in front of your player. Once you can place a single block in the Minecraft world, you can build anything you can possibly imagine, automatically!

1. Start Minecraft, IDLE, and if you are working on a PC or a Mac, start the server, too. You should have had a bit of practice with starting everything up by now, but refer to Adventure 1 if you need any reminders.

2. Open IDLE, the Python Integrated Development Environment (IDE). This is your window into the Python programming language and where you type and run all your Python programs.

3. Choose File ⇨ New File from the menu. Save this program by choosing File ⇨ Save As and name the file `block.py`. Remember to store your programs inside the `MyAdventures` folder, otherwise they won't work.

4. Import the modules you need for this adventure. You use an extra module called `block`, which holds all the constant numbers for all the block types that Minecraft supports. Do this by typing

```
import mcpi.minecraft as minecraft
import mcpi.block as block
```

5. Connect to the Minecraft game by typing

```
mc = minecraft.Minecraft.create()
```

6. Get your player's position into the `pos` variable. You use this position to calculate the coordinates of a space in front of your player, where you are going to create your new block:

```
pos = mc.player.getTilePos()
```

7. Now create a block in front of the player, using coordinates that are relative to your player's position. You can read all about **relative coordinates** after this section. By using `pos+3` in your program it ensures that the stone block doesn't appear right on top of your player! Do this by typing

```
mc.setBlock(pos.x+3, pos.y, pos.z, block.STONE.id)
```

8. Choose File ⇨ Save to save your program and then run it by choosing Run ⇨ Run Module from the Editor menu.

You should now see a block of stone very close to your player! (If you don't see the block of stone, you may have to turn your player round to see it.) You have just programmed the Minecraft world to create a block in front of you. From these simple beginnings, you can now create some really interesting structures automatically by programming Minecraft.

CHALLENGE

Stone isn't a very interesting block. Look at the blocks in Appendix B and experiment by changing the STONE in this program to other blocks. Some of the blocks don't work on all platforms, so Appendix B lists which platforms they work on.

GLOWING_OBSIDIAN for example works on the Raspberry Pi, but not on the PC/Mac versions. Some blocks are affected by gravity, so experiment with WATER and SAND for some interesting effects!

Relative coordinates refer to a set of coordinates such that their position is relative to some other point (or in Minecraft, your player). For example, `pos.x`, `pos.y+10`, `pos.z+3` is a location inside the Minecraft world 10 blocks above and 3 blocks south of your player: In other words, the coordinates are relative to the position of your player. As your player moves around the Minecraft world, the relative coordinates change as well.

Absolute coordinates refer to a set of coordinates that uses numbers at a fixed location to represent the location of a point (or in the case of Minecraft, a block). The coordinates `x=10`, `y=10`, `z=15` are an example of absolute coordinates. Every time you use these coordinates you refer to a block at location 10, 10, 15 inside the Minecraft world, which is always the same location.

CHALLENGE

If you have already done Adventure 2, load and run your `whereAmI.py` program and move to a location in the Minecraft world that has some free space. Jot down the x, y and z coordinates where your player is standing. Modify your `block.py` program to `setBlock()` at that **absolute coordinate**, and run the program to see what it does. How do you think relative coordinates and absolute coordinates might help in your programs?

Building More Than One Block

From this basic beginning, you can build anything! You can now extend your program to build more than one block. When you are building with Minecraft blocks, the only thing you need to remember is that you need to use some simple maths to work out the coordinates of each block that you want to create.

You are now going to extend your `build.py` program to create five more blocks in front of your player, using one `setBlock()` for each block that you want to create. The program you're about to write creates a structure that looks a bit like the dots on a dice. To do this, work through the following steps:

1. Start by choosing File ⇨ Save As from the Editor menu and saving your program as `dice.py`.

2. Add these lines to the end of the program:

```
mc.setBlock(pos.x+3, pos.y+2, pos.z,   block.STONE.id)
mc.setBlock(pos.x+3, pos.y+4, pos.z,   block.STONE.id)
mc.setBlock(pos.x+3, pos.y,   pos.z+4, block.STONE.id)
mc.setBlock(pos.x+3, pos.y+2, pos.z+4, block.STONE.id)
mc.setBlock(pos.x+3, pos.y+4, pos.z+4, block.STONE.id)
```

3. Save the program and run it. You should see a simple structure that looks like six dots on a dice, in front of your player! (See Figure 3-2.)

FIGURE 3-2 The Minecraft dice in front of the player shows six stone dots.

CHALLENGE

Modify the `dice.py` program so that some of the space around the stone dots is filled in with a white block, so that it looks more like the square face of a dice. Experiment with setting different blocks to `STONE` or `AIR` to create different numbers on the dice. Remember that there is a detailed list of blocks in Appendix B.

Using for Loops

Building with individual blocks allows you to build anything you like, but it's a bit like drawing a complex picture on a computer screen by hand, one dot at a time. What you need is some way to repeat blocks, so that you can build bigger structures without increasing the size of your program.

Fortunately, like any programming language, Python has a feature called a loop. You encountered loops already in Adventure 2 with the `while True:` game loop. A loop is just a way of repeating things multiple times in a programming language like Python. The loop you use here is called a `for` loop, sometimes called a counted loop because it counts a fixed number of times.

Building Multiple Blocks with a for Loop

To understand how a `for` loop works, use the Python Shell to try one out by following these steps:

1. Click the Python Shell window, just to the right of the last `>>>` prompt.

2. Type the following and press the Enter key on the keyboard:

   `for a in range(10):`

   Python won't do anything yet because it is expecting the program statements that belong to the loop (these are often called the loop body).

3. The Python Shell automatically indents the next line for you by one level, so that Python knows that your `print()` statement belongs to the `for` loop. Now type this `print()` statement:

   `print(a)`

Just as you did with the `while` loop you used to build your game loop in Adventure 2, you must indent the program statements that belong to the `for` loop, so the Python language knows that only these statements should be repeated every time the loop runs.

4. Press the Enter key twice. Your first press marks the end of the `print()` statement; your second tells the Python Shell that you have finished the loop.

You should now see the numbers 0 to 9 printed on the Python Shell screen.

DIGGING INTO THE CODE

The `for` loop that you just used has some interesting features:

```
for a in range(10):
  print(a)
```

The `a` in this case is called the loop control variable. This means it is the variable that is used to hold the value of the loop every time it runs the code in the loop body. The first time it runs, it has the number 0 in it, the second time it has the number 1 in it, and so on.

The `range(10)` tells Python that you want it to generate a sequence of ten numbers from 0 to 9, through which the `for` loop will count.

The colon (`:`) at the end is just like the colon that you used in earlier adventures with your `while` loop and your `if` statements. The colon marks where the body code begins. The body code is the code that (in this case) is to be repeated 10 times.

Any Python statements inside the loop (in other words, the statements that are indented one level from the `for` statement) are able to access the variable `a` and this variable holds a different value each time round the loop.

You can use the loop control variable `a` anywhere in the program statements inside the loop body for any purpose. You don't have to call the variable `a` all the time. You can think up any name you like for it, and it is good practice to think up variable names that are more descriptive, so that others who read your program can more easily understand it. A better name here for the variable instead of `a` would be `count` or `number_of_times`.

Building a Huge Tower with a for Loop

How would you like to build an enormous tower out of blocks inside the Minecraft world? Now that you know all about `for` loops, you can. Just follow these steps:

1. Start writing a new program by choosing File ⇨ New File from the menu. Choose File ⇨ Save As from the menu, and name it `tower.py`.

2. As usual, import the modules you need:

   ```
   import mcpi.minecraft as minecraft
   import mcpi.block as block
   ```

3. Connect to the Minecraft game:

   ```
   mc = minecraft.Minecraft.create()
   ```

4. If you build your tower where your player is standing it is easier to find, so your first job is to identify the position of your player by typing

```
pos = mc.player.getTilePos()
```

5. Your tower is going to be 50 blocks high, so start building it with a `for` loop that counts 50 times. Don't forget the colon (:) at the end of the line:

```
for a in range(50):
```

6. The next line is indented because it belongs to the body of the `for` loop. The y coordinate controls height within the Minecraft world, so add the loop control variable `a` onto the player's y position. This tells the program to build at an increasing height in the Minecraft world each time round the loop:

```
mc.setBlock(pos.x+3, pos.y+a, pos.z, block.STONE.id)
```

7. Save the program and run it. Has it worked? Your `for` loop should have created a massive tower in front of your player, similar to the one in Figure 3-3. Start counting—is it 50 blocks high?

FIGURE 3-3 This huge tower was created inside the Minecraft world using a `for` loop.

DAVID SAYS...

In the previous code, the `for` loop cycles around 50 times, and each time round the loop, it runs the indented lines below it, such that the `a` variable has a value one bigger than the previous time round the loop. It adds the value in the `a` variable (the loop control variable) onto the `pos.y` variable (which is the player's height above bedrock). This then creates a tower 50 blocks high!

Clearing Some Space

Sometimes, finding enough space in the Minecraft world to build your structures can be a bit frustrating. There are usually a lot of trees and mountains around your player, meaning there is often not enough space to build big structures. You can solve this problem by writing a program that clears some space for you to build whatever you want.

Using setBlocks to Build Even Faster

All the blocks in the Minecraft world have a block identity (id) number, and this includes the blank spaces that you see in front of you, called `block.AIR.id`. So, if you make sure every block in a large area is set to `block.AIR.id`, it clears a nice space ready for building other objects. The id number (which is the block type number discussed earlier) is listed in Appendix B for the most common blocks you use. For example, `block.AIR.id` is 0 and `block.STONE.id` is 1. Remember, the empty space you see in the Minecraft world is really just a block with a block id of `block.AIR.id`—it is a 1 metre cube space filled with air!

Computers are very fast, but the more program statements you use inside a `for` loop, the longer the program takes to run. It takes a little while for the Minecraft game to interpret your request to set a block inside the world, change the block type, and update the display on the screen. You could always write a big loop that sets hundreds of blocks in front of you to `block.AIR.id` to clear some space, and that would work, but it would be really slow. Fortunately there is a better way to set a lot of blocks in one go, and it is called `setBlocks()`. (Note the extra `s` at the end of the name.) `setBlock()` sets one block; `setBlocks()` sets a whole 3D area of blocks in one go!

The Minecraft programming interface has a `setBlocks()` statement that you can use to give all the blocks inside a three-dimensional (3D) rectangular space the same block id. Because this is a single request to the Minecraft game, Minecraft can optimise how it does this work, meaning it runs much quicker than if you used a `setBlock()` inside a `for` loop like you did with the tower.

Because `setBlocks()` works on a 3D area, it needs two sets of coordinates—the coordinates of one corner of the 3D rectangle, and the coordinates of the opposite corner. Because each 3D coordinate has three numbers, you need six numbers to completely describe a 3D space to Minecraft.

You are now going to write a useful little utility program that you can use any time you want to clear a bit of space in front of you to do some building:

1. Start a new program by choosing File ⇨ New File from the menu.

2. Save the program using File ⇨ Save As and choose the name `clearSpace.py`.

3. Import the modules that you need:

   ```
   import mcpi.minecraft as minecraft
   import mcpi.block as block
   ```

4. Connect to the Minecraft game:

   ```
   mc = minecraft.Minecraft.create()
   ```

5. You want to clear space in front of the player, and you use relative coordinates to do this. First get the player's position:

   ```
   pos = mc.player.getTilePos()
   ```

6. Now clear a space that is 50 by 50 by 50 blocks. The bottom-left corner of your space is the position of your player, and the top-right corner will be 50 blocks away in the x, y and z dimensions:

   ```
   mc.setBlocks(pos.x, pos.y, pos.z, pos.x+50, pos.y+50, ↵
      pos.z+50, block.AIR.id)
   ```

7. Save your program.

The fantastic thing about the program you've just created is that it allows you to walk to any location inside Minecraft and clear a 50 by 50 by 50 area any time you like; just run the program by choosing Run ⇨ Run Module from the menu, and the trees and mountains and everything nearby magically vanish before your eyes!

Move around the Minecraft world and re-run your program to clear lots of space in front of your player.

Reading Input from the Keyboard

Another useful thing you can do to your `clearSpace.py` program is to make it easy to change the size of the space that is cleared. That way, if you are only going to build a small structure, you can clear a small space but if you know you are going to build lots of big structures, you can clear a huge space first.

To do this, you use a new Python statement called `input()` to read a number from the keyboard first. You can then go to any part of the Minecraft world, run your program and simply type in a number representing the size of the space you want to clear; your program clears all that space for you. This means you don't have to keep modifying your program every time you want to clear a different size of area in the Minecraft world.

There are two main versions of Python—Python 2 and Python 3. The Minecraft programming interface now works on both versions. However, Python 2 uses `raw_input()` to read from the keyboard, whereas Python 3 uses `input()`. The programs in this book all use Python 3; if you see programs on the Internet designed for use with Python 2, you see `raw_input()` used instead.

Now that you understand what `input()` does, it's time to add it to your program. To do this, you have to make only two small modifications to your `clearSpace.py` program. Follow these steps:

1. Use `input()` to ask the user to type a number that represents the size of the space to clear, and store that number inside a variable called `size`. Just like in Adventure 2, where you used `str()` to convert something to a string, here you use `int()` to convert the string from `input()` into a number that you can perform calculations with. Try this line without the `int()` to see what happens! Type only the new lines that are marked in **bold**:

```
pos = mc.player.getTilePos()
size = int(input("size of area to clear? "))
```

2. Modify the `setBlocks()` line so that instead of using the number 50, it uses your new variable `size`:

```
mc.setBlocks(pos.x, pos.y, pos.z,
             pos.x + size, pos.y + size, pos.z + size,
             block.AIR.id)
```

3. Save your program and run it by choosing Run ⇨ Run Module from the menu.

Now move to somewhere in the Minecraft world where there are lots of trees or mountains. Type a number into the Python Shell Window when prompted—perhaps choose 100 or something like that—and press the Enter key on the keyboard. All the trees and mountains near your player should magically disappear and, as in Figure 3-4, you will have a nice space to build other structures!

Keep this little utility program, as it will be useful later when you need to clear a bit of space in the Minecraft world.

FIGURE 3-4 After running `clearSpace.py` you have a great clear area to build more exciting structures!

Building a House

When playing Minecraft in survival mode, one of the first things you need to is build a shelter for your player to protect him from the dangers lurking in the Minecraft night. What if you could build a house with the touch of a button? Fortunately, when programming with Minecraft, you can turn complex tasks into just that—the touch of a button.

In the `clearSpace.py` program, you learned how to set a large number of blocks to the same block type, by using just one programming statement. Now you are going to learn how to use the same techniques to build a house really quickly.

One way to build a house might be to build each wall using a separate `setBlocks()`. For that, you need to use four separate `setBlocks()` and quite a lot of maths to work out all the coordinates of every corner of every wall. Fortunately, there is a quicker way to build hollow rectangular structures: All you have to do is build a huge cuboid space, and then use `setBlocks()` again with slightly different coordinates to carve out the inside with the `AIR` block type.

Before you go any further, you need take some time to make sure you understand the maths associated with the design of the house you are going to build, as you need to get the coordinates right to write the program. Figure 3-5 shows a sketch of the house design, labelled with all the important coordinates that you use to build it. When you are building something complex, it is important to sketch it out on paper and work out all the important coordinates first. This is a very special house because your Python program calculates the size and position of the doorway and windows automatically. A little later you see a little later why this is important.

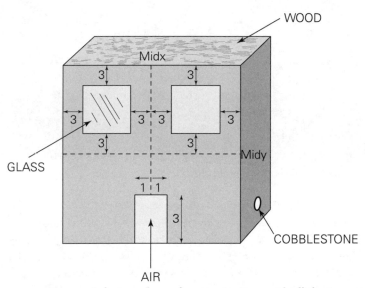

FIGURE 3-5 A design of your house on paper, with all the important coordinates worked out

To watch a tutorial on how to build your house, visit the companion website at www. wiley.com/go/adventuresinminecraft2e and choose the Adventure 3 Video.

Now that you have a design for your house, try to build it by following these steps:

1. Start a new program by choosing File ⇨ New File from the menu.

2. Save this program by using File ⇨ Save As from the menu, and call your program `buildHouse.py`.

3. Import the required modules:

```
import mcpi.minecraft as minecraft
import mcpi.block as block
```

4. Connect to the Minecraft game:

```
mc = minecraft.Minecraft.create()
```

5. Use a constant for the size of your house. You use this SIZE constant quite a lot in your house builder code. Using a constant here, instead of using the number 20 all over your code, makes it much easier to alter the size of your house later:

```
SIZE = 20
```

Remember that it is a programmer's convention that you put constants in uppercase. There is no rule in the Python language that says you have to do this, but it helps you to remember that this is a constant and you intend it not to be changed while the program is running.

6. Get the player's position so you can build the house just nearby:

```
pos = mc.player.getTilePos()
```

7. Store the x, y and z coordinates of the player in new variables. This makes the next few program statements easier to type and read and helps when you come to do some other clever construction tasks with your house design later on. The x variable is set to two blocks away from the player position, so that the house is not built right on top of the player:

```
x = pos.x+2
y = pos.y
z = pos.z
```

8. Calculate two variables called `midx` and `midy`, which are the midpoints of the front of your house in the x and y directions. This makes it easier for you to work out the coordinates of the windows and doorway later on, so that if you change

the size of your house, the windows and doorway will change their position too and fit properly.

```
midx = x + SIZE/2
midy = y + SIZE/2
```

9. Build the outer shell of the house as a huge rectangular 3D area. You can choose any block type here, but cobblestone is a good one to start with, making it an old house:

```
mc.setBlocks(x, y, z,
             x + SIZE, y + SIZE, z + SIZE,
             block.COBBLESTONE.id)
```

10. Now carve out the inside of the house by filling it with air. Note how you have used the simple maths from your design to work out the coordinates of the air inside the house, as relative coordinates to the outer corners of the cobblestone of the house:

```
mc.setBlocks(x + 1, y, z + 1,
             x + SIZE - 1, y + SIZE - 1, z + SIZE - 1,
             block.AIR.id)
```

11. Carve out a space for the doorway, again using the AIR block type. You won't use a normal Minecraft door here, because this is a huge house. Instead you create a large doorway that is three blocks high and two blocks wide. Your doorway needs to be in the middle of the front face of the house, so midx gives you that middle x coordinate:

```
mc.setBlocks(midx - 1, y, z,
             midx + 1, y + 3, z,
             block.AIR.id)
```

12. Carve out two windows using the block type GLASS. As this is a large house, you build the windows three blocks from the outer edge of the house and three blocks from the middle point of the front of the house. If you change your SIZE constant and run the program again, all the calculations in the program automatically adjust the positioning of everything and the doorway and windows will be in the right place so it still looks like a house.

```
mc.setBlocks(x + 3, y + SIZE - 3, z,
             midx - 3, midy + 3, z,
             block.GLASS.id)
mc.setBlocks(midx + 3, y + SIZE - 3, z,
             x + SIZE - 3, midy + 3, z,
             block.GLASS.id)
```

13. Add a wooden roof:

```
mc.setBlocks(x, y + SIZE - 1, z,
             x + SIZE, y + SIZE, z + SIZE,
             block.WOOD.id)
```

14. Now, add a woollen carpet:

```
mc.setBlocks(x + 1, y - 1, z + 1,
             x + SIZE - 2, y - 1, z + SIZE - 2,
             block.WOOL.id, 14)
```

You'll see there is an extra number at the end of `setBlocks()`. This number sets the colour of the carpet; in this case, it is number 14, which is red. This is explained in the following Digging into the Code sidebar.

Save your program, then move to somewhere in your Minecraft world where there is a bit of space and run your program by choosing Run ⇨ Run Module from the menu. You should see your house miraculously materialise in front of your eyes! Walk inside and explore it. Look up at the roof and through the windows, and marvel at how quickly you built this house from scratch! (See Figure 3-6.)

Don't forget that `buildHouse.py` always builds the house relative to your player's position. Move around the Minecraft world and run `buildHouse.py` again to build another house. You can build houses all over your Minecraft world—how cool is that?

FIGURE 3-6 This house was built automatically by a Python program.

DIGGING INTO THE CODE

When you built your carpet, you used an extra number with `setBlocks()`:

```
mc.setBlocks(x1, y1, z1, x2, y2, z2, block.WOOL.id, 14)
```

Let's dig into that and work out what it means.

`WOOL` is a really interesting block type because it has what is called 'extra data'. This means that not only can you ask for the block to be wool but you can also use this extra data to change the appearance of the `WOOL` block. There are other blocks in the Minecraft world that have extra data, too, and each type of block uses it in a different way. For `WOOL`, the "extra data" number selects the colour of the block. This useful feature makes `WOOL` a versatile block to build with, because you can choose any colour from a palette of supported colours, allowing you to make your designs much more colourful and realistic.

At the end of this adventure is a table listing the numbers and their associated colours for the `WOOL` block. Appendix B also lists various other block types that have an extra data value that you can change. TNT has a really interesting extra data value, which makes it possible to explode by 'arming' it.

If you have seen other Minecraft programs on the Internet, you might be wondering why in this book blocks are always referred to like this: `block.WOOL.id`. Why do you always put the `.id` at the end of the block? And why is it that other programs on the Internet don't do this? This is because `setBlock()` and `setBlocks()` sometimes don't work when the 'extra data' field is used, unless you put the `.id` at the end of the block. So, to keep everything simple and consistent in this book, we decided always to use `.id` with blocks so that every time you use it, it looks the same. You don't always have to put the `.id` at the end, but it makes sense to put it there so you don't have to remember when you have to use it and when you don't.

Try changing the `SIZE` constant in your program to a bigger number, such as 50, and running your program again. What happens to your house when you do this? Try changing `SIZE` to a small number like 10. What happens to your house now? Why do you think this happens when the number stored in the `SIZE` constant is very small?

Building More Than One House

Building one house is fun, but why stop there? Thinking back to your `tower.py` program from earlier in this adventure, it's easy to write a `for` loop that repeats program statements a fixed number of times. So, it must therefore be possible to build a whole street of houses, or even a whole town, just by looping through your house-building program many times.

Before you do this, though, you're going to improve your house-building program a little, to make sure it doesn't get too big and complex to manage.

Using Python Functions

One of the things you might want to do later is build a whole town with houses of many different designs. The program for a whole town could become quite big and complex, but fortunately there is feature inside the Python programming language that helps you package up that complexity into little chunks of reusable program code. It is called a **function.**

With a Python **function** you can group related Python program statements and give them a name. Whenever you want to run those program statements as a group, you just use the name of the function with brackets after it.

You might not realise it, but you have been using functions all the way through this book, ever since you posted a message to the Minecraft chat with `mc.postToChat("hello")` in the very first adventure. `postToChat()` is a function, which is just a group of related program statements that are run whenever you use the word `postToChat()` inside your program.

Before you change your working `buildHouse.py` program to use a function for the house, try out some functions at the Python Shell to make sure you understand the idea:

1. Click the Python Shell window to bring it to the front.

2. Type the following into the Shell window, which defines a new function called `myname`:

```
def myname():
```

The `def` means 'define a new function and here is its name'. Just like earlier with the `while`, `if` and `for` statements, you must put a colon (`:`) at the end of the line so that Python knows to expect you to provide other program statements as part of the body of this function.

3. The Python Shell automatically indents the next line for you, so that Python knows they are part of the function. Type a few lines of `print` statements that print your name and information about yourself. Don't be surprised that nothing happens as you type each line; that is correct. Be patient, all will become clear in a moment!

```
print("my name is David")
print("I am a computer programmer")
print("I love Minecraft programming")
```

4. Press the Enter key on the keyboard twice, and the Python Shell recognises that you have finished typing in indented statements.

5. Ask the Python Shell to run this function by typing its name with brackets after it:

```
myname()
```

6. Try typing `myname()` a few more times to see what happens.

At first it might seem a little strange that you typed instructions into the Python Shell but nothing happened. Normally when you type at the Python Shell, things happen as soon as you press the Enter key, so why didn't it work this time? This time, you did something different, however: You "defined" a new function called `myname` and asked Python to remember the three `print` statements as belonging to that function. Python has stored those `print` statements in the computer memory, rather than running them straight away. Now, whenever you type `myname()` it runs those stored statements, and you get your three lines of text printed on the screen.

Functions are very powerful, and allow you to associate any number of Python program statements to a simple name, a little bit like a mini-program. Whenever you want those program statements to run, you just type the name of the function.

Let's put this to good use by defining a function that draws your house. Then, whenever you want a house made from cobblestone, all you have to do is type `house()`, and it is built automatically for you!

1. So that you don't break your already working `buildHouse.py`, choose File⇨ Save As from the Editor menu, and call the new file `buildHouse2.py`.

2. At the top of the program after the `import` statements, define a new function called `house`:

```
def house():
```

3. Move the `midx`, `midy` and all of your `setBlocks()` statements so that they are indented under the `def  house():` line. Here is what your program should now look like. Be careful to get the indents correct:

```
import mcpi.minecraft as minecraft
import mcpi.block as block
mc = minecraft.Minecraft.create()
SIZE = 20
def house():
    midx = x + SIZE/2
    midy = y + SIZE/2
    mc.setBlocks(x, y, z, x+SIZE, y+SIZE, z+SIZE, ↵
        block.COBBLESTONE.id)
    mc.setBlocks(x+1, y+1, z+1, x+SIZE-1, y+SIZE-1, ↵
        z+SIZE-1, block.AIR.id)
    mc.setBlocks(x+3, y+SIZE-3, z, midx-3, midy+3, z, ↵
        block.GLASS.id)
    mc.setBlocks(midx+3, y+SIZE-3, z, x+SIZE-3, midy-3, z, ↵
        block.GLASS.id)
    mc.setBlocks(x, y+SIZE, z, x+SIZE, y+SIZE, z+SIZE, ↵
        block.SLATE.id)
    mc.setBlocks(x+1, y+1, z+1, x+SIZE-1, y+1, z+SIZE-1, ↵
        block.WOOL.id, 7)
pos = mc.player.getTilePos()
x = pos.x
y = pos.y
z = pos.z
house()
```

4. Notice how, in the last statement of your program, you have just put the name `house()`. This line runs the code that is now stored in the computer's memory, which was set up by the `def  house():` statement.

5. Save your program, move to a new location and run your program. You should see a house get built in front of you.

You might be thinking at this point, "so what?" You changed your program by moving some program statements around and it just does exactly the same thing! Sometimes, when you are writing computer programs, it is necessary to improve the layout or structure of the program first, before you can do more amazing things with it afterwards. That is just what you have done here. You have restructured your program slightly, so that it is now easier to reuse your house-building code many times.

CHALLENGE

The `house()` function always builds the house relative to the coordinates stored in `x`, `y` and `z`. Add some extra statements at the end of your program that change the `x`, `y` and `z` variables and then insert another `house()` to see what happens. How many houses do you think you could build like this?

DIGGING INTO THE CODE

In your new program, by putting all of your `setBlocks()` statements into the function `house()`, there is an extra little bit of magic that is taking place.

The variables `x`, `y` `z`, and the constant `SIZE` are all called **global** variables. They are global because they are first given a value inside the main program (the non-indented part). Because they are global, it means they can be used anywhere in the program, including inside the `house()` function. So, if you did some experiments and drew a few different houses, by changing the value of `x`, `y` and `z` in the main program, because these variables are global and can be used anywhere in the whole program, this works.

In Adventure 5 you learn that global variables can make a large program very hard to fix when it goes wrong, and there is a better way to share information with functions. However, for now, this use of global variables is good enough and your program is small enough that it doesn't cause a problem.

A **global** variable is a variable that can be used anywhere in the program. Any variables (and also constants) defined without a left-hand indent are global and can be accessed from anywhere in the program. So, if you use a = 1 and it has no left-hand indent, you can use that variable anywhere in that program.

However, any variables that are defined with some left-hand indent are not global (often called local variables). So, if you use a = 1 inside the indented region under a def statement (that is *inside* the function) then that variable cannot be accessed from code anywhere except from within the indented region of that function. There is more to learn about global variables, but that's all you need to know about them at this point.

Building a Street of Houses with a for Loop

You are now ready to put together all the things you have learned in this chapter and build a huge street of houses. If you were building all of these houses manually by choosing items from the inventory, it might take you hours to build them, and you might make mistakes in building them or make some of them slightly smaller or larger by accident. By automating the building of houses and other structures with Minecraft programming, you can speed things up and make sure that they are perfectly built to a very precise size!

To build lots of houses, you need to add a for loop to your program as follows:

1. So that you don't break your existing buildHouse2.py program, use File ➪ Save As from the menu and save a new file called buildStreet.py.

2. At the end of the program, add a for loop above the final house() along with a line that changes the x position where the house is built. Each house is built SIZE blocks away from the previous house. The new lines are marked in **bold**:

```
for h in range(5):
    house()
    x = x + SIZE
```

Save your program, then move to a place in the Minecraft world where there is a bit of space, and run the program. As shown in Figure 3-7, you should get a huge street of five houses as far as the eye can see! Walk your player into each of the houses and make sure that they have been built properly.

FIGURE 3-7 A street of five identical houses built automatically with a Python program

CHALLENGE

How could you modify your loop so that instead of building your houses in a row, it builds them upwards to create a huge tower block? Try it. Turn your tower block builder into a function called `tower()` and then use a loop to build a few tower blocks inside your Minecraft world.

Depending on where your player is standing when you build your houses, and how much other terrain is around, like trees and mountains, you might get some interesting effects on some of your houses. One of them might chop off half of a tree, or be partly built into a mountain. You might even get some interesting subsidence if your houses end up being built on top of the sea! You might like to modify your `house()` function to build a layer of bedrock under the house so that it is always on solid ground.

Adding Random Carpets

At this point, you should have a huge number of houses inside your Minecraft world, and things are looking pretty awesome. From a small number of lines of Python code, you've built some large engineering structures already!

However, you're probably thinking that having a street of identical houses is starting to look a little boring. How can you make the houses slightly different to add interest to your street?

One way to do this is to write a few different `house()` functions like `cottage()`, `townHouse()` and even `maisonette()`, and modify your program to use these different functions at different places to add some variety to your street designs.

Another way to make your structures more interesting is to slightly change part of them, such as the carpets, in a way that is different every time you run the program. This way even you, the programmer, won't know quite what you have created until you explore all the houses!

Generating Random Numbers

Computers are very precise machines. In many aspects of everyday life, we all rely on computers to be predictable and to do the same thing every time a program is run. When you pay £10 into your bank account, you want to make sure that exactly £10 makes it into the part of the computer's memory that holds your balance, every time, without fail. So the concept of randomness might seem quite unusual to such a precise system.

However, one area where randomness is really important is in game design. If games did everything exactly the same every time, they would be too easy to play—not fun or challenging at all. Almost every computer game you play has some kind of randomness in it to make things slightly different each time and hold your interest.

Fortunately for your Python programming, the Python language has a built-in module that generates **random numbers** for you so you don't have to write the code for this yourself; just use this built-in random number generator instead.

To make sure you know what these random numbers look like, try this out at the Python Shell:

1. Click the Python Shell window to bring it to the front.

2. Import the `random` module so that you can use the built-in random function, by typing:

    import random

3. Ask the program to generate a random number between 1 and 100 and print it to the screen:

    print(random.randint(1,100))

    You should see a number between 1 and 100 appear on the screen. Type the `print` statement again. What number do you get this time?

4. Now use a `for` loop to print lots of random numbers. Make sure you indent the second line so that Python knows that the `print` statement is part of the `for` loop:

```
for n in range(50):
  print(random.randint(1,100))
```

The two numbers inside the brackets of the `randint()` function tell it the range of numbers you want it to generate; 1 is the smallest number you should expect it to generate, and 100 the largest.

A **random number** is usually generated from a random number sequence—a list of numbers designed not to have any obvious pattern or repeating sequence.

Computers are very precise machines and often do not generate truly random numbers; instead, they generate pseudo-random numbers. These numbers might seem to be part of a random sequence, but there is a pattern to them. You can read more about random numbers at `http://en.wikipedia.org/wiki/Random_number_generation` and find out more about real random numbers at `www.random.org`.

Laying the Carpets

Earlier in this adventure you used an extra number in the `setBlocks()` function to make the colour of the woollen carpet red, using the extra data of `WOOL`. The allowed range of extra data numbers for `WOOL` is between 0 and 15—in other words, there are 16 colours you can choose from. Now use the following steps to change your house-building program to generate a random number and use that as the colour of `WOOL` for the carpet in the house:

1. Save your `buildStreet.py` with File ⇨ Save As from the menu, and call it `buildStreet2.py`.

2. Add this import statement at the top of the program to gain access to the random number generator:

   `import random`

3. Change your `house()` function so that it generates a random carpet colour each time it is used. As `WOOL` can have an extra data value ranging between 0 and 15, that is the range of random numbers you need to generate. Store the random number in a variable called `c` so that the carpet-building line doesn't become too

long and hard to read, and make sure that both of these lines are indented correctly, as they are both part of the `house()` function:

```
c = random.randint(0, 15)
mc.setBlocks(x+1, y+1, z+1, x+SIZE-1, y+1, z+SIZE-1, ↵
block.WOOL.id, c)
```

4. Save your program.

Now you need to find somewhere in your Minecraft world that has plenty of space to build more houses! Move around the world and find somewhere to build, and then run your new program. It should generate another street of houses, but this time, when your player explores inside the houses, the carpet in each house should be a different, random colour. See Figure 3-8 to see what these new houses look like, but your player needs to actually go into each house and look at the carpets so that you can check they are indeed all different!

FIGURE 3-8 Each house has a random carpet colour.

CHALLENGE

Define a `house2()` function that draws a different type of house. Use randomness in the main `for` loop to create one of two houses based on a random number. Every house you build will be random. Extend this program to build three different types of house. The more different types of house you build, the more interesting your street becomes. You could even experiment with negative coordinates like `y=-5` to build a basement or even a swimming pool inside your house!

DAVID SAYS...

To a large extent, the sort of huge structures you can build in Minecraft is limited only by your imagination. There is a limit to the height of the Minecraft world, of course, and that restricts the height of the tallest structure you can build. And some buildings in real life have slanting or curved structures. For example, look at the design of The Shard, currently the tallest building in the European Union at `www.the-shard.com/`. This amazing building would be possible to build in Minecraft, but because it has slanted edges it is more difficult to build.

Be patient and start with simple structures that are mainly rectangular in shape. In Adventure 6, Martin introduces you to some extra special helper functions that are capable of building angled lines and curves. After that, there will be no limit to the type of buildings you can build in your Minecraft world!

There are two other restrictions on how big you can build things in Minecraft—how much memory the computer has, and how far you can see in front of you. A larger structure takes up more computer memory; the size of the Minecraft world has edges to it, so that the amount of memory required to store it is practical. Secondly, your player can only see a certain distance, especially so on the Raspberry Pi, which has a very limited viewing distance.

Quick Reference Table

Command	Description

`import mcpi.block as block`
 	
`b = block.DIRT.id`
	Importing and using the block name constants

`mc.setBlock(5, 3, 2, block.DIRT.id)`	Setting/changing a block at a position

`block.AIR.id`
 	
`block.STONE.id`
 	
`block.COBBLESTONE.id`
 	
`block.GLASS.id`
 	
`block.WOOD.id`
 	
`block.WOOL.id`
 	
`block.SLATE.id`
	Useful block types for houses

`mc.setBlocks(0,0,0,5,5,5,block.DIRT.id)`	Setting/changing lots of blocks in one go

All of the new Python and Minecraft statements you learned in this chapter are listed in the reference section in Appendix B.

You can find a complete list of block id numbers on the Minecraft wiki: `http://minecraft.gamepedia.com/Blocks`. Minecraft extra data values are taken from `https://minecraft.gamepedia.com/Data_values`.

`Wool` is a very useful block type to build with, as you discovered when laying the random carpets in your street of houses. Here is a reference to the different colours that can be used with the `block.WOOL.id` block type. Look back at your `buildStreet2.py` program to see how to provide this extra data to the Minecraft API.

0 white	1 orange	2 magenta	3 light blue
4 yellow	5 lime	6 pink	7 grey
8 light grey	9 cyan	10 purple	11 blue
12 brown	13 green	14 red	15 black

Further Adventures in Building Anything

In this adventure, you've learned how to create single blocks and whole areas of blocks inside the Minecraft world using a single line of a Python program. You've built some pretty impressive structures already. You've learned that with functions you can split up your program into smaller logical units and, with `for` loops, repeat things over and over again. With this knowledge you should be able to build almost any structure you could possibly imagine!

- Using the techniques learned in this adventure, write one function for each of the six faces of a dice. Write a loop that spins round a random number of times, showing a different dice face each time round. Use `random.randint()` to stop on a random pattern, and challenge yourself and your friends to try and guess the number the Minecraft dice will stop on.

- Make a list of other things you could randomise about your street. Perhaps do some research by walking down your own street and seeing how the houses differ from each other. Define more house functions, one for each type, and try to build more complex streets with houses in lots of different styles.

- Get together with some friends and join all your different house-building programs into one big program. Use it to build a whole community of houses of different styles inside your world. Marvel, as you walk around your new town, at how much variety there is in house design!

Achievement Unlocked: **Designer of remarkable buildings and builder of amazing huge structures inside Minecraft!**

In the Next Adventure. . .

In Adventure 4, you learn how to sense and interact with blocks, including how to detect what type of block you are standing on and how to detect (and what to do) when blocks have been hit by the player. You use all this new knowledge to build an exciting treasure hunt game!

Adventure 4

Interacting with Blocks

ONE WAY YOU can make a Minecraft game more interesting is to make it change what it does based on what is going on around your player. As you move around the game world, the choices that you are faced with depend on what you've already done, which makes the game slightly different every time you play it. The Minecraft API allows you to interact with blocks by finding out what block type you are standing on and detecting when you hit a block with your sword.

In this adventure, you first learn the basics of interacting with blocks by writing a magic bridge program. This bridge is special, because as you walk on water or walk into the sky, a bridge magically appears in front of you to keep you safe. Soon your Minecraft world will fill up with bridges. Version 2 of your magic bridge builder uses a Python list to remember where you built the bridge and makes it do a disappearing act right before your eyes when you land on safe ground again!

Finally, you learn how to sense that a block has been hit and then build an exciting treasure hunt game using your magic bridge to find and collect treasure that appears randomly in the sky, complete with a homing beacon and a score.

In this adventure you work just like a real software engineer, building up a large program one function at a time, and finally stitching it all together at the end to make an exciting larger program. Fasten your seatbelt and take careful note of the instructions. It's going to be an exciting journey into the sky!

Finding Out What You Are Standing On

You learned in Adventure 2 that it is possible to track your player's position by reading the coordinates with `getTilePos()`. These coordinates represent the x, y and z coordinates in the Minecraft world where your player, Steve, is located at the moment. You used these coordinates to sense whether Steve was standing on a magic doormat or, using geo-fencing, whether he was standing in a field.

However, unless your programs maintain a detailed map of exactly where every block is in the Minecraft world, just sensing by position is not going to be flexible enough for you, as your programs become more sophisticated. You could always keep a detailed map of your own — but why go to all that trouble when Minecraft must already have that information in the computer's memory to display the 3D world on the screen?

Fortunately, the Minecraft API also includes a `getBlock()` function. This function gives you full access to the in-memory world map of Minecraft and, by using coordinates, you can use it to tell you about every block — not just the block where Steve is located but every block at every position in the Minecraft world.

You also saw in Adventure 3 that it is possible, through block types, to change any block in the Minecraft world. Fortunately, `setBlock()` and `getBlock()` work together as a pair, so if you use `setBlock()` with a block id and then use `getBlock()` immediately after that, you get the same block id back.

Soon you are going to build another exciting game inside Minecraft, but your program will be quite big. The best way to build a big program is to build little programs and then stick them all together once you know they work. Let's start by bringing this idea to life with a simple program that tells you if your player is standing on something safe or not.

Finding Out if Your Feet Are on the Ground

Start Minecraft and IDLE and, if you are working on a PC or a Mac, start the server, too. You should have had a bit of practice with starting everything by now, but refer to Adventure 1 if you need any reminders. You are now going to build a program that gives you important information about your player's exact location. You need to find out if his feet are on the ground before you can build your magic bridge into the sky.

1. Create a new window by choosing File ➪ New File. Save your new program as `safeFeet.py`. Remember to store your programs inside the `MyAdventures` folder, otherwise they will not work.

2. Import the necessary modules. You need the normal `minecraft` module and, because you are interacting with blocks, also the `block` module. You need a small time delay to slow things down, so also import the `time` module:

```
import mcpi.minecraft as minecraft
import mcpi.block as block
import time
```

3. Connect to the Minecraft game:

```
mc = minecraft.Minecraft.create()
```

4. Because you plan to use parts of this program in a bigger program later, you are going to write the bulk of the code inside a function called `safeFeet()`. This makes it easier for you to reuse this code later. The first thing this function does is to get the position of your player, Steve:

```
def safeFeet():
    pos = mc.player.getTilePos()
```

5. `getBlock()` gets the block id of the block at the coordinates you provide. Because `pos.x`, `pos.y` and `pos.z` are the coordinates of your player, you must use `pos.y-1` to get the block directly below Steve's feet:

```
b = mc.getBlock(pos.x, pos.y-1, pos.z) # note: pos.y-1 ↵
    is important!
```

6. You now use a simple method to work out whether your player is safe or not. If he is standing on air or water then he is not safe. Otherwise, he is safe. It is simpler to check the block types for the 'not safe' condition, as there are a few hundred blocks you would need to check for the 'safe' condition. This is quite a long piece of code, so make sure you type it in all on one line:

```
if b == block.AIR.id or b == block.WATER_STATIONARY.id ↵
    or b == block.WATER_FLOWING.id:
```

7. If the block is one of the unsafe blocks, post a message to the Minecraft chat saying that your player is not safe. Otherwise, he is safe.

Make sure you get the indents correct here, otherwise the program doesn't work. Remember that all of the code inside the function is indented one level, and any code inside an `if` or an `else` is indented by another level. The `if` and the `else` statements should line up with each other as they are related and logically at the same level.

```
    mc.postToChat("not safe")
else:
    mc.postToChat("safe")
```

8. This is now the end of the `safeFeet()` function. Leave a blank line to remind yourself that it is the end of the function, and start the `while` of the game loop without any indent. As in your earlier programs, you put a short delay and, finally, use the new `safeFeet()` function which does all the work.

```
while True:
    time.sleep(0.5)
    safeFeet()
```

Now choose File ➪ Save to save your program and then run it by choosing Run ➪ Run Module from the Editor menu.

What happens as your player moves around the Minecraft world? You should see the words 'safe' or 'not safe' appear on the Minecraft chat as appropriate, as shown in Figure 4-1. Try flying in the air and swimming in the sea to see what happens.

FIGURE 4-1 The `safeFeet` program shows you are not safe while you are in the sky.

In your `safeFeet.py` program, just like other programs, you used a short time delay in your main game loop. This is not always necessary, and later you work on programs that are slowed down so much by the time delay that they don't work properly. When posting messages to the Minecraft chat, however, it is actually useful to slow things down a bit; otherwise the chat fills up very quickly. Try shortening the delay or removing it altogether to see what happens.

Building Magic Bridges

In the previous program, you wrote code that sensed the block directly under your player and posted a message on the chat. This is an interesting tiny step towards a bigger program, but let's see if you can now turn this experiment into something real by stitching it together with some of the techniques you learned in Adventure 3 with the `setBlock()` function.

By making a small change to `safeFeet.py`, you can turn it into a magic bridge builder that places a glass bridge under your feet wherever you walk, making sure that your player never falls into the sea or falls out of the sky! You reuse this new function in a later program in this adventure, so make sure you name it correctly.

1. Choose File ⇨ Save As and rename your `safeFeet.py` program as `magicBridge.py`.

2. Change the name of the `safeFeet()` function so that it is now called `buildBridge()`, and modify the `if/else` statement as marked in bold by removing the `mc.postToChat()` and replacing it with a `mc.setBlock()`. Every time your player's feet are unsafe, this builds a glass bridge under him. Be careful of the long line in the `if` statement:

```
def buildBridge():
  pos = mc.player.getTilePos()
  b = mc.getBlock(pos.x, pos.y-1, pos.z)
  if b == block.AIR.id or b == block.WATER_FLOWING.id ↵
    or b==block.WATER_STATIONARY.id:
    mc.setBlock(pos.x, pos.y-1, pos.z, block.GLASS.id)
```

The `else` and the `mc.postToChat()` have been removed from the code, as they are no longer needed.

3. If you build the bridge too slowly, your player falls off, so you need to remove the time delay from the game loop. Make sure you use the new `buildBridge()` function:

```
while True:
  buildBridge()
```

4. Save your program by choosing File ⇨ Save from the Editor menu.

Run your program and walk around the world, jumping up into the sky and walking on water. As your player walks around, whenever his feet are not on safe ground, a magic glass bridge appears to keep him from falling, as in Figure 4-2. It is now possible for him to walk on water. It's a miracle!

This program works very nicely on the Raspberry Pi. On the PC and on the Mac, the response time isn't quite as quick, and as a result of this the player may keep falling because the blocks aren't placed quickly enough. Take your time, and don't start running around too fast expecting the bridge to keep you safe all the time! You can experiment with faster and slower delays to improve this game, or you can try creep mode (hold down the Shift key on the keyboard while moving) to walk forward slowly.

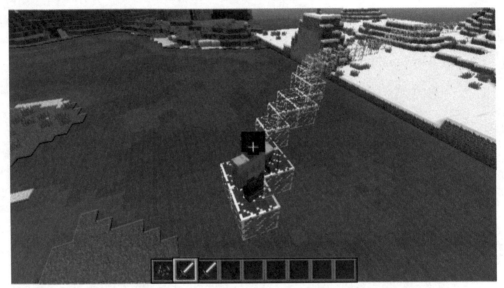

FIGURE 4-2 The `magicBridge.py` program builds a glass bridge, allowing your player to walk on water.

In the `magicBridge.py` program, you removed the time delay from the main loop. What happens if you put this time delay back in? Experiment with different delay values somewhere between the range of 0.1 to 2 seconds, and see how this affects the usability of your magic bridge. What value provides the best usability?

DIGGING INTO THE CODE

Let's just pause for a minute, as there is a little bit of magic to do with functions that hasn't quite been explained properly yet.

You have been using functions since the start of this book. `mc.postToChat()` is a function, as is `mc.getTilePos()`, and they are both part of the Minecraft API. You have also defined your own functions with `def`, such as in Adventure 2 when you designed a `house()` function of your own. But what really is happening when you use these functions in your code?

I've been cheating a little up until now and saying "now use this function," but the proper way to talk about what is happening here is to say that when you put `house()` or `buildBridge()` in your code, you can say that you **call** your function. But what really happens?

All the time your Python program is running, the computer remembers which statement it is working on at any time, a bit like an invisible finger pointing to the line in the code that is running. Normally, this invisible finger moves down the page from top to bottom. When you use a loop, this invisible finger jumps back to the top of the loop and runs down the code again a number of times.

When you call a function, some extra magic is happening behind the scenes. Python remembers where this invisible finger was (imagine that it sticks a little coloured tab at that point in the program) and then jumps into your function, such as your `buildBridge()` function. When it gets to the end of the `buildBridge()` function, it jumps back to where it left that little coloured sticky note and continues from there again.

Using functions in your programs is useful for many reasons, two of the most important ones being:

- You can split a large program up into lots of smaller programs.
- You can re-use the code inside a function from lots of different places in the same program.

Both of these reasons will make your programs easier to read and easier to modify.

When you **call** a function, Python remembers where it has got to in your program and temporarily jumps into the function at the point you defined it with `def`. When the end of the function is reached, Python jumps back to just after where it was when it jumped into that function.

Using Python Lists as Magic Memory

In all of the programs you have written up until now, you have used some form of variable to store information that changes as the program runs. Each of these variables has a name and a value, and if you want your programs to remember more than one thing, you use more variables.

However, these variables are a fixed size and each can store only one thing (for example, a number or a string of text). In many of the programs you will write as a Minecraft programmer you need to store an undefined number of items. You won't always know how many items you will want to store in a program.

Fortunately, like any modern programming language, Python has a feature called a list, which can store varying amounts of data as the program runs.

A **list** is a type of variable in a programming language that can store any number of items of data. You can add new items to the list, count the length of the list, access items at particular positions, remove items from anywhere in the list and do many other things. Lists are a very useful way of storing collections of similar items that belong together, such as a list of numbers that need sorting, a list of members in a user group or even a list of blocks in a Minecraft game.

Experimenting with Lists

The best way to understand lists is to experiment with them in the Python Shell.

Make sure you are careful with the brackets in this section. There are two types of brackets in use. The round brackets ( ) and the square brackets [ ]. Don't worry. The difference between these two types of brackets become clear as you work through this section.

1. Bring the Python Shell window to the front by clicking it. Click the mouse to the right of the last >>> prompt, which is where you start typing your interactive commands. Don't forget that you must stop your existing program running by choosing Shell ⇨ Restart Shell from the Python Shell menu, or pressing CTRL then C. If your previous program is still running, this next section doesn't work!

2. Create a new empty list, and show what is in the list:

```
a = [] # an empty list
print(a)
```

3. Add a new item to the list, and print it again:

```
a.append("hello")
print(a)
```

4. Add a second item to the list, and print it again:

```
a.append("minecraft")
print(a)
```

5. Check how long the list is:

```
print(len(a))
```

6. Look at items at specific positions within the list. These positions are called **indexes**:

```
print(a[0]) # the [0] is the index of the first item
print(a[1]) # the [1] is the index of the second item
```

7. Remove one word from the end of the list, and show that word and the remaining list:

```
word = a.pop()
print(word)
print(a)
```

8. Check how long the list is, and check how long the word string is:

```
print(len(a))
print(len(word))
```

9. Remove the final item from the list, show the item and the list, and show the length of the list:

```
word = a.pop()
print(word)
print(a)
print(len(a))
```

Figure 4-3 shows the output of these experiments in the Python Shell.

An **index** is a number that identifies which item in a list of items to access. You specify the index in square brackets like a[0] for the first item and a[1] for the second item. Indexes in Python are always numbered from 0, so 0 is always the first item in a list. In the steps just completed, you *indexed* into the list.

```
●  ●  ●                      Python 3.6.1 Shell
Python 3.6.1 (v3.6.1:69c0db5050, Mar 21 2017, 01:21:04)
[GCC 4.2.1 (Apple Inc. build 5666) (dot 3)] on darwin
Type "copyright", "credits" or "license()" for more information.
>>> a = []
>>> print(a)
[]
>>> a.append("hello")
>>> print(a)
['hello']
>>> a.append("minecraft")
>>> print(a)
['hello', 'minecraft']
>>> print(len(a))
2
>>> print(a[0])
hello
>>> print(a[1])
minecraft
>>> w = a.pop()
>>> print(w)
minecraft
>>> print(a)
['hello']
>>> print(len(a))
1
>>> print(len(w))
9
>>> w = a.pop()
>>> print(w)
hello
>>> print(a)
[]
>>> print(len(a))
0
>>> |

                                                    Ln: 35  Col: 4
```

FIGURE 4-3 Experimenting with Python lists in the Python Shell

The length of a list changes as you add new items to it and remove items from
it. What happens if you try to access an item in the list that does not exist? Try
this at the Python Shell and see what happens:

b = []

print(b[26])

How do you think you could prevent this from happening in your programs?
(Note there is more than one right answer to this question. You could do some
research on the Internet to find out the different ways you can prevent this
problem in your programs.)

When you pop an item from a list, you remove the last item from that list.

Building Vanishing Bridges with a Python List

You are now going to use your new knowledge about lists to write a bridge builder program, where the bridge vanishes once your player's feet are safely on the ground again. This program is similar to the `magicBridge.py` program, so you could save that as a new name and edit it, but the full program is shown here to make it easier to explain each of the steps. Use copy and paste from your `magicBridge.py` program if you want to save a little bit of typing.

To see a tutorial on how to build and play the vanishing bridge game, visit the companion website at www.wiley.com/go/adventuresinminecraft2e and choose the Adventure 4 video.

1. Create a new file by choosing File ⇨ New File, and save it as `vanishingBridge.py` by choosing File ⇨ Save As from the Editor menu.

2. Import the necessary modules:

```
import mcpi.minecraft as minecraft
import mcpi.block as block
import time
```

3. Connect to the Minecraft game:

```
mc = minecraft.Minecraft.create()
```

4. Create a bridge list that is empty. There are no blocks in your bridge at the moment, so it always starts empty:

```
bridge = []
```

5. Define a `buildBridge()` function that builds the bridge for you. You use this `buildBridge()` function in the final program in this adventure, so make sure you name this function correctly. Most of the code at the start of this function is the same as in the `magicBridge.py` program, so you could copy that if you want to save some typing time. Be careful to get the indents correct:

```
def buildBridge():
  pos = mc.player.getTilePos()
  b = mc.getBlock(pos.x, pos.y-1, pos.z)
  if b == block.AIR.id or b == block.WATER_FLOWING.id ↵
    or b == block.WATER_STATIONARY.id:
    mc.setBlock(pos.x, pos.y-1, pos.z, block.GLASS.id)
```

6. When you build part of the bridge, you have to remember where you built the block, so that the block can be removed later when your player's feet are safely on the ground. You use another list to keep the three parts of the coordinate together, and add this to the bridge list. See the following Digging into the Code sidebar for a fuller explanation of what is going on here:

```
coordinate = [pos.x, pos.y-1, pos.z]
bridge.append(coordinate)
```

7. To make your bridge vanish when your player is no longer standing on it, you need an `else` statement to check whether he is standing on glass. If he is not, your program starts deleting blocks from the bridge. The program has to check that there is still some bridge left, otherwise it raises an error if you try to pop from an empty list. The `elif` is short for `else if`, and the `!=` means 'not equal to'. Be careful with the indents here: The `elif` is indented once, as it is part of the `buildBridge()` function; the next `if` is indented twice as it is part of the `elif`:

```
elif b != block.GLASS.id:
  if len(bridge) > 0:
```

8. These next lines are indented three levels because they are part of the `if` that is part of the `elif` that is part of the `buildBridge()` function! Phew!

Remember that earlier you appended a list of three coordinates to the bridge list? Here, you have to index into that list with `coordinate[0]` for x, `coordinate[1]` for y and `coordinate[2]` for z. Adding the `time.sleep()` also makes the bridge vanish slowly, so that you can see it happening:

```
coordinate = bridge.pop()
mc.setBlock(coordinate[0], coordinate[1],
coordinate[2], block.AIR.id)
time.sleep(0.25)
```

9. Finally, write the main game loop. As in your earlier experiments, you might like to try different delay times in the game loop to improve the usability of the bridge builder. Remember that this game loop is part of the main program (the `while True:` is not indented at all), so check the indentation very carefully:

```
while True:
    time.sleep(0.25)
    buildBridge()
```

Save your program with File ⇨ Save and then run it with Run ⇨ Run Module. Walk your player around the Minecraft world, walk him off a ledge or into a lake and, then turn and walk him back onto safe ground again. What happens? Figure 4-4 shows the bridge starting to vanish once Steve is on safe ground.

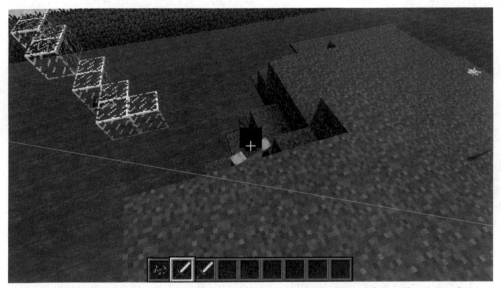

FIGURE 4-4 The bridge magically vanishes once your player is safely on the ground.

DIGGING INTO THE CODE

Earlier, when you experimented with lists at the Python Shell, you added text strings to your list. In the `vanishingBridge.py` program, there is an extra little bit of Python magic that is worth explaining.

Python lists can store any type of data, such as text strings, numbers and even lists. You have used this magic already in your program, perhaps without realising it.

continued

continued

The following line creates a list with three items in it (the x, y and z coordinates of a block you have just placed):

```
coordinate = [pos.x, pos.y-1, pos.z]
```

By putting values between the `[ ]` brackets, you are creating the list with values already in it, rather than creating an empty list. You could have done the same like this:

```
coordinate = []
coordinate.append(pos.x)
coordinate.append(pos.y-1)
coordinate.append(pos.z)
```

Later, when your program retrieves the coordinates of a block to delete, it pops off a list (of coordinates) from your bridge list:

```
coordinate = bridge.pop()
```

The list that is stored in the coordinate variable has three items inside it: `coordinate[0]` is the x position of the block; `coordinate[1]` is the y position of the block; and `coordinate[2]` is the z position of the block.

Figure 4-5 shows what this 'list of lists' actually looks like.

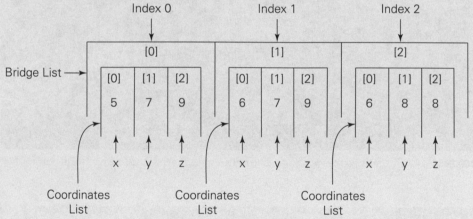

FIGURE 4-5 A bridge is a list of coordinates, and each coordinate is a list.

DAVID SAYS:

Python actually has a number of different variable types for storing collections of items, in addition to the lists that you have just used. Professional Python programmers would probably use a feature called a **tuple** in this program for storing the coordinates. I didn't want to introduce too many concepts here in one go, but Martin introduces a tuple in Adventure 9. If you like, you can do some research on the Internet about tuples, and find out how they are different from lists and what additional benefits they bring to a Python program.

Sensing That a Block Has Been Hit

The last sensing ability that you need in your tool-bag for this adventure is the ability to sense when your player hits a block. Block-hit detection enables you to create some really exciting games and programs of your own because it allows your player to interact directly with each and every block inside the Minecraft world. To hit a block you need to right-click while you're holding a sword.

Start a new program for this adventure, as it begins life as a little self-contained experiment but later makes its way into your final game of this adventure.

1. Create a new file by choosing File ➪ New File from the Editor menu. Choose File ➪ Save As and name the new file `blockHit.py`.

2. Import the necessary modules:

   ```
   import mcpi.minecraft as minecraft
   import mcpi.block as block
   import time
   ```

3. Connect to the Minecraft game:

   ```
   mc = minecraft.Minecraft.create()
   ```

4. Work out the position of the player and move very slightly to one side. Use this as the position of the diamond that you are going to create — this is your magic treasure:

   ```
   diamond_pos = mc.player.getTilePos()
   diamond_pos.x = diamond_pos.x + 1
   mc.setBlock(diamond_pos.x, diamond_pos.y, diamond_pos.z,
               block.DIAMOND_BLOCK.id)
   ```

5. Define a function called `checkHit()`. You reuse this function in your final program, so make sure you name it correctly:

   ```
   def checkHit():
   ```

6. Ask the Minecraft API for a list of events that have happened. This is just a normal Python list, like the one you used in your `vanishingBridge.py` program earlier:

   ```
   events = mc.events.pollBlockHits()
   ```

7. Process each event in turn, using a `for` loop. See the following Digging into the Code sidebar for a more detailed explanation of this new form of the `for` loop:

   ```
   for e in events:
     pos = e.pos
   ```

8. Ask your program to check whether the position of the block the player just hit with his sword is the same as the position of the diamond. If it is, ask it to post a message to the Minecraft chat:

```
if pos.x == diamond_pos.x and pos.y == diamond_pos.y ↵
    and pos.z == diamond_pos.z:
    mc.postToChat("HIT")
```

9. Finally, write your game loop. For now, you use a time delay of one second to limit how quickly messages can appear on the Minecraft chat, but you might like to experiment with different time delays to get the best usability from your program. Check your indentation very carefully here:

```
while True:
    time.sleep(1)
    checkHit()
```

Save your program with File ➪ Save and run it using Run ➪ Run Module from the Editor menu.

Move your player around a bit until you can see the diamond. Now, hit it on each of its faces with a sword. What happens? As Figure 4-6 shows, when you hit the diamond, the message 'HIT' appears on the Minecraft chat.

FIGURE 4-6 A block has been hit.

If you accidentally use the wrong mouse button and delete your treasure, you're never able to hit it! You have to either rerun the program to create new treasure or manually build a block of treasure in the same place before you can hit it. This is because the block type AIR does not process block-hit events.

CHALLENGE

Modify your `blockHit.py` program so that it also reads the `e.face` variable from the event that it is returned in the `for` loop. This `e.face` variable is a different number depending on which of the block's six faces has been hit. Start by displaying `e.face` on the Minecraft chat and then hitting each face to work out which numbers are used for which faces. Finally, modify your program to display a different message for each of the six faces of your diamond block.

DIGGING INTO THE CODE

In the block-hit detection program, you used a `for` loop, but you used a style of it that you have not used before. Let's look a little bit into this extra magic, as it is quite a powerful feature of Python.

The normal `for` loop you have used before looks like this:

```
for i in range(6):
  print(i)
```

`range(6)` is actually a function that generates a list of numbers `[0,1,2,3,4,5]`.

The for/in statement in Python loops through all items in a list, storing the first item in the loop control variable (`i` in the previous example), running the loop body, storing the next item in the loop control variable and doing this until the list is exhausted.

This means that if you have a list with anything in it, you can loop through all the items in the list in the same way. Try this at the Python Shell:

```
for name in ["Becky", "Keira", "Phil", "Holly"]:
  print("hello " + name)
```

continued

continued

You can also loop through the characters of a text string like this:

```
name = "Becky"
for ch in name:
  print(ch)
```

Writing a Treasure Hunt Game

For most of this adventure, you have been learning skills and building snippets of program code to test out and experiment with various sensing features in Minecraft. It's now time for you to knit all of that code into a complete game. The game you are going to write is called 'Sky Hunt', a treasure hunt in which you have to find diamond blocks hanging randomly in the sky using a homing beacon and hit them to get points.

There is a twist to this game though: Every time you move forward you leave a trail of gold, and this costs you one point off your score per gold block. If you run around aimlessly looking for the treasure, your score rapidly decreases and even becomes negative! You have to use your Minecraft navigation skills to look for the diamond blocks quickly, and try to get to them in as few moves as possible.

When you find each piece of treasure you score points, and the trail of gold magically melts away (possibly leaving holes in the ground for you to trip over, so watch out!).

This program is mostly made up of reusable parts from all the other little experimental programs you have already written in this adventure. You can cut and paste bits of your other programs and modify them to save typing time if you want, but I have included the full program here to make sure you know what is needed.

Professional software engineers often start with a simple framework program built with just print statements and test this first to make sure the structure is correct. Then they add and test new features to it gradually. In this section, you are also going to be a real software engineer and write and test this program in steps. First, let's get the framework of the game loop in, and some dummy functions that you can flesh out as you go along.

Writing the Functions and the Main Game Loop

Use the following steps to write the functions and the main game loop:

1. Start a new file with File ⇨ New File from the menu. Save it with File ⇨ Save As and call it `skyHunt.py`.

2. Import the necessary modules:

```
import mcpi.minecraft as minecraft
import mcpi.block as block
import time
import random
```

3. Connect to the Minecraft game:

```
mc = minecraft.Minecraft.create()
```

4. Set a score variable that keeps track of your score as the game plays. You also use a RANGE constant to set how difficult the game is, by setting how far away from the player the random treasure is placed. Set this to a small number to start with, while you are testing, and make the number bigger later when your program is completed:

```
score = 0
RANGE = 5
```

5. As you are going to develop and test this program in steps, first write some dummy functions for each of the features of the program. Python functions need at least one statement in them, so you can use the Python `print` statement here to print a message. This just acts as a placeholder for code you write later:

```
treasure_x = None # the x-coordinate of the treasure

def placeTreasure():
  print("placeTreasure")

def checkHit():
  print("checkHit")

def homingBeacon():
  print("homingBeacon")

bridge = []

def buildBridge():
  print("buildBridge")
```

6. Now write the main game loop. You run this loop quite fast when the game is running (10 times per second) so that the gold block trail is accurate enough to walk along in the sky, but slow it down to once per second while you are testing it. Inside this game loop you use your dummy functions, which you write soon.

```
while True:
  time.sleep(1)

  if treasure_x == None and len(bridge) == 0:
    placeTreasure()

  checkHit()
  homingBeacon()
  buildBridge()
```

7. Save your program with File ⇨ Save and then click Run ⇨ Run Module from the menu to run it. You should not have any errors in the program, and for now it should just print some messages once per second on the Python Shell window. You now have the framework of your program in place, ready for you to start adding new code to it, bit by bit.

Placing Treasure in the Sky

The first function you need to write is the one that places treasure at a random position in the sky. You use three global variables for the coordinates of the treasure, and their initial value is None. The None value is a special Python value, indicating that the variable is in memory but has nothing stored in it. You use this in your game loop to check whether a new piece of treasure needs to be built.

1. Create the global variables to track the position of the treasure, add the lines in bold:

```
treasure_x = None
treasure_y = None
treasure_z = None
```

2. Fill in the placeTreasure() function (and take out the print statement you put in earlier) with this code:

```
def placeTreasure():
  global treasure_x, treasure_y, treasure_z
  pos = mc.player.getTilePos()
```

3. Use the `random` function to place the treasure at a position no more than RANGE blocks away from the player, but set the y coordinate so that it is somewhere above the player (which will probably place it in the sky):

```
treasure_x = random.randint(pos.x,   pos.x+RANGE)
treasure_y = random.randint(pos.y+2, pos.y+RANGE)
treasure_z = random.randint(pos.z,   pos.z+RANGE)
mc.setBlock(treasure_x, treasure_y, treasure_z, ↵
   block.DIAMOND_BLOCK.id)
```

Run your program and test that a piece of treasure is created up in the sky, near where your player is standing.

Collecting Treasure When It Is Hit

Now you use the code from the `blockHit.py` program with a few small modifications to detect when the treasure is hit by your player's sword.

1. Remove the `print` statement from the `checkHit()` function and replace it with the code shown here. The `score` and `treasure_x` variables have to be listed as global variables here because the `checkHit()` function changes their values. Python requires you to list inside a function any global variables that it changes the value of. If you don't do this, your program doesn't work:

```
def checkHit():
  global score
  global treasure_x
```

2. Read through any block-hit events and check whether the position matches the position of your treasure:

```
events = mc.events.pollBlockHits()
for e in events:
  pos = e.pos
  if pos.x == treasure_x and pos.y == treasure_y ↵
    and pos.z == treasure_z:
    mc.postToChat("HIT!")
```

3. Now you are going to tell your program to add points to the `score` for hitting the treasure and then delete the treasure so it disappears. Finally, you must remember to set `treasure_x` to `None` (so that `placeTreasure()` can create a new random piece of treasure later). Be careful with the indents here, as this code is part of the body of the `if` statement:

```
score = score + 10
mc.setBlock(treasure_x, treasure_y, treasure_z,
            block.AIR.id)
treasure_x = None
```

Save and run your program, and check that when your player hits the treasure it disappears. You should also find that when you hit the treasure and it disappears, a new piece of treasure is created at a random position close to your player.

Adding a Homing Beacon

The homing beacon displays the score and the approximate distance to the treasure every second on the Minecraft chat. Here is how to add this.

1. Create a `timer` variable. As the main game loop eventually runs 10 times per second, you have to count 10 loops for every second. This `timer` helps you to do that. If you change the speed of the game loop, you have to adjust this TIMEOUT value as well. Make sure you put this code just above the `homingBeacon()` function (note, there is no indent at all here):

    ```
    TIMEOUT = 10
    timer = TIMEOUT
    ```

2. Remove the `print()` from inside the `homingBeacon()` function and list the `timer` as a global variable, as this function will want to change its value:

    ```
    def homingBeacon():
      global timer
    ```

3. Treasure is present in the sky if the `treasure_x` variable has a value in it. You have to check here whether treasure has been created; otherwise you get homing beacon messages on the Minecraft chat when there is no treasure to find:

    ```
      if treasure_x != None:
    ```

4. This function is called 10 times per second from the game loop, so you only want to update the homing beacon every 10 times:

    ```
        timer = timer - 1
        if timer == 0:
          timer = TIMEOUT
    ```

5. When the `timer` times out (every 10 calls to this function, or once every second), calculate a rough number that tells you how far away from the treasure you are. The `abs()` function finds the absolute value (a positive value) of the difference between two positions. By adding all the positive differences together, you get a number that is bigger when you are further away from the treasure, and smaller when you are nearer to it. Check your indents here, as this code all belongs to the body of the most recent `if` statement:

```
    pos = mc.player.getTilePos()
    diffx = abs(pos.x - treasure_x)
    diffy = abs(pos.y - treasure_y)
    diffz = abs(pos.z - treasure_z)
    diff = diffx + diffy + diffz
    mc.postToChat("score:" + str(score) + ↩
      " treasure:" + str(diff))
```

Save and run your program and make sure that the homing beacon and score are displayed on the Minecraft chat. Because you are still testing and developing your program, the game loop is set to run 10 times slower than normal, so you should see messages on the Minecraft chat every 10 seconds at the moment. Make sure this is the case by counting from 1 to 10 in your head. You will still see some of the dummy functions printing out on the Python Shell window every second for now because your program is not quite finished.

Adding Your Bridge Builder

You now add the bridge builder from your earlier `vanishingBridge.py` program. You only need to modify it a little, so that it checks whether your player is standing on gold and, if not, creates a gold trail.

1. Make sure your `buildBridge()` function looks like the following. The important lines that have changed from your `vanishingBridge.py` program are marked in **bold**:

    ```
    bridge = []

    def buildBridge():
      global score
      pos = mc.player.getTilePos()
      b = mc.getBlock(pos.x, pos.y-1, pos.z)

      if treasure_x == None:
        if len(bridge) > 0:
          coordinate = bridge.pop()
          mc.setBlock(coordinate[0],
                      coordinate[1],
                      coordinate[2],
                      block.AIR.id)
        mc.postToChat("bridge:" + str(len(bridge)))
        time.sleep(0.25)
    ```

```
      elif b != block.GOLD_BLOCK.id:
        mc.setBlock(pos.x, pos.y-1, pos.z, block.GOLD_BLOCK.id)
        coordinate = [pos.x, pos.y-1, pos.z]
        bridge.append(coordinate)
        score = score - 1
```

2. Congratulations! You have finished writing your program. As the game is ready to be played properly now, modify the `time.sleep(1)` in the game loop to sleep every 0.1 seconds. This runs the game loop 10 times per second. The timer in `homingBeacon` counts 10 of these and therefore only displays a message on the Minecraft chat every second.

Save and run your program. Check that the gold trail disappears after you collect the treasure and that your score goes down for every gold block that you spend.

Now all you have to do is enjoy the game! See how hard it is to get a good score by collecting the treasure?

Figure 4-7 shows the score and homing beacon display on the Minecraft chat.

FIGURE 4-7 The homing beacon showing vital statistics as you play Sky Hunt

Command	Description
`b = mc.getBlock(10, 5, 2)`	Getting the block type at a position

`hits = mc.events.pollBlockHits()`
`for hit in hits:`
`  pos = hit.pos`
`  print(pos.x)`
	Finding out which blocks have been hit

`a = [] # an empty list` `a = [1,2,3] # an initialised list`	Creating lists
`a.append("hello")`	Adding to the end of a list
`print(a)`	Printing the contents of a list
`print(len(a))`	Working out the size of a list
`print(a[0]) # 0=first, 1=second`	Accessing items in a list by their index
`print(a[-1])`	Accessing the last item in a list
`word = a.pop() # remove last item` `print(word) # item just removed`	Removing the last item from a list
`for item in a:` `  print(item)`	Looping through all items in a list

Further Adventures in Interacting with Blocks

In this adventure, you have learned how to use `getBlock()` to sense the block that your player is standing on, and how to use `events.pollBlockHits()` to respond when your player hits any face of any block. You've built a fantastic and complete game within Minecraft, complete with scoring!

- Set the RANGE constant to a larger number so that treasure is created further away from your player. This makes your game more difficult to play, so try to add a new feature that displays 'cold', 'warm' or 'hot' on the Minecraft chat depending on the distance your player is from the treasure.

- Design a better scoring scheme to make it possible to get a reasonable positive score as you play the game normally. Do lots of testing and work out what the best score increment is for finding the treasure, and what the best score penalty is for spending a gold block.

- Research Pythagoras' theorem on the Internet, and see if you can code a better distance estimator to make the `homingBeacon()` function more accurate. (Psst! Martin covers a little bit about this in Adventure 6, so you could sneak a peek at that adventure and see if you can work it out!)

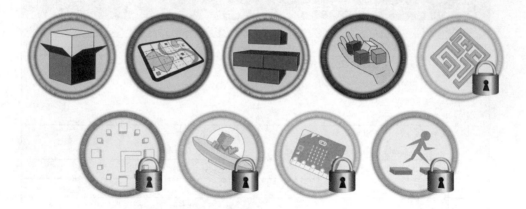

Achievement Unlocked: Expert in defying the laws of gravity and walking on water—two miracles achieved in one adventure!

In the Next Adventure. . .

In Adventure 5, you learn how to read data from files to automatically build large, complex structures like Minecraft mazes. You use your new skills to build a huge 3D duplicating machine that can duplicate large objects all over the Minecraft world. Trees will never again be safely rooted to the ground!

Using Data Files

IT'S WHEN YOU can start to process large amounts of data that computer programming gets really exciting. Your program then becomes a set of rules that govern how that data is read, processed and visually represented—the data becomes the really important part.

In this adventure, you first look at how to create text files that define mazes. The mazes will then be automatically built in the Minecraft world for you and your friends to solve; you'll wonder how such a small Python program can build something so big in the Minecraft world.

You are then going to develop this simple idea into a complete virtual 3D scanning and printing facility called the duplicator room. Anything you build inside the duplicator room can be saved to a file, recalled later and teleported to any location in your Minecraft world, and even loaded into Minecraft worlds on other computers! You will be able to build your own library of objects and build them in Minecraft so quickly that your friends will all want duplicating machines of their own!

Reading Data from a File

Computer programs are generally quite unintelligent—they repeatedly follow instructions that you give them. If you don't change any input to your program, it will do exactly the same thing every time you run it. The Minecraft programs you have been making have been quite interactive because they change what they do depending on what happens in the game world, which is the input to the program.

Interesting Things You Can Do with Data Files

Another interesting way to make computer programs do different things every time you run them is to store the input data in a text file and have the computer read that file when it starts. You can then create any number of text files and even have a menu so you can choose which file to open depending on what you want to do with the program. This is called a data-driven program because it is mostly the data in the external text file that defines what the program does.

If you think about it, many of the programs you already use on your computer use data files. The word processor you use to type up your homework stores your homework in a data file; when you take a photo with a digital camera it is stored in a data file; and your image editor program reads that photo from the data file. Even Minecraft uses data files behind the scenes for tasks like saving and loading the world, and for the texture packs used to build all of the different blocks in the world from. Using data files with a program is a much more flexible way of working because it means that the program can be used for lots of different things without forcing you, the user, to modify the program every time you want it to do something slightly different. You can also share those data files with your friends, if they have the same programs as you.

DAVID SAYS: An early example program that I wrote that demonstrates the use of data files with Minecraft is a program on my blog, called the Minecraft BMP builder (http://blog.whaleygeek.co.uk/minecraft-pi-with-python/), which reads an image from a bitmap picture file (BMP file) and builds it block by block inside the Minecraft world. With it, I built a huge Raspberry Pi logo that is so big it looks a bit foggy when you look up at it! This program can read any BMP image file and then build that image out of blocks inside the Minecraft world, without any need to modify the program.

Your first step in writing a data-driven program is to learn how to use Python to open and read text files from the computer filing system.

Making a Hint-Giver

To learn how to open and read text files, you are going to write a simple hint-giver program. This program reads a file you have prepared of useful Minecraft hints and tips and displays one of the hints on the Minecraft chat at random intervals. You're going to need a text file with tips in it, so your first task is to create this file. You can create this file in the normal Python editor, just like you do with your Python programs.

Start up Minecraft, IDLE, and if you are working on a PC or a Mac, start up the server, too. You should have had a bit of practice with starting everything by now, but refer to Adventure 1 if you need any reminders.

1. In IDLE, create a new text file by choosing File ➪ New File from the menu. Save the file as `tips.txt`.

2. Now list four or five tips, using one line of text for each tip. Here are a few example Minecraft tips, but it's much more fun if you make up your own. Make sure you press the Enter key at the end of each line, so that this creates a **newline** inside the file for each line. (You find out more about newlines later in this adventure.)

```
Build yourself a house before the mobs come and get you
Use flowing water to fill underwater channels
Build up with sand then knock out the bottom block
Use both first-person and third-person views
Double tap space bar to fly into the sky
```

3. Save this file in your `MyAdventures` folder. You don't run this file, as it is not a Python program but a text file you're going to tell your Python program to use.

A **newline** is a special invisible character that the computer uses to mark the end of a line of text.

It is also sometimes called a *carriage-return*, which is historic from the days of mechanical typewriters. Whenever you wanted to type on the next line of the page, you would use the carriage return, which would make the carriage return to the left of the page and then down by one line.

Now you have a data file with tips in it—in other words, input data—it's time to write the program that processes that input data. This program read a random tip from the file and display it after a random interval on the Minecraft chat. Then, while you are playing your game, helpful tips will pop up on the chat.

1. Start a new file with File ➪ New File and then save it as `tipChat.py`.

2. Import the necessary modules:

```
import mcpi.minecraft as minecraft
import time
import random
```

3. Connect to the Minecraft game:

```
mc = minecraft.Minecraft.create()
```

4. Set a constant for the filename, so that you can easily change it to read a different file later:

```
FILENAME = "tips.txt"
```

5. Open the file in read mode (see the following Digging into the Code for a fuller explanation of this line):

```
f = open(FILENAME, "r")
```

6. Read all the lines of the file into a list called `tips`. Remember that you have already used lists in Adventure 4 (magic bridge builder):

```
tips = f.readlines()
```

7. Close the file when you have finished with it. It is good practice to always close a file when you have finished with it, because when the file is open it cannot be used by other programs, such as the editor you used to enter the text into the file in the first place:

```
f.close()
```

8. Now write a game loop that waits a random length of time between three and seven seconds:

```
while True:
  time.sleep(random.randint(3,7))
```

9. Now tell the program to choose a random message from the `tips` list and display it on the chat. You need to use the `strip()` function to strip out unwanted newline characters. You'll be looking at newline characters later on, so don't worry too much about understanding this for now.

```
msg = random.choice(tips)
mc.postToChat(msg.strip())
```

Save and run your program. What happens? As you walk around the Minecraft world and play your game, every so often a tip pops up on the chat, just like in Figure 5-1. Note how the Minecraft chat builds up messages on the screen, and gradually they disappear over time.

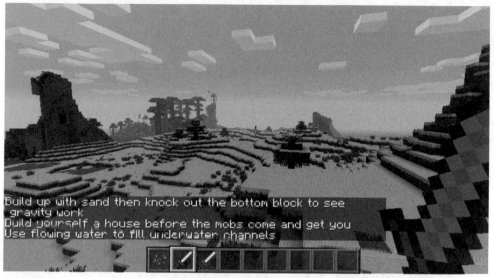

FIGURE 5-1 Random tips pop up on the chat as you play Minecraft.

CHALLENGE

Add more Minecraft tips to your `tips.txt` file based on your experience playing Minecraft. Give your `tips.txt` and your `tipChat.py` program to a friend who is learning Minecraft and let them use it to quickly learn how to do amazing things in the game. You could even write a whole series of `tips.txt` files with different topics and different amounts of detail depending on the ability of the player, and publish them on a small website for others to use along with your `tipChat.py` program.

DIGGING INTO THE CODE

In the `tipChat.py` program, a little bit of magic happens in the following line:

```
f = open(FILENAME, "r")
```

The `open()` function opens the file named in the `FILENAME` constant—but what does that `"r"` at the end mean? When you open a file, you have to tell the `open()` function what level of access you want to that file. In this case, the `"r"` means that you only want to read the file. If you accidentally try to write to the file, you get an error message. This protects your files by preventing accidental damage. If you want to open a file and write to it, you can use a `"w"` instead (or if you want to read and write a file at the same time, use `"rw"`).

continued

continued

Secondly, what is f? f is just another variable, but it stores a file handle. A file handle is just something to "grab hold of" the file with—it is a kind of virtual reference to the real file inside your computer's filing system. Whenever you want to do anything with the open file, use f to refer to it. This is very handy because, like any other variable you have used before, you can have multiple file variables to allow multiple files to be open at the same time like this:

```
f1 = open("config.txt", "r")
f2 = open("levels.txt", "r")
f3 = open("score.txt", "rw")
```

The variables f1, f2 and f3 can be used in the rest of your program to correctly identify which file you want to read from or write to.

Building Mazes from a Data File

Now that you know how to make your programs read from data files, you are ready to get a bit more adventurous. You know from earlier adventures that it is easy to place blocks in the Minecraft world. What if you could build blocks using lists of blocks stored in a data file? That's exactly what you are going to do here: You are going to build a complete 3D maze in Minecraft, where the maze data is stored in an external file! But first, you need to decide how the maze data will be represented inside the file.

To watch a tutorial on how to build and play your maze game, visit the companion website at www.wiley.com/go/adventuresinminecraft2e and choose the Adventure 5 Video.

The mazes that you design are 3D because they are built in the Minecraft 3D world, but really they are just 2D mazes built out of 3D blocks—there is only one layer to your maze. This means that the data file needs to store x and z data for each block in the maze, so it is rectangular.

You need to decide how blocks themselves are represented in the data file. You use walls and air. To keep things simple, use a 1 to represent a wall and a 0 to represent air. You can always change the block types inside your Python program that are used for walls later.

Understanding CSV Files

For this program, you use a special type of text file called a CSV file, to represent your mazes as files in your computer's filing system.

CSV is a very simple and widely used format. Here is a sample of a CSV file that stores part of a table from a database with details about Minecraft gamer characters. In this CSV file, the first row (or line) in the file has the names of the fields, and all other lines have data separated by commas:

```
Name,Handle,Speciality
David,w_geek,Coding in Python
Roma,physics_gurl,Designing big buildings
Ryan,mr_teck,Minecraft robots
Craig,rrrrrrr,TNT expert
```

This CSV file has one header row, which has three field names called `Name`, `Handle` and `Speciality`. There are four data rows, each with three fields of data.

When designing complex structures in software, sometimes it is useful to use other tools to help you. As a software engineer, a spreadsheet is one of the tools that I regularly find a use for when designing and representing data. Spreadsheets provide a fantastic way to represent tables of data that can be exported in a CSV file format, and then loaded into programs. You could try designing a maze in your favourite spreadsheet program by setting all the columns to be very narrow, using formulas to display a white square whenever you put a `0` and using a yellow square whenever you put a `1`. Once you have visualised your maze this way, export it as `maze.csv` and run your program to see if you and your friends can solve it!

For your maze data file, you don't need a header row because each column in the table represents the same type of data; that is, it stores a number 0 for a space and a number 1 for a wall. You can download this sample maze file from the companion website, but here it is if you want to type it in:

1. Create a new text file by choosing File ⇨ New File. Use File ⇨ Save As and name the file `maze1.csv`. Make sure you save this file in your `MyAdventures` folder.

2. Type in the following lines very carefully, making sure there are exactly the same number of columns on each line. If you look very carefully at this data you should already be able to see the structure of this maze! There are 16 numbers per line and 16 lines, so perhaps use a pencil to tick off each line as you type it in so you don't lose your place:

```
1,1,1,1,1,1,1,1,1,1,1,1,1,1,1,1
0,0,0,0,0,0,0,0,0,0,0,0,0,0,0,1
1,1,1,1,1,1,1,1,0,1,0,1,1,0,0,1
1,0,0,1,0,0,0,0,1,0,1,0,1,0,0,1
1,1,0,1,0,1,1,0,0,0,0,0,1,0,1,1
1,1,0,1,0,1,1,1,1,1,1,1,0,0,1,1
1,1,0,0,0,1,1,1,1,0,0,0,0,1,1
1,1,1,1,1,0,0,0,0,0,1,1,1,1,1
1,0,0,0,0,1,0,0,0,0,0,0,0,0,0,1
1,0,1,1,1,0,0,0,0,0,1,1,1,1,1
1,0,0,0,0,0,0,0,0,0,0,0,0,0,0,1
1,0,1,1,1,1,1,1,1,0,1,1,1,1,1
1,0,1,0,0,0,0,0,1,0,0,0,0,0,0,1
1,0,1,0,1,1,1,0,1,1,1,1,1,0,1
1,0,0,0,0,0,0,0,1,0,0,0,0,0,0,1
1,1,1,1,1,1,1,1,1,0,1,1,1,1,1
```

3. Save this file. You will use it once you have written the Python program that reads and processes the data in this file.

Building a Maze

Now that you have a data file describing your maze, the final step is to write the Python program that reads data from this file and builds the maze in Minecraft using blocks.

1. Start a new file with File ⇨ New File and then use File ⇨ Save As to save it as `csvBuild.py`.

2. Import the necessary modules:

```
import mcpi.minecraft as minecraft
import mcpi.block as block
```

3. Connect to the Minecraft game:

```
mc = minecraft.Minecraft.create()
```

4. Define some constants. The GAP constant is the block type that is used in the spaces. This is normally air, but you could experiment with different block types to make the maze interesting. The WALL constant is the block type that the walls of the maze are built with, so choose this carefully as some block types won't work very well as walls. The FLOOR constant is used to build the layer that the maze stands on:

```
GAP = block.AIR.id
WALL = block.GOLD_BLOCK.id
FLOOR = block.GRASS.id
```

Don't use SAND for the floor layer. If you do, depending on where the maze is built, the floor might start to fall away under your player's feet!

5. Open the file containing your maze data. The FILENAME constant is used so that it is easy for you to change the filename later to read in different maze files:

```
FILENAME = "maze1.csv"
f = open(FILENAME, "r")
```

6. Get the player position and work out the coordinates of the bottom corner of the maze. Adding 1 to the x and z makes sure that the maze doesn't get built on top of your player's head. You could vary the y coordinate to build the maze in the sky if you wanted to:

```
pos = mc.player.getTilePos()
ORIGIN_X = pos.x+1
ORIGIN_Y = pos.y
ORIGIN_Z = pos.z+1
```

7. The z coordinate varies at the end of each line of data, so start it off at the origin of the maze. It varies a little later on in the program:

```
z = ORIGIN_Z
```

8. Loop around every line of the file. See Digging into the Code, which explains what the readlines() function does. The for loop is actually looping through every line in the file, one by one. Each time round the loop, the line variable holds the next line that has been read from the file:

```
for line in f.readlines():
```

9. Split the line into parts, wherever there is a comma. See Digging into the Code, which explains what the `split()` function does. Remember that all of the lines that are part of the body of the `for` loop have to be indented one level:

```
data = line.split(",")
```

10. Look at this step very carefully: You now have another `for` loop. This is called a **nested loop**, because one loop is nested inside another. Your program has to reset the x coordinate at the start of every new row of the maze, so this has to be done outside of the `for` loop that draws a whole row:

```
x = ORIGIN_X
for cell in data:
```

11. Each number read in from the row is actually read in as a piece of text (a string), so for this program to work, you have to put quotes ("") around the number. This `if`/`else` statement chooses whether to build a gap or a wall, based on the number just read back from the CSV file. A 0 builds a gap, and anything else builds a wall. Make sure your indentation is correct here: The `if` statement is indented twice because it is part of the `for cell in data` loop, which is part of the `for line in f.readlines()` loop. The b variable here is useful as it makes the program a bit smaller and simpler. (Try rewriting this part without using the b variable to see what I mean!)

```
if cell == "0":
    b = GAP
else:
    b = WALL
mc.setBlock(x, ORIGIN_Y, z, b)
mc.setBlock(x, ORIGIN_Y+1, z, b)
mc.setBlock(x, ORIGIN_Y-1, z, FLOOR)
```

12. Update the x coordinate at the end of the `for cell` loop. This must be indented so that it lines up with the previous `mc.setBlock()` as it is still part of the body of the `for cell in data` loop.

```
x = x + 1
```

13. Update the z coordinate at the end of the loop that processes each row of data (this must be indented one level only, as it is part of the `for line in f.readlines()` loop).

```
z = z + 1
```

Save your program and double-check that all the indentation is correct. If the indentation is wrong, the program doesn't work correctly, and you get some very strange-shaped mazes!

Run your program and a fantastic (and quite hard to solve) maze will be built in front of you. Walk around the maze and see if you can solve it without breaking down any walls or flying. Figure 5-2 shows what the maze looks like from ground level.

FIGURE 5-2 A ground level view of the maze inside Minecraft

If you get stuck, you can always cheat a bit and fly into the sky to get a 3D bird's-eye view of the maze, as shown in Figure 5-3.

FIGURE 5-3 A bird's-eye view of the maze inside Minecraft

DAVID SAYS...

If you accidentally leave some blank lines at the end of your data file, these lines are read in and interpreted by your Python program. Fortunately it doesn't make your program crash, but you might see some redundant extra blocks at the end of the maze as a result.

DIGGING INTO THE CODE

In earlier adventures, you experimented with Python lists and learned that a list is just a collection of zero or more items stored in numbered slots. Many functions built into the Python language provide data in the form of a list, and you have just met two new ones in the maze builder program.

This line of code is the first one:

```
for line in f.readlines():
```

Remember that `f` is a file handle—something you can grab hold of to gain access to an open file. Usefully, the `file` type in Python has a `readlines()` function built into it. This simply reads every line of the file. You may also remember from earlier adventures that, when it's given a list, the `for` statement in Python loops through all the items in the list.

All the `for` statement does is read every line in the file, and then loop through them one at a time. Each time around the `for` loop, the `line` variable (the loop control variable) holds the next line of data.

There is a second point in your program where you used another Python list but might not have realised it. It was in this line:

```
data = line.split(",")
```

The `line` variable holds a string of text that is the complete line read from the CSV file. All string variables have a built-in function called `split()` that takes that string and splits it into a list. The `","` inside the brackets tells the `split` function which character to split on.

Imagine you have a line variable with three words separated by commas like this:

```
line = "one,two,three"
data = line.split(",")
```

The result of this is that the data variable contains a list with three items in it, like this:

```
['one','two','three']
```

CHALLENGE

Design your own maze files in other CSV data files with lots of winding passages, dead ends and loops to make the mazes hard to solve. Challenge your friends to find their way through the maze. You might want to plant some random treasure (for example, DIAMOND_BLOCK) throughout the maze and at the exit so that your friends can prove they have walked through the whole maze, or you could even build a huge maze that takes up most of the Minecraft world! How could you store the positions of the treasure in the maze file?

When I was designing the programs for this chapter, I had to modify the maze program slightly as sometimes it was very hard to solve. For example, what happens if you remove the line from the program that builds the floor? Try building the walls with some other block types, such as CACTUS or WATER_FLOWING and see what happens. I went through many versions of this program before finding block types that I was happy with for the walls and the floor!

CHALLENGE

There is a bug hidden in this program for you to find. If the last number on a line is zero, then for some reason the maze builder still builds a gold block wall there. Why do you think this happens? Try to fix this bug yourself. Hint: You already solved a similar problem in the tipChat.py program.

In this adventure you have been using the `readlines()` and `split()` functions to process CSV files. Python is a very large and established programming language and has lots of features already built in. You could have a look at the built in CSV reader module that is accessible with `import csv` as it is a more powerful method of what we have learnt here. However, I like to build programs up in small steps as it helps me understand how things work, which is why I have used `readlines()` and `split()` in this book.

Building a 3D Block Printer

Building mazes is great fun, but there is so much more you can do with data files now that you know the basics! Why stop at building with only two block types on a single layer? You are now going to use your maze program as the basis of your very own 3D printer and 3D scanner that will duplicate trees, houses—in fact, anything you can build in Minecraft—and "print" them all around the Minecraft world at the touch of a button! This is a block builder really, but I like to call this a 3D printer because of the way you can sometimes see the blocks building up row at a time, just like how a computer printer prints onto a piece of paper row at a time, or how a 3D printing machine builds up structures a layer at a time.

You're getting quite good at building programs now, and each new program you build is larger than the last one. Just like in the previous adventure, where you built your program out of functions, you are going to build this program up in steps.

DAVID SAYS...

The technique of writing the different features of a program as functions and then stitching them all together into a bigger program is a very common development technique used by professional software engineers. It relies on the principle that a big program is just a collection of small programs. Providing that the design of the overall program is correct from the start, the detail inside each of the support functions can be filled in gradually as you build and test your program. I always like to have demos handy so that if someone comes up to me and says, "Wow, what's this great program you are writing?" I can very quickly show them something that works.

Hand-Crafting a Small Test Object to 3D Print

In your maze program, data was stored in a CSV file, where each line in the file represents a line of blocks inside the Minecraft world. Each column inside that line (separated by commas) corresponds to one block in that line of blocks. This is a 2D structure because it stores a block for each x and z coordinate of a rectangle region. The mazes you have built here are really only 2D mazes, as they only have one layer. They are just built inside the 3D Minecraft world by using 3D blocks.

To build 3D shapes, you need to build up in the y dimension too. If you think of a 3D object as just multiple layers or slices, then your 3D program is not all that different from your maze program. All you need to do for a cube that is 5 by 5 by 5 blocks in size is to store five layers of information.

There is a problem with this. Your Python program doesn't know how many lines to expect until it has processed the whole file. It could assume a certain size, but it would be nice to design a flexible CSV file format that can work with any size of object.

To solve this problem, you add some metadata in the first line of the file that describes the size of the object.

Metadata is data about data. If the data in your file is the block types to build, then the metadata (data about that data) can be things like how big the object is, what it is called and who designed it. In the same way that the metadata for a photo stored on your computer describes the date and time it was taken and the name of the camera, the metadata in your 3D printer describes other useful information about your 3D objects.

You are now going to create a sample object that is a tiny 3D cave so that you can test the 3D printing capabilities of your program. You can download this sample object as shown in Figure 5-4 from the companion Wiley website by downloading the `CodeFiles.zip` file, or just type it in here like you did with your maze.

Make sure that you put blank lines between each layer of the object. They are there to help you see where each layer begins, but the Python program you write expects them to be there, and it doesn't work if you leave them out.

FIGURE 5-4 You build a small stone cave by writing a CSV data file.

Use copy and paste from the Editor menu as much as you can in these steps to cut down the amount of typing you need to do and to reduce the possibility of you typing the wrong number of lines.

1. Start a new file with File ⇨ New File, and save it as `object1.csv`.

2. Type the first metadata line that describes the size of the object. Your test object is 5 by 5 by 5. The first number is the x-size (width), the second number is the y-size (height) and the third number is the z-size (depth):

   `5,5,5`

3. Type the first layer of the test object, making sure that you leave a blank line before the first line of data. You need all the block positions filled in on the bottom layer, which is why every number is set to a 1:

   ```
   1,1,1,1,1
   1,1,1,1,1
   1,1,1,1,1
   1,1,1,1,1
   1,1,1,1,1
   ```

4. You are building a hollow cube with an open front, so put in three layers with that format. Make sure you put a blank line before these numbers:

```
1,1,1,1,1
0,0,0,0,1
0,0,0,0,1
0,0,0,0,1
1,1,1,1,1
```

5. Use copy and paste to put in two more identical hollow layers below this one, making sure you leave exactly one blank line between each square section of numbers.

6. Finally, put a solid top on the object. To do this, use copy and paste to copy the rows of data from step 3, again making sure that there is a blank line before the first row of numbers of this layer.

Save your file, but don't run it—you can't run it as it is not a Python program but a data file that will be used by the program you are now going to write.

Writing the 3D Printer

Now that you have written your test data, it is time to write the 3D printer program that builds the hollow cave inside the Minecraft world. This program is very similar to your maze program, but this one has three nested loops: one loop for each of the x, y and z dimensions.

This is probably one of the most detailed programs you have written while working through this book. Work through it carefully, step by step, and you'll be amazed by the final results! If you get stuck, check your indents very carefully, and remember that all of the program listings for all of the programs in this book are downloadable from the companion Wiley website at www.wiley.com/go/adventuresinminecraft2e.

1. Start a new file with File ➪ New File, and use File ➪ Save As from the menu to save it as print3D.py.

2. Import the necessary modules:

```
import mcpi.minecraft as minecraft
import mcpi.block as block
```

3. Connect to the Minecraft game:

```
mc = minecraft.Minecraft.create()
```

4. Create a constant that is the name of your data file. You can easily change this later on if you want to read different files with different objects in them:

```
FILENAME = "object1.csv"
```

5. Define a print3D() function. You reuse this function later on in the final project, so make sure you name it correctly:

```
def print3D(filename, originx, originy, originz):
```

6. Just as you did with your maze builder program, open the file in read mode and read in all the lines into a Python list:

```
f = open(filename, "r")
lines = f.readlines()
```

7. The first item in the list is at index 0. This is the first line of the file that holds the metadata. Split this line into parts by using the split() function. Then store those three numbers into the variables sizex, sizey and sizez. You have to use the int() function here because when you read lines from a file they come in as strings, but you need them to be numbers so you can calculate with them later:

```
coords = lines[0].split(",")
sizex = int(coords[0])
sizey = int(coords[1])
sizez = int(coords[2])
```

8. Set a lineidx variable to remember the index of the line in the lines[] list that you are processing. Because your program scans through the lines list reading out data for different layers of the 3D object, you can't use this as the loop control variable:

```
lineidx = 1
```

9. The first for loop scans through each of the vertical layers of the data read in from the file. The first few lines of the file are for the layer that is built at the lowest y layer. You can put a postToChat here so that the progress of the printing process is visible inside Minecraft:

```
for y in range(sizey):
    mc.postToChat(str(y))
```

10. Skip over the blank line between each layer in the file by adding 1 to the lineidx variable. Remember that these blank lines are only in the file so that it is easier for people to read it, but your program has to skip over them.

```
lineidx = lineidx + 1
```

11. Start a nested `for` loop that reads out the next line in the file and splits it whenever there is a comma. Be careful of the indentation here; the `for` has to be indented two levels (one for the function and one for the `for` y loop) and the code inside this `for` x loop needs to be indented three levels.

```
for x in range(sizex):
    line = lines[lineidx]
    lineidx = lineidx + 1
    data = line.split(",")
```

12. Now start your third `for` loop that scans through each of the blocks in the line just read and builds them inside Minecraft. The `for` z loop is indented three levels and the body of the loop is indented four times, so take very special care of the indentation; otherwise you'll end up with some very strange-shaped objects!

```
for z in range(sizez):
    blockid = int(data[z])
    mc.setBlock(originx+x, originy+y, originz+z, ↵
        blockid)
```

13. Finally, type the lines of the main program, which are not indented at all. These lines read the player position and then ask the `print3D()` function to print your 3D object just to the side of where you're standing:

```
pos = mc.player.getTilePos()
print3D(FILENAME, pos.x+1, pos.y, pos.z+1)
```

Save your program and run it to see what happens! Run around to different locations inside Minecraft and run the program. Every time you run the program, a hollow stone cave should be built just near your player! Figure 5-5 shows how easy it is to build lots of stone caves very quickly.

CHALLENGE

Create some more CSV files with 3D objects in them, change the FILENAME constant in the `print3D.py` program and run it to stamp your objects all over your Minecraft world. As your objects become more sophisticated, think of some different ways that you could design them before entering the numbers into the file. You might find some way of drawing the objects in a spreadsheet program. Or perhaps you could even buy a big box of plastic construction bricks and design your objects in the physical world first, then take them apart layer by layer and enter the block numbers into your CSV file.

FIGURE 5-5 3D printing lots of stone caves inside Minecraft

Building a 3D Block Scanner

Your 3D printer is already very powerful. You can create a big library of CSV files for different objects you want to build, and then, whenever you need to, just run your `print3D.py` program with a different `FILENAME` constant to stamp the object all over your Minecraft world.

However, building larger and more complex objects becomes very difficult if you have to enter all the numbers into the CSV file by hand. Minecraft itself is the best program for building complex objects—so, what if you could use Minecraft to create these CSV data files for you? Here, you are going to run up to a tree and hug it, and then make an identical copy of the tree so you can duplicate it all over the Minecraft world. Fortunately, 3D scanning works a bit like 3D printing in reverse, so this not quite as hard as you might think.

1. Start a new file with File ⇨ New File, save it with File ⇨ Save As and call the program `scan3D.py`.

2. Import the necessary modules:

    ```
    import mcpi.minecraft as minecraft
    import mcpi.block as block
    ```

3. Connect to the Minecraft game:

    ```
    mc = minecraft.Minecraft.create()
    ```

4. Create some constants for the name of the CSV file you want to scan to and the size of the area that you want to scan:

```
FILENAME = "tree.csv"
SIZEX = 5
SIZEY = 5
SIZEZ = 5
```

5. Define a `scan3D()` function. You use this function in a later program, so make sure it is named correctly:

```
def scan3D(filename, originx, originy, originz):
```

6. Open the file, but this time open it in write mode using the `"w"` file mode inside the `open()` function:

```
f = open(filename, "w")
```

7 The first line of the file has to contain the metadata, so write the x, y and z sizes in the first line. See Digging into the Code to understand what the `"\n"` at the end of the line is and why you need it.

```
f.write(str(SIZEX) + "," + str(SIZEY) + ","
        + str(SIZEZ) + "\n")
```

8. The scanner program is just the reverse of the printing program, again using three nested loops. Here is this part of the program all in one go, so that it is easy for you to get the indents correct. See Digging into the Code for an explanation of how the comma-separated lines are created:

```
for y in range(SIZEY):
    f.write("\n")
    for x in range(SIZEX):
        line = ""
        for z in range(SIZEZ):
            blockid = mc.getBlock(originx+x,
                                  originy+y,
                                  originz+z)
            if line != "":
                line = line + ","
            line = line + str(blockid)
        f.write(line + "\n")
f.close()
```

9. Finally, the main program is not indented at all. This just reads the player position, calculates a cube space, where the player is standing at the centre of that space, and asks the `scan3D()` function to scan that whole space to your CSV file.

```
pos = mc.player.getTilePos()
scan3D(FILENAME, pos.x-(SIZEX/2), pos.y, pos.z-(SIZEZ/2))
```

Save your program. Double-check that all your indentation is correct before you run it.

Now run up to a tree and hug it (stand as close as you can to its trunk), and run your `scan3D.py` program. What happens?

Did anything happen at all? Remember that this program scans an object to a CSV file, so you have to look at the CSV file `tree.csv` which is in the `MyAdventures` folder, to see what numbers have been stored in it. Open the file `tree.csv` by choosing File ⇨ Open from the editor window and choosing All Files in the file type drop-down menu. Figure 5-6 shows a section of the `tree.csv` file that I captured after hugging a tree on my computer! Because the scanning space is quite small, you might regularly get only half a tree scanned, but you can always change the `SIZE` constants to scan a bigger area.

WARNING

Because the scanning process takes some time to complete, you may see the file appear on your computer before all of the data has been saved to it—so wait a few seconds before opening it to make sure the scanning process has finished.

```
5,5,5

0,0,0,0,0
0,0,17,0,0
0,0,0,0,0
0,0,0,0,0
78,78,78,78,78

0,0,0,0,0
0,0,17,0,0
0,0,0,0,0
0,0,0,0,0
0,0,0,0,0

18,18,18,18,18
18,18,17,18,18
18,18,18,18,18
18,18,18,18,18
0,0,0,0,0
```

FIGURE 5-6 Contents of CSV file after hugging and scanning a tree

DAVID SAYS...

Remember that the direction that your player is facing is not necessarily the direction that is scanned, so make sure you look around the area. The 3D scanner scans from where your player is standing, through increasing values in coordinates. So, if you are standing at 0,0,0, the 3D scanner scans from there through to coordinates that are larger such as 4,4,4. Look back at the diagram in Adventure 2 where you first learnt about coordinates to understand which direction each part of the coordinate represents.

IDLE normally shows only files that end in the `.py` extension in its Open and Save windows, but you can see your `.csv` files by choosing Files of Type ⇨ All Files.

TIPS & TRICKS

Now that you have a 3D scanner and a 3D printer, modify your 3D printer program to use a `FILENAME` constant of `tree.csv`, and then run around in the Minecraft world and keep running `print3D.py`. You should be able to print trees all over the place. Try printing some trees up in the sky and under water to see what happens. How quickly can you build a whole forest of trees this way?

DIGGING INTO THE CODE

In the `scan3D.py` program, you used a special character in the `write()` function that needs to be explained:

```
f.write("\n")
```

The `\n` character (called "backslash n") is a special non-printable character that Python allows you to use inside quotes. All it means is 'move to the next line'. The n character is used because it stands for 'newline'. The backslash character is used to distinguish this letter n from a normal letter n.

In the `scan3D.py` program, you designed the file format so that there was a blank line between each layer of the object data to make it easy for people to read and edit the CSV data file. `f.write("\n")` just puts in this blank line for you.

Later in the `scan3D.py` program, there is some interesting code to do with building up the line variable. Here are the important parts of that code:

```
for x in range(SIZEX):
  line = ""
  for z in range(SIZEZ):
    blockid = mc.getBlock(originx+x, originy+y, originz+z)
    if line != "": # line is not empty
      line = line + ","
    line = line + str(blockid)
```

The parts that are **bold** are part of a very common coding pattern that is regularly used for building comma-separated values. When the x loop starts, the line variable is set to an empty string. Every time the z loop generates another value, it first checks whether the line is empty. If it isn't, it adds a comma. Finally it adds on the `blockid` of this block. The `if` statement is necessary to prevent a comma appearing at the start of the line before the first number, which would confuse the `print3D.py` program when it read it back in.

Building a Duplicating Machine

You now have all the building blocks of programs you need in order to design and build your own 3D duplicating machine that will be envy of all your friends. With it, you will be able to jump into the Minecraft world and make a magic duplicating room materialise, in which you can build any object you like. You can then save these objects to files, load them into the room to edit them or magically duplicate them all over the Minecraft world. Finally, you can escape from the world and make the duplicating room vanish completely, leaving no traces of your magic behind you.

Just like in some of the earlier adventures, you are going to use your existing programs and stitch them together into a much bigger program. Because this program has a number of features, you are going to add a menu system to it so it is easy to control.

Writing the Framework of the Duplicating Machine Program

The first thing to do is to write the framework of the program that makes it all hang together. You start with some dummy functions that just print their name when you call them, and gradually fill in their detail using your existing functions from other programs. You may remember that this is the same way you built up your treasure hunt game in Adventure 4.

1. Start a new file with File ⇨ New File and save it as `duplicator.py`.

2. Import the necessary modules:

   ```
   import mcpi.minecraft as minecraft
   import mcpi.block as block
   import glob
   import time
   import random
   ```

3. Connect to the Minecraft game:

   ```
   mc = minecraft.Minecraft.create()
   ```

4. Set some constants for the size of your duplicating machine. Don't set these too big, or the duplicator will take too long to scan and print objects. Also set an initial default position for your duplicating room:

   ```
   SIZEX = 10
   SIZEY = 10
   SIZEZ = 10
   roomx = 1
   roomy = 1
   roomz = 1
   ```

5. Define some dummy functions for all the features that this program needs to have. You fill in the detail of these soon:

```python
def buildRoom(x, y, z):
    print("buildRoom")

def demolishRoom():
    print("demolishRoom")

def cleanRoom():
    print("cleanRoom")

def listFiles():
    print("listFiles")

def scan3D(filename, originx, originy, originz):
    print("scan3D")

def print3D(filename, originx, originy, originz):
    print("print3D")
```

6. The dummy menu function is special because it returns a value at the end of the function. For now, you can generate a random option and return it so that it is possible to test the early versions of your program, but soon you write a proper menu here. You are writing a dummy menu so that you can test the structure of your program first, and you soon fill this in with a proper menu:

```python
def menu():
    print("menu")
    time.sleep(1)
    return random.randint(1,7)
```

7. Write the main game loop that displays a menu and then uses the function required for that feature. See Digging into the Code for more information about how the anotherGo variable is used:

```python
anotherGo = True
while anotherGo:
    choice = menu()
    if choice == 1:
        pos = mc.player.getTilePos()
        buildRoom(pos.x, pos.y, pos.z)
    elif choice == 2:
        listFiles()
    elif choice == 3:
        filename = input("filename?")
        scan3D(filename, roomx+1, roomy+1, roomz+1)
```

```
    elif choice == 4:
       filename = input("filename?")
       print3D(filename, roomx+1, roomy+1, roomz+1)
    elif choice == 5:
       scan3D("scantemp", roomx+1, roomy+1, roomz+1)
       pos = mc.player.getTilePos()
       print3D("scantemp", pos.x+1, pos.y, pos.z+1)
    elif choice == 6:
       cleanRoom()
    elif choice == 7:
       demolishRoom()
    elif choice == 8:
       anotherGo = False
```

Save your test program and run it. What happens? Figure 5-7 shows what happened when I ran this program on my computer. You can see that the program is telling you what it is doing—it is choosing a random item from the menu, and then it is using the function that handles that menu option. As each function at the moment in your program only prints its name, that is all that you see. You see a different sequence of words on your screen to those in Figure 5-7 because the menu() function chooses a random choice each time it is used.

```
menu
filename?tree.csv
scan3D
menu
filename?tree.csv
scan3D
menu
filename?tree.csv
scan3D
menu
scan3D
print3D
menu
listFiles
menu
buildRoom
menu
scan3D
print3D
menu
filename?
```

FIGURE 5-7 The results of running your test program

A **return** is a way of passing back a value from a function when it jumps back to the program that used the function in the first place.

For example, when you ask for a random number, you use the function `random.randint()`. This function returns a value, which you can store in a variable like this: `a = random.randint(1,100)`. The `return` in Python just allows you to use this same technique of passing back a value from your own functions.

The input() function reads a line of text entered at the keyboard. If you put a string between the brackets, that string is used as a prompt, so `name = input("What is your name?")` both asks a question and gets the response.

When you use input() to read from the keyboard, it always returns a string of text. If you want to enter a number (for example, in your menu system), you have to use the int() function to convert it to a number. Some Python programmers like to do this all on one line, like this: `age = int(input("What is your age?"))`.

Throughout this book you have been using Python version 3. If you use another computer it might have Python version 2 installed. There are a few differences between the two, and one of these is that in Python version 2, you need to use raw_input() instead of input() as used in Python 3. This book uses Python 3.

DIGGING INTO THE CODE

You have used **boolean** variables before in other adventures, but it is worth looking at how the anotherGo variable is used in the duplicator.py program. Here are the important parts:

```
anotherGo = True
while anotherGo:
  choice = menu()
  if choice == 8:
    anotherGo = False
```

This is a common programming design pattern for a loop that runs at least once, asks you if you want another go and, if you don't, it quits the loop. There are many different ways to achieve this same goal in Python, but using a boolean variable is quite a good way to do this, as it is very clear how the program works.

You won't be using it in this book, but Python has a statement called break that can be used to break out of loops. You could do some research on the Internet to see how you could rewrite this loop to use a break statement instead, which would remove the need for the boolean variable.

Displaying the Menu

A menu system is a very useful feature to add to your programs if they have lots of options for you to choose from. This menu system prints all the available options and then loops around, waiting for you to enter a number in the correct range. If you enter a number that is out of range, it just prints the menu again to give you another try.

Modify the menu function and replace it with the following (make sure that you get the indentation correct):

```python
def menu():
  while True:
    print("DUPLICATOR MENU")
    print(" 1. BUILD the duplicator room")
    print(" 2. LIST files")
    print(" 3. SCAN from duplicator room to file")
    print(" 4. LOAD from file into duplicator room")
    print(" 5. PRINT from duplicator room to player.pos")
    print(" 6. CLEAN the duplicator room")
    print(" 7. DEMOLISH the duplicator room")
    print(" 8. QUIT")
    choice = int(input("please choose: "))
    if choice < 1 or choice > 8:
      print("Sorry, please choose a number between 1 and 8")
    else:
      return choice
```

Save the program and run it. What does your program do differently from the one with the dummy menu? Figure 5-8 shows what the real menu looks like.

```
DUPLICATOR MENU
 1. BUILD the scanner room
 2. LIST files
 3. SCAN from scanner room to file
 4. LOAD from file into scanner room
 5. PRINT from scanner room to player.pos
 6. CLEAN the scanner room
 7. DEMOLISH the scanner room
 8. QUIT
please choose: |
```

FIGURE 5-8 The menu system

By writing the framework of the program with the menu system and all the dummy functions, and then filling in the details of the functions one by one and re-testing, you are working in exactly same way as a modern software engineer when he or she develops computer programs. It is good practice to write your programs in small steps, making a change and then testing that change, until you eventually have a complete program. This also means that it never takes you more than two minutes to demonstrate your program to anyone who taps you on your shoulder and asks you to show them your new awesome program!

Building the Duplicator Room

The duplicator room is going to be built out of glass, and it has a missing front on it so that your player can easily climb into it and create and delete blocks.

Replace the `buildRoom()` function with the following code. Be careful of the long lines that use `setBlocks()`, but note that I have not used the ↵ arrow here, because Python allows you to split these across multiple lines (see Digging into the Code for an explanation of why you can sometimes split lines and sometimes cannot):

```
def buildRoom(x, y, z):
    global roomx, roomy, roomz
    roomx = x
    roomy = y
    roomz = z
    mc.setBlocks(roomx, roomy, roomz,
        roomx+SIZEX+1, roomy+SIZEY+1, roomz+SIZEZ+1,
        block.GLASS.id)
    mc.setBlocks(roomx+1, roomy+1, roomz,
        roomx+SIZEX, roomy+SIZEY, roomz+SIZEZ,
        block.AIR.id)
```

Save your program and test it again. Test option 1 on the menu to make sure that you can build the duplicator room. Run to another location in the Minecraft world and choose option 1 again to see what happens! Figure 5-9 shows the duplicator room after it has just been built.

Demolishing the Duplicator Room

When you have run your duplicator program many times, you probably end up with lots of old duplicator rooms built all over the Minecraft world. Only the latest one that you have created is actually a working room, and after some time your world fills up so much that you won't know which room is the right one! To solve this problem, you're adding a feature to your program that demolishes the duplicator room so that your Minecraft world doesn't get cluttered with all these old rooms!

FIGURE 5-9 The duplicator room built in front of you

DIGGING INTO THE CODE

Python uses indentation (spaces or tabs) on the left side to identify which groups of program statements belong together. Whenever you use loops or `if-else` statements, or even functions, you have been using indentation to group program statements that belong together. Python is unusual in its use of indents to group statements into blocks; many other languages—such as C and C++—use special characters such as { and } to group the program statements together. You have to be extra-careful with Python indentation as a result; otherwise your program doesn't work properly!

Most of the time, Python doesn't allow you to split long lines, which is why in this book you often see the ↵ arrow instructing you that this is a long line that should not be broken. However, there are two other ways in Python that you can cope with long lines.

Firstly, you can use a line continuation character—if the last character at the end of a line is a backslash character (like this: \) then you can continue on the next line.

```
a = 1
if a == 1 or \
a == 2:
  print ("yes")
```

The second method that you can sometimes use to split long lines is to split them at a point where it is obvious to Python that the line has not finished. For example, if you are setting initial values in a list, or using a function, you can break the lines when Python knows from the other parts of the line that there must be more code to follow. Here are two examples of where Python allows you to split a long line into shorter lines because the open brackets tell Python that the line has not finished until a matching close bracket is seen:

```
names = ["David",
"Steve",
"Joan",
"Joanne"
]


mc.setBlocks(x1, y1, z1,
x2, y2, z2, block.AIR.id)
```

Demolishing the duplicator room is just like using your `clearSpace.py` program from Adventure 3. All you need to know is the outer coordinates of the room. Because the room is one block bigger all around the outside of the duplicating space defined by `SIZEX`, `SIZEY` and `SIZEZ`, this is quite simple to do with a little bit of maths.

Modify the `demolishRoom()` function to look like this.

```
def demolishRoom():
  mc.setBlocks(roomx, roomy, roomz,
    roomx+SIZEX+1, roomy+SIZEY+1, roomz+SIZEZ+1,
    block.AIR.id)
```

Save your program and run it again. Now it's easy to build or demolish your duplicator room. Just use option 1 on your menu to build it and option 7 to demolish it.

Scanning from the Duplicator Room

You have written this part of the program before, in your `scan3D.py` program, so you can use that with some small modifications.

1. Replace the `scan3D()` function with the following code. This code is almost identical to the `scan3D.py` program, but the line in bold has been added to make it show the progress of the scanning on the Minecraft chat. Scanning a big room can take a long time, so it is nice to have some indication of how far

through the process your program has got. You can use copy and paste to bring in the code from your earlier program to save some typing time here:

```python
def scan3D(filename, originx, originy, originz):
    f = open(filename, "w")
    f.write(str(SIZEX) + "," + str(SIZEY) + "," + ↵
      str(SIZEZ) + "\n")
    for y in range(SIZEY):
        mc.postToChat("scan:" + str(y))
        f.write("\n")
        for x in range(SIZEX):
            line = ""
            for z in range(SIZEZ):
                blockid = mc.getBlock(originx+x, originy+y, ↵
                  originz+z)
                if line != "":
                    line = line + ","
                line = line + str(blockid)
            f.write(line + "\n")
    f.close()
```

2. Save the program and test it again by jumping into the duplicating room, building something and then choosing option 3 from the menu. Open up the file that it creates to check that the object has been scanned properly. Figure 5-10 shows a portion of a scanned file. Note that there are lots of zeros; this is because it has scanned all the AIR blocks as well.

```
10,10,10

0,0,0,0,0,0,0,0,0,0
0,0,0,0,0,0,0,0,0,0
0,0,0,0,0,0,0,0,0,0
0,0,0,0,0,0,0,0,0,0
0,0,0,0,1,0,0,1,1,0
0,0,0,0,1,1,1,1,1,0
0,0,0,0,0,0,0,0,0,0
0,0,0,0,0,0,0,0,0,0
0,0,0,0,0,0,0,0,0,0
0,0,0,0,0,0,0,0,0,0

0,0,0,0,0,0,0,0,0,0
0,0,0,0,0,0,0,0,0,0
0,0,0,0,0,0,0,0,0,0
0,0,0,0,0,0,0,0,0,0
0,0,0,0,0,0,0,0,0,0
0,0,0,0,1,0,0,0,0,0
```

FIGURE 5-10 The contents of the scanned file

Cleaning the Duplicator Room

Fancy a spring clean? Sometimes it is useful to have a fresh start and just clear the room. You could do this by demolishing the room and rebuilding it, but it's really easy to add a clean feature, as it is only the coordinates that differ from the demolish Room() function.

1. Modify the `cleanRoom()` function so that it looks like the following code. Note how the start coordinates are all bigger than the edge of the room, and the end coordinates are not as far over as in the `demolishRoom()` function. This way, it clears the inner space of the room without destroying its walls:

```
def cleanRoom():
  mc.setBlocks(roomx+1, roomy+1, roomz+1,
    roomx+SIZEX, roomy+SIZEY, roomz+SIZEZ, block.AIR.id)
```

2. Save your program and run it again. Create something inside the room and then choose option 6 to test whether you can clear the room quickly.

Printing from the Duplicator Room

Printing (duplicating) the object that is in the room is really easy, because you have already written the `print3D.py` program that does this, and it is identical. Here it is again so you can see it all in one place:

```
def print3D(filename, originx, originy, originz):
  f = open(filename, "r")
  lines = f.readlines()
  coords = lines[0].split(",")
  sizex = int(coords[0])
  sizey = int(coords[1])
  sizez = int(coords[2])
  lineidx = 1
  for y in range(sizey):
    mc.postToChat("print:" + str(y))
    lineidx = lineidx + 1
    for x in range(sizex):
      line = lines[lineidx]
      lineidx = lineidx + 1
      data = line.split(",")
      for z in range(sizez):
        blockid = int(data[z])
        mc.setBlock(originx+x, originy+y, originz+z, ↵
          blockid)
```

Save the program and run it again. Test that you can build something in the room, run to somewhere in the Minecraft world and then choose option 5 from the menu. The contents of the room are scanned then printed just to the side of where your player is standing. You should be able to run to anywhere in the Minecraft world and duplicate your objects many times. Try duplicating objects in the sky and under water to see what happens! Figure 5-11 shows the results of running this program.

FIGURE 5-11 A stone shape in the room and printed next to your player

Listing Files

Your last task is to write a useful little function that lists all the files in your filing system that are CSV files. You could just use the File Manager, but it is nice to add this feature to your program so that you have everything you need in one place:

1. Modify the `listFiles()` function to use the `glob.glob()` function to read in a list of all files and print them. See Digging into the Code for an explanation of how this works.

   ```
   def listFiles():
     print("\nFILES:")
     files = glob.glob("*.csv")
     for filename in files:
       print(filename)
     print("\n")
   ```

2. Save the program and run it again. Scan a few objects into CSV files and then choose option 2 from the menu to make sure that they are all listed. Figure 5-12 shows the files I created when I ran this on my computer.

```
DUPLICATOR MENU
 1. BUILD the scanner room
 2. LIST files
 3. SCAN from scanner room to file
 4. LOAD from file into scanner room
 5. PRINT from scanner room to player.pos
 6. CLEAN the scanner room
 7. DEMOLISH the scanner room
 8. QUIT
please choose: 2

FILES:
blocks.csv
maze1.csv
object1.csv
tree.csv


DUPLICATOR MENU
 1. BUILD the scanner room
 2. LIST files
 3. SCAN from scanner room to file
 4. LOAD from file into scanner room
 5. PRINT from scanner room to player.pos
 6. CLEAN the scanner room
 7. DEMOLISH the scanner room
 8. QUIT
please choose:
```

FIGURE 5-12 Viewing the list of CSV files you have created

DIGGING INTO THE CODE

`glob.glob()`—what a funny name for a function. So funny that you have to put it twice!

The name `glob` is used twice because the first one is the name of the module (the `glob` module) that it was imported from at the top of your program. The second use of `glob` is the name of the function `glob` inside the module `glob`.

But what does `glob` do, and why is it called `glob`?

It is simply short for the words "global command" and stems from the early days of the design of the Unix operating system. You can read about the history behind the name `glob` on the Wikipedia page at `http://en.wikipedia.org/wiki/Glob_(programming)`.

All it does is collect a list of files that match a pattern (or a **wildcard**). When you use `glob.glob("*.csv")`, Python searches the current directory in the computer's filing system and generates a list of all the files that end in `".csv"`.

So, if you have the files `one.csv`, `two.csv` and `three.csv` in your `MyAdventures` folder, using `glob.glob("*.csv")` returns a Python list that looks like this:

```
['one.csv', 'two.csv', 'three.csv']
```

Remember that `for` loops through all items in a list, which is why these next lines of code are really useful:

```
for name in glob.glob("*.csv")
  print(name)
```

A **wildcard** is a special character that can be used to select lots of similar names or words. It's like a joker or a 'wild card' in a pack of playing cards; it can represent anything you want it to be.

In Python, the wildcard is often used to select lots of similarly named files in the filing system, such as 'all CSV files'. This can be done with `glob.glob("*.csv")`; the * character marks the wildcard position, and `glob.glob()` matches any file in the filing system that ends with the letters `.csv`.

CHALLENGE

If in your `duplicator.py` program, you type a filename that does not exist, the program crashes with an error and leaves your duplicating room in the Minecraft world. Make your program more robust by researching on the Internet how you can detect that a file does not exist so that your program does not crash. Extend the data that is written to the file so that the extra data is also stored and retrieved in the file. This makes it possible to store WOOL blocks with different colours and to scan and build multi-coloured creations.

Quick Reference Table

Command	Description

`f = open("data.txt", "r")`
`tips = f.readlines()`
`f.close()`
`for t in tips:`
`  print(t)`
	Reading lines from a file

`f = open("scores.txt", "w")`
`f.write("Victoria:26000\n")`
`f.write("Amanda:10000\n")`
`f.write("Ria:32768\n")`
`f.close()`
	Writing lines to a file

`import glob`
`names = glob.glob("*.csv")`
`for n in names:`
`  print(n)`
	Getting a list of matching filenames

`a = "\n\n  hello  \n\n"`
`a = a.strip()`
`print(a)`
	Stripping unwanted white space from strings

Further Adventures in Data Files

In this adventure, you learnt how to read from and write to data files. This opens up endless opportunities for saving and restoring parts of the Minecraft world, and even bringing in large amounts of real-world data from other sources, such as websites. You built your own 3D mazes with lots of winding tunnels and dead ends, and finished by building a fully functional 3D scanner and printer, complete with a full menu system. This technique of writing a menu system is useful for many other programs, too!

There are many sources of "live data" on the Internet. One data source that I found when researching for this book was the Nottingham City Council car park data here: `http://data.nottinghamtravelwise.org.uk/parking.xml`. This data is updated every five minutes and tracks cars as they enter and exit the car parks. I have written a Python program and put it on my github page that processes this data and prints out useful information here: `https://github.com/whaleygeek/pyparsers`. See if you can use this to write a Minecraft game that builds car parks with cars in them, inside your Minecraft world. Your game could be a car-parking challenge where you have to run around the Minecraft world and try to find a spare parking space in a limited time!

Everything you ever wanted to know about 3D mazes is explained in detail on this fantastic web page: `http://www.astrolog.org/labyrnth/algrithm.htm`. This page includes lots of example multilayer 3D mazes that are stored in normal text files. Look through the site and see if you can find a file for a multi-layer maze, and modify your maze program to use the techniques you learned with your 3D duplicating machine to build a huge multilayered maze. You might even experiment with some of the suggestions on this website to write a Python program that automatically generates mazes for you!

Achievement Unlocked: **Shattering the laws of physics and magically materialising and dematerialising huge objects all over the Minecraft world at the push of a button.**

In the Next Adventure. . .

In Adventure 6, you learn how to build complex 2D and 3D objects by writing Python programs. You learn how to keep time with the Minecraft clock, build polygons and other multi-sided shapes with just a few lines of Python code—and set off on an exciting expedition to the Pyramids!

Adventure 6
Building 2D and 3D Structures

ONE OF THE great things about programming in Minecraft is that in addition to looking at your creations on a 2D screen you can actually bring them to life in a virtual 3D world. You can walk around them, go inside them, make them bigger—even blow them up if you like! By using the ideas originally created to display 3D objects on a 2D screen, you can code 3D objects in Minecraft, turning the ordinary into the extraordinary.

In this adventure you find out how to use the `minecraftstuff` module to create 2D lines and shapes, which, when combined with a little maths, allow you to program a clock so big you can stand on its hands as they go round (see Figure 6-1). After you have mastered creating 2D shapes, you then learn how to combine them to create enormous 3D structures in seconds.

FIGURE 6-1 A massive Minecraft clock

The minecraftstuff Module

minecraftstuff is an extension module to the Minecraft API, which was written for *Adventures in Minecraft* and contains all the code you need to draw shapes and control 3D objects. It has a set of functions called MinecraftDrawing, which allows you to create lines, circles, spheres and other shapes. Because this complicated code is in a separate module it makes it simpler for you to create the code, and it's easier to understand too. Modules are a way of splitting up a program into smaller chunks. When programs get too big, they are more difficult to read and harder to understand, and it takes longer to track down problems.

The minecraftstuff module is included in the "Adventures in Minecraft" starter kit that you installed in Adventure 1, and you can import it into a Minecraft program in the same way as you import the minecraft and block modules.

The minecraftstuff module can do a lot more than what is covered in *Adventures in Minecraft*, so be sure to have a look at the documentation (https://minecraft-stuff.readthedocs.io) and experiment with it.

If you are not using a starter kit, there are also installation instructions, although you have to change how the minecraftstuff module is imported, as for convenience it is included in the mcpi folder of the starter kit.

Creating Lines, Circles and Spheres

When you combine a lot of small, simple things, you can create something as large and complex as you want. In this adventure, you're going to use lots of lines, circles, spheres and other shapes to produce a really big Minecraft structure. In this part of the adventure, you create a new program, import the modules you need and set up the `minecraft` and `minecraftdrawing` modules. Later, you use the functions in the modules to draw lines, circles and spheres.

Start up Minecraft and Python IDLE. You should have had a bit of practice with starting everything up by now, but refer to Adventure 1 if you need any reminders.

1. Start by opening IDLE and creating a new file. Save the file as `LinesCirclesAndSpheres.py` in the `MyAdventures` folder.

2. Import the `minecraft`, `block`, `minecraftstuff` and `time` modules by typing the following lines:

   ```
   import mcpi.minecraft as minecraft
   import mcpi.block as block
   import mcpi.minecraftstuff as minecraftstuff
   import time
   ```

3. Create the connection to Minecraft:

   ```
   mc = minecraft.Minecraft.create()
   ```

4. Use the `minecraftstuff` module to create a `MinecraftDrawing` object by typing

   ```
   mcdrawing = minecraftstuff.MinecraftDrawing(mc)
   ```

DIGGING INTO THE CODE

`MinecraftDrawing` is a class in the `minecraftstuff` module. Classes are part of a special method of programming called object-oriented programming (OOP) which is a way of grouping similar functions and data together—in this case, Minecraft drawing functions and data—so they are easier to understand and use. When you use a class and give it a name (such as `mcdrawing`) you create an object. This is known as instantiation. An object is similar to a variable but rather than just holding values (or data), it also has functions!

continued

continued

OOP is a complex subject and volumes of books have been written about what it is and how to use it successfully; there is, however, a useful introduction to using classes in Python at `en.wikibooks.org/wiki/A_Beginner's_Python_Tutorial/Classes`.

You can look at the code in `minecraftstuff` by using IDLE to open the `minecraftstuff.py` file in the `MyAdventures/mcpi` folder.

Drawing Lines

The `MinecraftDrawing` object has a function named `drawLine()`, which when **called** and **passed** two positions (x, y, z) and a block type as parameters it creates a line of blocks between those positions—just like the `setBlocks()` function you first learnt about in Adventure 3.

DEFINITIONS

When a function needs information to run — such as `setBlock()`, which needs an x, y, z and a block type — these values are known as **parameters**. When a program uses that function, it is said to be **called** and **passed** parameters.

The following code uses the `drawLine` function to create a line of blocks like that shown in Figure 6-2:

```
drawLine(x1, y1, z1, x2, y2, z2, blockType, blockData)
```

Now update your program so that it uses the `drawLine()` function to create three lines in Minecraft — one straight up, one across and one diagonal from the player's position. Add the following code to the bottom of the `LinesCirclesAndSpheres.py` program:

1. Find the position of the player by typing the following code:

   ```
   pos = mc.player.getTilePos()
   ```

2. Draw a vertical line of 20 blocks from the player's position straight upwards, by typing

   ```
   mcdrawing.drawLine(pos.x, pos.y, pos.z,
                      pos.x, pos.y + 20, pos.z,
                      block.WOOL.id, 1)
   ```

FIGURE 6-2 The `drawLine()` function creates a line of blocks between two sets of x,y,z points.

3. Now draw a horizontal line of 20 blocks by typing

```
mcdrawing.drawLine(pos.x, pos.y, pos.z,
                   pos.x + 20, pos.y, pos.z,
                   block.WOOL.id, 2)
```

4. Draw a diagonal line of 20 blocks across and up:

```
mcdrawing.drawLine(pos.x, pos.y, pos.z,
                   pos.x + 20, pos.y + 20, pos.z,
                   block.WOOL.id, 3)
```

5. Because you will be adding to this program, add a time delay so there is a gap between each section. The gap lets you can see what is happening:

```
time.sleep(5)
```

6. Save the file and run the program. You should have created three lines of blocks, each in a different colour of wool: one running vertically from the player's position, the second running horizontally and the third running diagonally between them.

DIGGING INTO THE CODE

The `drawLine()` function uses the Bresenham line algorithm to create the line. Have a look at `https://en.wikipedia.org/wiki/Bresenham's_line_algorithm` to learn more about the algorithm.

Drawing Circles

You don't have to stick to lines—you can also use `MinecraftDrawing` to create circles, by using the `drawCircle()` function, passing a centre point for the circle, a radius and a block type. You can create a circle by using the following code to call the `drawCircle` function:

```
drawCircle(x, y, z, radius, blockType, blockData)
```

To create the circle shown in Figure 6-3, add the following code to the bottom of the `LinesCirclesAndSpheres.py` program:

1. Find the current position of the player by typing the following code:

   ```
   pos = mc.player.getTilePos()
   ```

2. Draw a circle, starting 20 blocks above the player and with a radius of 20 blocks:

   ```
   mcdrawing.drawCircle(pos.x, pos.y + 20, pos.z, 20,
                        block.WOOL.id, 4)
   ```

3. Add a time delay so you can see what's happening in the program and to give you a chance to move the player:

   ```
   time.sleep(5)
   ```

4. Save the file and run the program.

FIGURE 6-3 `drawCircle` creates a circle using a radius around a centre position (x,y,z)

The lines are drawn again first; you then have five seconds to move the player before the circle is drawn directly above the player.

Drawing Spheres

The `drawSphere()` function is similar to `drawCircle()` in that you work with a centre point, a radius and a block type. You can create a sphere by using the following code to call the `drawSphere()` function:

```
drawSphere(x, y, z, radius, blockType, blockData)
```

To create the sphere shown in Figure 6-4, add the following code to the bottom of the `LinesCirclesAndSpheres.py` program:

1. Find the current position of the player by typing

    ```
    pos = mc.player.getTilePos()
    ```

2. To draw a sphere starting 20 blocks above the player, with a radius of 15 blocks, type

    ```
    mcdrawing.drawSphere(pos.x, pos.y + 20, pos.z, 15,
                         block.WOOL.id, 5)
    ```

3. Save the file and run the program.

The lines and circles are drawn again, giving you five seconds to move the player before the sphere is redrawn.

You can download the complete code for lines, circles and spheres from the *Adventures in Minecraft* companion website at www.wiley.com/go/adventuresinminecraft2e.

FIGURE 6-4 `drawSphere` creates a sphere using a radius around a centre position (x,y,z)

Spheres are great for creating explosions in Minecraft. By drawing a sphere of `AIR`, you can remove all the blocks around the centre of the sphere, creating a 'hole' in the world.

CHALLENGE

Now that you've seen how simple it is to create basic shapes, try creating your own 3D art masterpiece in code, using lines, circles and spheres.

Creating a Minecraft Clock

After seeing how to create circles and lines in Minecraft, perhaps you can see how you would create the clock in Figure 6-1. The face is simply a large circle, and each of the hands is a line. Now comes the difficult part—working out where to put the lines and how to make them move.

To see a tutorial on how to create the Minecraft Clock, visit the companion website at www.wiley.com/go/adventuresinminecraft2e.

In this part of the adventure, you use **trigonometry** to work out where to point the hands by turning the angle of the hand into the x and y coordinates on the clock face (see Figure 6-5). You're going to make the hands seem to move by first drawing them with blocks then removing them by drawing them with AIR and then drawing them again in a new position.

FIGURE 6-5 Finding where to point the hands on a clock face

Trigonometry is the branch of mathematics that deals with the relationships between angles and the lengths of sides in triangles. Visit en.wikipedia.org/wiki/Trigonometry to learn more.

To create your clock, follow these steps:

1. Create a new program for the Minecraft clock by opening IDLE and creating a new file. Save the file as `MinecraftClock.py` in the `MyAdventures` folder.

2. Import the `minecraft`, `block`, `minecraftstuff`, `time`, `datetime` and `math` modules by typing the following code:

    ```
    import mcpi.minecraft as minecraft
    import mcpi.block as block
    import mcpi.minecraftstuff as minecraftstuff
    import time
    import datetime
    import math
    ```

3. Create a function, `findPointOnCircle()`. When you pass this function the centre of the circle and the angle of the clock's hands, the function returns the position of the clock's hands as shown in Figure 6-5.

    ```
    def findPointOnCircle(cx, cy, radius, angle):
        x = cx + math.sin(math.radians(angle)) * radius
        y = cy + math.cos(math.radians(angle)) * radius
        x = int(round(x, 0))
        y = int(round(y, 0))
        return(x, y)
    ```

4. Connect to `Minecraft` and create the `MinecraftDrawing` object:

    ```
    mc = minecraft.Minecraft.create()
    mcdrawing = minecraftstuff.MinecraftDrawing(mc)
    ```

5. Find the player's current position by typing

    ```
    pos = mc.player.getTilePos()
    ```

6. Now you're going to create variables for the centre of the clock (which is 25 blocks above the player's position), the radius of the clock face and the length of the clock hands:

    ```
    clockMiddle = pos
    clockMiddle.y = clockMiddle.y + 25
    CLOCK_RADIUS = 20
    HOUR_HAND_LENGTH = 10
    MIN_HAND_LENGTH = 18
    SEC_HAND_LENGTH = 20
    ```

7. Draw the clock face using `drawCircle()`:

    ```
    mcdrawing.drawCircle(
        clockMiddle.x, clockMiddle.y, clockMiddle.z,
        CLOCK_RADIUS, block.DIAMOND_BLOCK.id)
    ```

8. The program is not finished, but you should run it now to check everything is working and that a large circle (the clock face) appears above the player.

Next you add the code to your program for the hands of your clock:

1. Start an infinite loop. All the code after this point will be inside this loop.

```
while True:
```

2. Ask your computer what the time is by using the function `datetime.`
`datetime.now()`. You then split the time into hours, minutes and seconds.
Because your clock is a 12-hour clock, not a 24-hour one, you need to specify
that if the time is after noon, 12 should be subtracted from the hour (so that, for
example, if the time is 14:00, it is shown as 2 o'clock). Do this by typing the
following code:

```
timeNow = datetime.datetime.now()
hours = timeNow.hour
if hours >= 12:
    hours = timeNow.hour - 12
minutes = timeNow.minute
seconds = timeNow.second
```

3. Draw the hour hand. The angle of this is 360 degrees divided by 12 hours, multiplied by the current hour. Find the x and y position for the end of the hand using
`findPointOnCircle()` and draw the hand using `drawLine()` by typing the
following:

```
hourHandAngle = (360 / 12) * hours

hourHandX, hourHandY = findPointOnCircle(
    clockMiddle.x, clockMiddle.y,
    HOUR_HAND_LENGTH, hourHandAngle)

mcdrawing.drawLine(
    clockMiddle.x, clockMiddle.y, clockMiddle.z,
    hourHandX, hourHandY, clockMiddle.z,
    block.DIRT.id)
```

4. Draw the minute hand, which is one block behind (z–1) the hour hand, by
typing:

```
minHandAngle = (360 / 60) * minutes

minHandX, minHandY = findPointOnCircle(
    clockMiddle.x, clockMiddle.y,
    MIN_HAND_LENGTH, minHandAngle)

mcdrawing.drawLine(
    clockMiddle.x, clockMiddle.y, clockMiddle.z-1,
    minHandX, minHandY, clockMiddle.z-1,
    block.WOOD_PLANKS.id)
```

5. Add the second hand, which is one block in front (z+1) of the hour hand:

```
secHandAngle = (360 / 60) * seconds

secHandX, secHandY = findPointOnCircle(
    clockMiddle.x, clockMiddle.y,
    SEC_HAND_LENGTH, secHandAngle)

mcdrawing.drawLine(
    clockMiddle.x, clockMiddle.y, clockMiddle.z+1,
    secHandX, secHandY, clockMiddle.z+1,
    block.STONE.id)
```

6. Wait for one second:

```
time.sleep(1)
```

7. Again your program is not finished, but you should run it to check that the hands appear. Have a look at what happens as the hands move.

You may have noticed that the hands of the clock aren't cleared away as they move. The next step is clearing the hands of the clock by drawing them again using AIR:

1. Clear the hour hand:

```
mcdrawing.drawLine(
    clockMiddle.x, clockMiddle.y, clockMiddle.z,
    hourHandX, hourHandY, clockMiddle.z,
    block.AIR.id)
```

2. Clear the minute hand:

```
mcdrawing.drawLine(
    clockMiddle.x, clockMiddle.y, clockMiddle.z-1,
    minHandX, minHandY, clockMiddle.z-1,
    block.AIR.id)
```

3. Clear the second hand:

```
mcdrawing.drawLine(
    clockMiddle.x, clockMiddle.y, clockMiddle.z+1,
    secHandX, secHandY, clockMiddle.z+1,
    block.AIR.id)
```

4. Run the program to see the result of your efforts: a massive Minecraft clock above the player. Make sure the player is on the correct side of the clock, though; otherwise time will be going backwards!

You can download the complete code for the Minecraft Clock from the companion website www.wiley.com/go/adventuresinminecraft2e but I strongly recommend that you type in the code yourself as you read through the steps. You'll learn a lot more that way!

DIGGING INTO THE CODE

The `findPointOnCircle()` function works out a point (x, y) on a circle from the centre position of the circle (cx, cy), the radius of the circle and the angle you've specified (refer to Figure 6-5).

1. The function is defined with `cx`, `cy`, `radius` and `angle` as input parameters:

```
def findPointOnCircle(cx, cy, radius, angle):
```

2. The point on the circle (x, y) is calculated using the `math` functions `sin()` and `cos()`, multiplied by the radius:

```
x = cx + math.sin(math.radians(angle)) * radius
y = cy + math.cos(math.radians(angle)) * radius
```

The `math.sin()` and `math.cos()` functions need radians to be passed to them. Radians are a different way of measuring angles (rather than the often used 0 – 360 degrees), so the `math.radians()` function is used to convert the angles into radians.

3. The x, y values calculated are decimals, but the function needs whole numbers, so the `round()` and `int()` functions are used to round the decimal number to its nearest whole number and convert it from decimal to integer:

```
x = int(round(x, 0))
y = int(round(y, 0))
```

4. The x and y values are then returned to the program:

```
return(x, y)
```

The `findPointOnCircle()` function returns two parameters (x, y), so when it is called two variables must be provided:

```
x, y = findPointOnCircle(cx, cy, radius, angle)
```

You create the hands of the clock using a three-step process:

1. Work out the angle of the hand by dividing 360° by 12 or 60 (depending whether it is an hour, minute or second hand) and then multiplying that by the number of hours, minutes or seconds:

```
hourHandAngle = (360 / 12) * hours
```

continued

continued

2. Find the coordinates (x, y) of the end of the hand using the `findPoint OnCircle()` function:

```
hourHandX, hourHandY = findPointOnCircle( ↵
    clockMiddle.x, clockMiddle.y,
    HOUR_HAND_LENGTH, hourHandAngle)
```

3. Draw a line from the middle of the clock to the end of the hand:

```
mcdrawing.drawLine( ↵
    clockMiddle.x, clockMiddle.y, clockMiddle.z,
    hourHandX, hourHandY, clockMiddle.z,
    block.DIRT.id)
```

CHALLENGE

The hour hand on real clocks tracks every minute of the hour. For example, if the time is 11:30, the hour hand is halfway between the 11 and the 12. The code for the Minecraft clock you've just created doesn't work this way—the hour hand remains pointing at 11 until 11:59:59 ticks over to 12:00:00.

See if you can make your Minecraft clock work like a real clock by changing how you calculate the hour angle.

Drawing Polygons

A polygon is any 2D shape made up of straight connecting sides. It can have any number of sides, from three (a triangle) upwards. As you can see from Figure 6-6, you can create any number of interesting polygons in Minecraft.

Although they are 2D shapes, you'll find polygons extremely useful for making 3D graphics because you can create virtually any 3D object by connecting lots of polygons together. When polygons are used together to create 3D objects, they are known as faces. You can create some awesome structures this way. Just look at Figure 6-7, which shows the skyline of Manhattan Island, created by lots of polygons (see how it's done at `www.stuffaboutcode.com/2013/04/minecraft-pi-edition-manhattan-stroll.html`).

FIGURE 6-6 Examples of polygons in Minecraft

FIGURE 6-7 Minecraft skyline of Manhattan Island, New York

A **face** is a single flat surface that is part of a larger object; for example, one side of a cube or the top of a drum.

You can create polygons (or faces) using the `drawFace()` function in `MinecraftDrawing`. The function expects a list of points (x, y, z) that, when connected in sequence, create a complete polygon. Passing a `True` or `False` in the filled parameter determines whether the face is filled, and the final parameter is the type of block the face should be made from (see Figure 6-8):

```
drawFace(points, filled, blockType, blockData)
```

Create a new program to experiment with the `drawFace()` function and create the triangle shown in Figure 6-8:

1. Open IDLE and create a new file. Save the file as `Polygon.py` in the `MyAdventures` folder.

2. Import the `minecraft`, `block` and `minecraftstuff` modules by typing

   ```
   import mcpi.minecraft as minecraft
   import mcpi.block as block
   import mcpi.minecraftstuff as minecraftstuff
   ```

FIGURE 6-8 `drawFace()` used to create a triangle from three points

3. Connect to minecraft and create the `MinecraftDrawing` object:

   ```
   mc = minecraft.Minecraft.create()
   mcdrawing = minecraftstuff.MinecraftDrawing(mc)
   ```

4. Get the player's current position:

```
pos = mc.player.getTilePos()
```

5. Use the `minecraftstuff.Points` class to create a list of points:

```
points = minecraftstuff.Points()
```

6. Then add three points (x, y, z) to the points, which, when joined together, create a triangle:

```
points.add(pos.x, pos.y, pos.z)
points.add(pos.x + 20, pos.y, pos.z)
points.add(pos.x + 10, pos.y + 20, pos.z)
```

7. Use the `MinecraftDrawing.drawFace` function to create the triangle polygon:

```
mcdrawing.drawFace(points, True, block.WOOL.id, 6)
```

8. Save the file and run the program to create the triangle polygon.

CHALLENGE

What other shapes can you make using `drawFace()`? How about a five-sided shape such as a pentagon?

Pyramids

Find a picture of a pyramid and take a good look at it. What do you notice? What shape are its sides? What do all the sides have in common? How many sides does it have?

As you probably know, each side of a pyramid (except the base) is always a triangle. The pyramids in Egypt had four sides (or five if you include the base), but they can have any number of sides from three upward. Did you also notice that the base of any pyramid will fit exactly into a circle! Take a look at Figure 6-9 to see what I mean.

You are now going to create a program, which by using the `drawFace()` and `findPointOnCircle()` functions, makes any size of pyramid, of any height, with any number of sides:

1. Open IDLE and create a new file. Save the file as `MinecraftPyramids.py` in the `MyAdventures` folder.

2. Import the `minecraft`, `block`, `minecraftstuff` and `math` modules by typing:

```
import mcpi.minecraft as minecraft
import mcpi.block as block
import mcpi.minecraftstuff as minecraftstuff
import math
```

FIGURE 6-9 A pyramid made of triangles, which fits exactly into a circle

3. Create the `findPointOnCircle()` function, which will be used to work out where each of the triangles which make up the pyramid will be placed:

```
def findPointOnCircle(cx, cy, radius, angle):
    x = cx + math.sin(math.radians(angle)) * radius
    y = cy + math.cos(math.radians(angle)) * radius
    x = int(round(x, 0))
    y = int(round(y, 0))
    return(x, y)
```

4. Connect to Minecraft and create the `MinecraftDrawing` object:

```
mc = minecraft.Minecraft.create()
mcdrawing = minecraftstuff.MinecraftDrawing(mc)
```

5. Set up the variables for your pyramid. The middle of the pyramid is the player's position. The values of these variables change the size (or radius), height and number of sides of the pyramid.

```
middle = mc.player.getTilePos()
RADIUS = 20
HEIGHT = 10
SIDES = 4
```

6. Loop through each side of the pyramid; all the code after this point is indented under the for loop:

```
for side in range(0, SIDES):
```

The bigger the pyramid, the longer the program takes to run and the longer Minecraft takes to show the pyramid in the game. If your pyramid is too tall it may also go over the maximum height of the game. So take it slowly and expand your values gradually. You can make enormous pyramids, but you may need to be patient; if they are really big they take a while to appear!

7. For each side of the pyramid, calculate the angles of the sides of the triangle and then use findPointOnCircle() to find the x, y, z coordinates. The angle is calculated by dividing 360 degrees by the total number of sides, multiplied by the number of the side which is being drawn, as you can see in Figure 6-10. Type the code as follows indented under the for loop:

```
point1Angle = int(round((360 / SIDES) * side,0))
point1X, point1Z = findPointOnCircle(
    middle.x, middle.z, RADIUS, point1Angle)

point2Angle = int(round((360 / SIDES) * (side + 1),0))
point2X, point2Z = findPointOnCircle(
    middle.x, middle.z, RADIUS, point2Angle)
```

8. Create the points of the triangle and use drawFace() to create the side of the pyramid as follows:

```
points = minecraftstuff.Points()
points.add(point1X, middle.y, point1Z)
points.add(point2X, middle.y, point2Z)
points.add(middle.x, middle.y + HEIGHT, middle.z)
mcdrawing.drawFace(points, True, block.SANDSTONE.id)
```

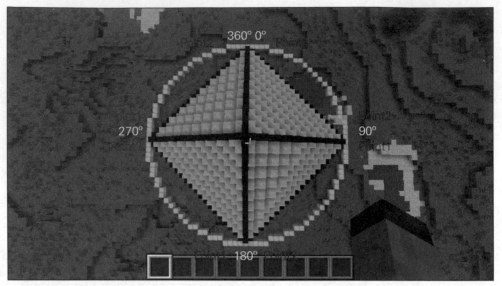

FIGURE 6-10 The angles of a four-sided pyramid

Sandstone (`block.SANDSTONE.id`) is a really useful block type to use for pyramids as it looks very similar to sand but has a very useful characteristic—it isn't affected by gravity and doesn't fall down if there are no blocks underneath it to hold it up. If you were to make the pyramid out of sand, the player would be buried in it and would have to spend ages digging himself out.

9. Save the file and run the program. A pyramid appears above the player—and traps him inside!

This program can create pyramids of any size and with any number of sides. Try changing the pyramid variables in the program and re-running it. Figure 6-11 shows a couple of impressive examples.

You can download the complete code for the Minecraft pyramid from the *Adventures in Minecraft* companion website at `www.wiley.com/go/adventuresinminecraft2e`.

CHALLENGE

The pyramid you've created doesn't have a base. Can you create a polygon that fits on the bottom of the pyramid? This should be easy for a four-sided pyramid but if you code it correctly, the same code should also work for a five-, six- or seven-sided pyramid.

FIGURE 6-11 Minecraft pyramids

Further Adventures with 2D and 3D Shapes

Using the `drawFace()` function, you can create any sort of **polyhedron**, which is a shape with flat faces (just like the pyramids you created earlier), so why not create some more?

You can find lots of polyhedron examples and good ideas at the following websites:

- Maths is Fun (`www.mathsisfun.com/geometry/polyhedron.html`)
- Kids Math Games (`www.kidsmathgamesonline.com/facts/geometry/ 3dpolyhedronshapes.html`)

Quick Reference Table

Command	Description

`mcdrawing.drawLine(0, 0, 0,`
`                10, 10, 10,`
`                block.DIRT.id)`
	Draw a line between two points

`mcdrawing.drawCircle(0, 0, 0,`
`                radius,`
`                block.DIRT.id)`
	Draw a circle

`mcdrawing.drawSphere(0, 0, 0,`
`                radius,`
`                block.DIRT.id)`
	Draw a sphere

`tri = minecraftstuff.Points()`
`filled = True`
`tri.add(0,0,0)`
`tri.add(10,0,0)`
`tri.add(5,10,0)`
`mcdrawing.drawFace(tri,`
`                filled,`
`                block.DIRT.id)`
	Draw a polygon or face (e.g. a triangle)

Achievement Unlocked: **3D master, creator of massive structures, all hail the pyramid builder!**

In the Next Adventure. . .

In the next adventure, you learn how to give Minecraft objects a mind of their own, make friends with a block and avoid an alien invasion.

Adventure 7

Giving Blocks a Mind of Their Own

COMPUTERS DON'T THINK. They aren't capable of having any thoughts at all; they can only ever do what programmers tell them to do. You can, however, make computers *look* like they are thinking and making decisions by themselves. By programming your computer to "understand" what's happening and giving it rules to "decide" what to do next, you can open a door to a lot of fun.

In this adventure, you are going to program a block friend who will follow you around, provided you don't get too far away. You are also going to create a flying saucer that chases you until it can get above you and beam you aboard.

You learn how to make a block move and follow the path it decides is best, as well as how to use the Python `random` module to make it look as if the computer is thinking. You also create shapes using the `MinecraftShape` functions in the `minecraftstuff` module (which is included in your starter kit).

Your Block Friend

Minecraft can be a lonely world. But your player doesn't have to be alone—you can create a block that will follow him around, talk to him and be his friend (see Figure 7-1).

FIGURE 7-1 Create a block friend to accompany your player on his Minecraft adventures.

To program a block friend you need to think like her! She will be happy if she's near your player, so she will want to follow him around and try to sit next to him. She'll stay happy as long as your player is close to her; if your player walks off, she will walk after him. If your player gets too far away, it will make the block friend sad and she will stop following him until he comes back and gives her a hug (by standing next to her).

The block friend program has two distinct parts:

- **The rules the block uses to decide what it should do next:** This part of the program makes the block friend decide whether to move toward your player (the target) or stay still.

- **The code that moves the block toward a target:** Once the block friend reaches her target, she uses the rules again to work out what to do next.

While the block friend is moving towards the target, she should be travelling "on top" of the land, not floating in the air or burrowing under the ground! You do this by using the function `mc.getHeight(x,z)` and passing it a horizontal position (x,z). It returns the vertical position (y) of the first block down from the sky that isn't `AIR`.

VIDEO

To see a tutorial on how to create the block friend, visit the companion website at `www.wiley.com/go/adventuresinminecraft2e`.

Start by creating a new program for the block friend:

1. Open IDLE, select File ⇨ New File to create a new program and save the file as `BlockFriend.py` in the `MyAdventures` folder.

2. Import the `minecraft`, `block`, `minecraftstuff`, `math` and `time` modules:

```
import mcpi.minecraft as minecraft
import mcpi.block as block
import mcpi.minecraftstuff as minecraftstuff
import math
import time
```

3. The first thing you need to do is create a function to calculate the distance between two points. Later you use this function to work out how far the block friend is from your player:

```
def distanceBetweenPoints(point1, point2):
    xd = point2.x - point1.x
    yd = point2.y - point1.y
    zd = point2.z - point1.z
    return math.sqrt((xd*xd) + (yd*yd) + (zd*zd))
```

4. Now you need to decide how far away your player needs to be for the block friend to stop following him. Create a constant to store the distance that you consider to be "too far away". I have chosen 15, meaning that when the block friend and the player are 15 blocks apart, the block friend stops following the player:

```
TOO_FAR_AWAY = 15
```

5. Create the `Minecraft` and `MinecraftDrawing` objects:

```
mc = minecraft.Minecraft.create()
mcdrawing = minecraftstuff.MinecraftDrawing(mc)
```

6. Create a variable to store the block's mood. For this adventure, the block is either happy or sad. Set it to `"happy"`:

```
blockMood = "happy"
```

7. Create the block friend, a few blocks away from the player, by getting the player's position, adding 5 to the x position and using the `getHeight()` function to find out the y position, so the block is sitting on top of the land:

```
friend = mc.player.getTilePos()
friend.x = friend.x + 5
friend.y = mc.getHeight(friend.x, friend.z)
mc.setBlock(friend.x, friend.y, friend.z,
            block.DIAMOND_BLOCK.id)
mc.postToChat("<block> Hello friend")
```

8. Create a target for the block friend. This is the position she will move towards. Initially, set the target as the block friend's current position, this is so the block friend doesn't try to move anywhere when the program starts:

```
target = friend.clone()
```

MARTIN SAYS:

To copy positions in Minecraft, you use the `clone()` function. This is because the positions returned by the Minecraft API are Python objects and they are different to normal variables. For example, if you had used the code `target = friend` and later changed the `friend.x` value in the `friend` object, the `target.x` value would be changed in `target` too.

9. Start an infinite loop, so the program will run forever. (Note that all the code after this point is indented under this loop.)

```
while True:
```

10. Get the player's position and calculate the distance between the player and the block friend using the `distanceBetweenPoints()` function:

```
pos = mc.player.getTilePos()
distance = distanceBetweenPoints(pos, friend)
```

11. Apply the rules you want the block friend to use to work out what to do next. If it's "happy", tell it to compare the distance between the friend and the "too far away" constant. If the distance is less than the "too far away" constant, set the target to be the position of the player. If it's greater than the "too far away" constant, change the block's mood to "sad" (see Figure 7-2):

```
if blockMood == "happy":
  if distance < TOO_FAR_AWAY:
    target = pos.clone()
  else:
    blockMood = "sad"
    mc.postToChat("<block> Come back. You are too far ↵
                   away. I need a hug!")
```

12. Indented inline with the `if` statement that checks if the block is "happy", you need to tell the program if the block friend is "sad", to wait until the player is within one block's distance (a hug) before changing the block's mood to "happy".

```
elif blockMood == "sad":
  if distance <= 1:
    blockMood = "happy"
    mc.postToChat("<block> Awww thanks. Lets go.")
```

<block> Come back. You are too far away. I need a hug!

FIGURE 7-2 The block friend is sad.

13. Run your program to test that when you walk away from your block friend she changes from happy to sad and back to happy when you give her a hug.

The block friend appears next to your player; if you walk too far away the friend asks you to come back.

Now that your block friend is talking to you to let you know how she feels, the next step is to update the program to make the block friend follow the player:

1. The block friend only needs to move, if her position is not the same as her target (the player):

   ```
   if friend != target:
   ```

2. Find all the blocks between the friend and her target by using the getLine() function in MinecraftDrawing:

   ```
   line = mcdrawing.getLine(
      friend.x, friend.y, friend.z,
      target.x, target.y, target.z)
   ```

The getLine() function works in the same way as drawLine() (see Adventure 6). However, instead of drawing the line in blocks, it returns a list of points (x, y, z) that make a line between the two sets of x, y, z coordinates passed as parameters.

3. Directly under the previous code, you need to tell your program to loop through all the blocks between the friend and the target, and move the block friend to the next block between the block friend and the player:

```
for nextBlock in line[:-1]:
    mc.setBlock(friend.x, friend.y, friend.z, block.AIR.id)
    friend = nextBlock.clone()
    friend.y = mc.getHeight(friend.x, friend.z)
    mc.setBlock(friend.x, friend.y, friend.z,
                block.DIAMOND_BLOCK.id)
    time.sleep(0.25)
target = friend.clone()
```

When the `for` loop finishes, the block friend has reached her target, so set the target to be the block friend's own current position. This way she won't try to move again.

The program moves the block friend by clearing her from her previous last position (which it does by setting the block to `AIR`), updating the block friend's position to be the next block in the line, then re-creating the block friend in that position.

MARTIN SAYS:

The speed the block friend travels is set by how long the program sleeps between each block move—`time.sleep(0.25)`. If this wait is too short, the block moves too quickly, and the player is never able to get away. If it's too long, the block moves so slowly it will drive you mad with frustration!

4. Put in a small delay at the end of the infinite loop so the program asks for the player's position once every 0.25 seconds:

```
time.sleep(0.25)
```

5. Run the program.

The block friend now follows the player until they get too far away from each other. When that happens, the block friend comes to a stop and your player has to go back and stand next to the block friend before she starts following again.

You can download the complete code for the block friend program from the *Adventures in Minecraft* companion website at www.wiley.com/go/adventuresinminecraft2e.

DIGGING INTO THE CODE

To calculate the distance between the block and the player, you create a function called `distanceBetweenPoints(point1, point2)`. This uses Pythagoras's theorem to calculate an accurate distance between two points. You may have investigated how Pythagoras's theorem would work in the challenge in "Adding a Homing Beacon" in Adventure 4.

The function calculates the distance by

1. Working out the difference between the x,y,z values in `point1` and `point2`:

```
xd = point2.x - point1.x
yd = point2.y - point1.y
zd = point2.z - point1.z
```

2. Calculating the squares of the difference between the points:

```
xd*xd
```

3. Adding together all the squares:

```
(xd*xd) + (yd*yd) + (zd*zd)
```

4. Returning the difference between the two points, which is the **square root** of the sum of the squares using the Python function `math.sqrt()`:

```
return math.sqrt((xd*xd) + (yd*yd) + (zd*zd))
```

Visit `www.mathsisfun.com/algebra/distance-2-points.html` to learn about Pythagoras's theorem and how to use it to calculate the distance between two points.

The block friend is moved towards the player by finding the blocks between the block friend and the player, and looping through those blocks:

```
for nextBlock in line[:-1]:
```

The `[:-1]` tells Python to loop through all the blocks in the `line` list until it gets to the last but one block. This way, when the block friend is moved towards the player, she stands next to the player and not on top of him.

The **square root** of a number is the value that can be multiplied by itself to give that number. For example, the square root of 9 is 3, because 3 x 3 = 9.

1. The block friend always moves at the same speed: one block about every 0.25 seconds, or 4 bps (blocks per second). However, a real friend would speed up the further away her target got. Try changing the program so that the further the block friend is from the player, the quicker she moves.

2. Revisit "Adding a Homing Beacon" in Adventure 4 and complete the challenge again, this time building a better distance estimator using the `distanceBetweenPoints()` function.

Using Random Numbers to Make Your Block Friend More Interesting

The problem with the block friend program you just created is that it is **predictable**; she's always going to do the same thing. After you've run the program only a couple of times, you'll know exactly what she's going to do and when, so things are going to get boring very quickly. To really give your block friend a 'mind', you need to give her an air of unpredictability.

When something is **predictable**, it means you are able to foresee what is going to happen before it does. This isn't great if you want it to act as if it's real. Real things are not always predictable.

By using random numbers, you can simulate unpredictability—in other words, make something look as if it's acting unpredictably. You do this by making a program choose to do things based on a **probability**; for example, you might tell it to do a particular action 1 every 100 times. By adding more rules based on different odds, you can make the program much more difficult to predict. Before changing the block friend program to use random numbers, let's explore the code to create random numbers and probability checks. You may remember random numbers being introduced in Adventure 3.

A **probability** is the measurement of how likely it is that something will happen, i.e. when flipping a coin there is a 50% (or 1 in 2) chance that it will land on heads.

The Python `random` module contains the function `random.randint(start Number, endNumber)` which is used to generate a random number between two specific numbers (`startNumber`, `endNumber`).

The following code prints a random number between 1 and 10 each time it is run. If you want to see the results, you should create a new Python program:

```
import random
randomNo = random.randint(1,10)
print(randomNo)
```

By adding an `if` statement to check when the random number is 10, you create a probability check that will be true approximately 1 time in every 10:

```
import random
if random.randint(1,10) == 10:
  print("This happens about 1 time in 10")
else
  print("This happens about 9 times out of 10")
```

If you were to run this program 100 times you would expect to see "This happens about 1 time in 10" printed about 10 times (see Figure 7-3), but you might only see it 9 or 11 times, or maybe even not at all. It's unpredictable!

If you were to run this program 1,000,000 times, how many times would you expect to see "This happens about 1 time in 10" printed? You would expect to see it 100,000 times, but you might not; you might not see it all, or you might see it 1,000,000 times!

If you use random numbers and a probability check in your block friend program, you can make it less predictable. You can even make the block friend "unfriend" your player!

Add some new rules to the block friend program so that if the block friend is "sad" there is a 1 in 100 chance she will decide she has had enough of waiting and will not follow your player if he comes back and gives her a hug:

1. Open IDLE and open the `BlockFriend.py` program from the `MyAdventures` folder.

2. Click File ⇨ Save As and save the file as `BlockFriendRandom.py`.

FIGURE 7-3 Creating random numbers to give your block friend an air of unpredictability

3. Add the `random` module to the `import` statements at the top of the program (the code in **bold**):

```
import mcpi.minecraft as minecraft
import mcpi.block as block
import mcpi.minecraftstuff as minecraftstuff
import math
import time
import random
```

4. Add a 1 in 100 random number test to change the block's mood to `"hadenough"` when the block is `"sad"`:

```
elif blockMood == "sad":
  if distance <= 1:
    blockMood = "happy"
    mc.postToChat("<block> Awww thanks. Lets go.")
  if random.randint(1,100) == 100:
    blockMood = "hadenough"
    mc.postToChat("<block> Thats it. I have had ↩
      enough.")
```

5. Run the program.

When your player gets too far away from the block friend, if you wait long enough (for a 1 in 100 chance to come true), the block friend decides she has had enough and 'unfriends' the player! Once that happens, the block friend says, "That's it. I have had enough", and will sit there forever.

CHALLENGE

Change the program again so that there is a 1 in 50 chance that if the block friend's mood is "hadenough" she forgives the player if he gives her a hug.

Bigger Shapes

In the block friend program, you made one block move around and follow the player. But what if you wanted to make a lot of blocks move around? Or how about a shape made out of moving blocks, like a car or an alien spaceship?

This is where things become much more difficult, because you need to keep track of lots of blocks. Each time you want to make it move you would need to set all the blocks to AIR and then re-create the blocks in their new position. If there are a lot of blocks, the shape stops moving properly and slows to a crawl.

The minecraftstuff module contains functions called MinecraftShape, which has been written especially to create shapes and move them around. It does this by keeping track of all the blocks that make up a shape; when the shape is moved, it only changes the blocks that have changed rather than changing all of them.

To use MinecraftShape, you have to tell it what the shape looks like by creating a list of blocks that make up the shape. Each of the blocks in the shape has a position (x, y, z) and a block type.

Figure 7-4 shows a simple shape made up of seven blocks, together with the positions of the blocks. In this case, "position" isn't the same as the position in Minecraft. You'll see that the centre of the wooden horse is 0,0,0 and each block is relative to the centre, so the block to the right is 1,0,0.

FIGURE 7-4 Block positions of a wooden horse Minecraft shape

Now you're going to create a program that uses `MinecraftShape` to create the wooden horse in Figure 7-4 and make it move:

1. Open IDLE, and click File ⇨ New File to create a new program. Save the file as `WoodenHorse.py` in the `MyAdventures` folder.

2. Import the `minecraft`, `block`, `minecraftstuff` and `time` modules:

```
import mcpi.minecraft as minecraft
import mcpi.block as block
import mcpi.minecraftstuff as minecraftstuff
import time
```

3. Create the `Minecraft` object:

```
mc = minecraft.Minecraft.create()
```

4. Tell `MinecraftShape` where in the Minecraft world to create the wooden horse. Get the player's position and add 1 to the z and y coordinates, so it isn't directly on top of the player:

```
horsePos = mc.player.getTilePos()
horsePos.z = horsePos.z + 1
horsePos.y = horsePos.y + 1
```

5. Create the wooden horse by using `MinecraftShape`, passing the Minecraft object and the position where the shape should be created as parameters:

```
horseShape = minecraftstuff.MinecraftShape(mc, horsePos)
```

6. Set the blocks in the wooden horse:

```
horseShape.setBlock(0,0,0,block.WOOD_PLANKS.id)
horseShape.setBlock(-1,0,0,block.WOOD_PLANKS.id)
horseShape.setBlock(1,0,0,block.WOOD_PLANKS.id)
horseShape.setBlock(-1,-1,0,block.WOOD_PLANKS.id)
horseShape.setBlock(1,-1,0,block.WOOD_PLANKS.id)
horseShape.setBlock(1,1,0,block.WOOD_PLANKS.id)
horseShape.setBlock(2,1,0,block.WOOD_PLANKS.id)
```

The position of the blocks is the same as shown in Figure 7-4.

7. Run the program. Voila! You should see a wooden horse appear next to the player.

8. Modify the `WoodenHorse.py` program to make the horse move by adding the following code to the bottom of the program:

```
for count in range(0,10):
    time.sleep(1)
    horseShape.moveBy(1,0,0)
horseShape.clear()
```

The `moveBy(x,y,z)` function tells the shape to "move by" the number of blocks in x, y, z. So in this example, the `horseShape` is moved by one block across (x). The `clear()` function removes the shape, setting all the blocks to `AIR`.

9. Run the program and watch the wooden horse gallop!

As well as `moveBy(x,y,z)` and `clear()`, you can also tell a shape to `move(x,y,z)` to any position in Minecraft. If the shape has been cleared you can re-create it with `draw()`.

You can download the complete code for the wooden horse from the *Adventures in Minecraft* companion website at www.wiley.com/go/adventuresinminecraft2e.

You'll find shapes useful now, because you're going to create an alien spaceship! Later, you use them again to create obstacles.

Alien Invasion

Aliens are about to invade Minecraft. A spaceship comes down from the sky directly above your player, who is in mortal danger—these aliens are *not* friendly and they won't give up until they have completed their mission.

In the next program, you use `MinecraftShape` and the programming techniques you used in the block friend program to create an alien spaceship (see Figure 7-5) which hovers above the surface of the world, chasing your player, trying to get above him. And when it succeeds, it beams him onboard.

FIGURE 7-5 Create an alien spaceship to spice up your Minecraft game!

You create the alien spaceship using `MinecraftShape`, just like in the wooden horse program with each block in the shape having its own relative position and block type. Figure 7-6 shows the positions of the shape's blocks from the side and from above.

Like the block friend program, the code for the alien invasion is in two parts. The first part is the rules to decide what the spaceship does next; the second part is the code that moves the alien spaceship towards the player.

When the alien spaceship is chasing the player, it taunts him by posting messages (like "you can't run forever") to the chat. The messages are picked at random from a list of taunts (see Figure 7-7).

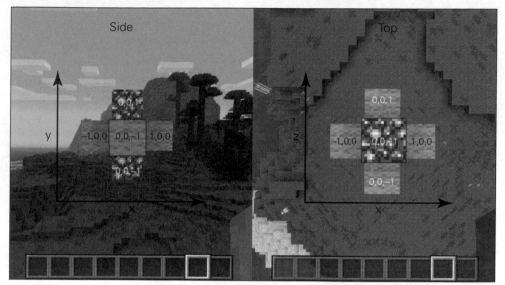

FIGURE 7-6 Alien spaceship block positions

 MARTIN SAYS...

The alien spaceship shows you how you can create three-dimensional shapes using the `MinecraftShape` object. The shapes can be as big, small, simple or complex as you like. This gives you lots of different options for using shapes in your Minecraft programs.

FIGURE 7-7 The alien spaceship gives chase.

The rules to decide what the alien spaceship does next is based on one of three modes:

- **Landing:** When the program starts, this is the spaceship's initial mode as the spaceship comes down from sky directly above the player.

- **Attack:** As soon as the spaceship lands, it starts to attack, constantly chasing the player until it is directly above him, from where it will "beam" the player inside.

- **Mission accomplished:** This mode is set after the player has been beamed inside the ship and the aliens are ready to return him to the ground. At this point the program finishes, and the player is beamed back.

Once the alien spaceship has captured the player, the program builds a dismal room in which to hold him and change his position to be inside it (see Figure 7-8). The aliens then post messages to the player before beaming him back by changing his position back to what it was and clearing the room.

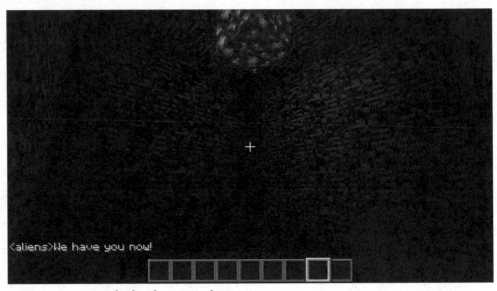

FIGURE 7-8 Inside the alien spaceship

Use the following steps to create the alien invasion program:

1. Open IDLE, click New ⇨ New File and save the file as `AlienInvasion.py` in the `MyAdventures` folder.

2. Import the `minecraft`, `block`, `minecraftstuff` and `time` modules:

```
import mcpi.minecraft as minecraft
import mcpi.block as block
import mcpi.minecraftstuff as minecraftstuff
import time
```

3. Create the `distanceBetweenPoints()` function:

```
def distanceBetweenPoints(point1, point2):
    xd = point2.x - point1.x
    yd = point2.y - point1.y
    zd = point2.z - point1.z
    return math.sqrt((xd*xd) + (yd*yd) + (zd*zd))
```

4. Create the constants for the program. HOVER_HEIGHT is the number of blocks the alien spaceship hovers over the player; ALIEN_TAUNTS is a list of the taunts that are posted to the chat while the aliens are chasing the player:

```
HOVER_HEIGHT = 15
ALIEN_TAUNTS = ["<aliens>You cannot run forever",
                "<aliens>Resistance is useless",
                "<aliens>We only want to be friends"]
```

You can change the aliens' taunts—see how creative you can be! Or add more if you like.

5. Create the `Minecraft` and `MinecraftDrawing` objects:

```
mc = minecraft.Minecraft.create()
mcdrawing = minecraftstuff.MinecraftDrawing(mc)
```

6. Set the aliens' starting position and mode, which will be 50 blocks directly above the player and "landing":

```
alienPos = mc.player.getTilePos()
alienPos.y = alienPos.y + 50
mode = "landing"
```

7. Create the alien spaceship using `MinecraftShape` (refer to Figure 7-6 for a reminder of how this is done):

```
alienShape = minecraftstuff.MinecraftShape(mc, alienPos)

alienShape.setBlock(-1,0,0,block.WOOL.id, 5)
alienShape.setBlock(0,0,-1,block.WOOL.id, 5)
alienShape.setBlock(1,0,0,block.WOOL.id, 5)
alienShape.setBlock(0,0,1,block.WOOL.id, 5)
alienShape.setBlock(0,-1,0,block.GLOWSTONE_BLOCK.id)
alienShape.setBlock(0,1,0,block.GLOWSTONE_BLOCK.id)
```

8. Create a `while` loop, which continues to loop while the mode is not `"missionaccomplished"` or, to put it another way, exits when the mode is `"missionaccomplished"`:

```
while mode != "missionaccomplished":
```

9. Get the player's position each time around the loop:

```
playerPos = mc.player.getTilePos()
```

10. The next section of code relates to the rules the program uses to decide what to do next—if the mode is `"landing"`, set the alien target (where the alien spaceship travels to) to be above the player's position and set the mode to `"attack"`:

```
if mode == "landing":
  mc.postToChat("<aliens> We do not come in peace - ↵
    please panic")
  alienTarget = playerPos.clone()
  alienTarget.y = alienTarget.y + HOVER_HEIGHT
  mode = "attack"
```

11. Otherwise, if the mode is `"attack"`, check to see whether the alien spaceship is above the player. If it is, beam him inside the ship and set the mode to `"missionaccomplished"`. Otherwise, if the player has got away, set the alien target to be the player's current position and post a taunt to the chat:

```
elif mode == "attack":
  #check to see if the alien ship is above the player
  if alienPos.x == playerPos.x and alienPos.z == ↵
    playerPos.z:
    mc.postToChat("<aliens>We have you now!")

    #create a room
    mc.setBlocks(0,50,0,6,56,6,block.BEDROCK.id)
    mc.setBlocks(1,51,1,5,55,5,block.AIR.id)
    mc.setBlock(3,55,3,block.GLOWSTONE_BLOCK.id)

    #beam up player
    mc.player.setTilePos(3,51,5)
    time.sleep(10)
    mc.postToChat("<aliens>Not very interesting at all - ↵
      send it back")
    time.sleep(2)

    #send the player back to the original position
    mc.player.setTilePos(
      playerPos.x, playerPos.y, playerPos.z)
```

```
#clear the room
mc.setBlocks(0,50,0,6,56,6,block.AIR.id)
mode = "missionaccomplished"

else:
    #the player got away
    mc.postToChat(
        ALIEN_TAUNTS[random.randint(0,len(ALIEN_TAUNTS)-1)])
    alienTarget = playerPos.clone()
    alienTarget.y = alienTarget.y + HOVER_HEIGHT
```

When the player is beamed aboard the spaceship, a room is built 50 blocks over the spawn position and the player's position is set to be inside the room. (Just like Doctor Who's Tardis, the inside is bigger than the outside!). Messages are then posted to the chat, before the player's position is set to be back where he started and the room is cleared.

The room into which the player is beamed is created in the sky above the spawn location, partly for convenience but also because it's likely to be well away from anything else. You can create the room anywhere you like, however, because as soon as the player leaves, it is cleared, returning the Minecraft world to the way it was before.

12. If the position of the alien spaceship is not equal to the target (set in the rules above), move the alien spaceship to the target by typing this code into the end of the program, indented under the `while` loop:

```
if alienPos != alienTarget:

    line = mcdrawing.getLine(
        alienPos.x, alienPos.y, alienPos.z,
        alienTarget.x, alienTarget.y, alienTarget.z)

    for nextBlock in line:
        alienShape.move(
            nextBlock.x, nextBlock.y, nextBlock.z)

        time.sleep(0.25)

    alienPos = alienTarget.clone()
```

13. At this point the program returns to the top of the `while` loop. When the mode has been set to `"missionaccomplished"` and the `while` loop finishes, the last line of the program makes the alien spaceship disappear:

```
alienShape.clear()
```

14. Run the program and watch out for the aliens who come down from the sky directly above you.

You can download the complete code for the alien invasion from the *Adventures in Minecraft* companion website at www.wiley.com/go/adventuresinminecraft2e.

DIGGING INTO THE CODE

Each time the aliens chase the player, a random taunt is picked from the constant ALIEN_TAUNTS and posted to the chat.

```
mc.postToChat(ALIEN_TAUNTS[random.randint(0,len(ALIEN_
TAUNTS)-1)])
```

ALIEN_TAUNTS is a list of strings; the random.randint() function is used to pick an item from the list, randomly picking a number between 0 and the length of the ALIEN_TAUNTS list minus 1.

1 is subtracted from the length of the list because—although len() returns the actual number of items in the list (i.e. 3)—You have to reference items starting at 0 (i.e. 0,1,2).

CHALLENGE

The alien spaceship is really simple. Try creating an amazing spaceship, one you really like. Change the spaceship so that when it lands it goes into "lurk" mode, where it stays close to the player but doesn't attack and then, based on a random probability, switches without warning to attack mode.

Further Adventures in Simulation

In this adventure you have used algorithms and rules to simulate a friend and an alien invasion—how about taking it further and simulating other things such as a flock of birds (or blocks), waves across the oceans in Minecraft or a complete cellular system such as Conway's Game of Life made out of blocks.

To find out more about Conway's Game of Life visit en.wikipedia.org/wiki/
Conway's_Game_of_Life.

Quick Reference Table	
Command	**Description**
`import random`	Imports the Python `random` module
`random.randint(start, end)`	Creates a random number between the start and end numbers
`import minecraftstuff`	Imports the `minecraftstuff` extensions module, which is included in the Starter Kit
`mc.getHeight(x,z)`	Gets the height (y coordinate) of the land (i.e. the first block down from the sky that isn't `AIR`) for a horizontal position (x,z)
`mcdrawing = minecraftstuff.` ↵ `MinecraftDrawing(mc)`	Creates the `MinecraftDrawing` object
`copyOfPosition = position.clone()`	Creates a copy (clone) of a Minecraft position
`mcdrawing.getLine(x1, y1, z1, x2, y2, z2)`	Gets all the blocks in a line between two points

`shape = minecraftstuff.` ↵
 	
 `MinecraftShape(mc, pos)`
 	
 `shape.setBlock(1,0,0,block.DIRT.id)`
 	
 `shape.setBlock(0,0,1,block.DIRT.id)`
	Creates a `MinecraftShape`

`shape.moveBy(x,y,z)`	Moves a `MinecraftShape` by the value in x,y,z
`shape.move(x,y,z)`	Moves a `MinecraftShape` to the position x,y,z
`shape.clear()`	Clears the `MinecraftShape`
`shape.draw()`	Draws the `MinecraftShape`

Achievement Unlocked: **Abducted by your own artificial intelligence!**

In the Next Adventure. . .

In the next adventure, you learn how to break out of the confines of the Minecraft virtual game world and even beyond the boundaries of your computer by linking Minecraft to real-world objects. You use a BBC micro:bit to build your own interactive game controller, learn how to use a banana as an input device, and build a complete mini-game based on tilt movements!

Adventure 8
Building a Game Controller with a BBC micro:bit

WHEN YOU PLAY in the Minecraft world, even with the programming interface, it is a virtual world. The only way you can interact with the game is by using your keyboard and mouse to direct the controls that the engineers designed.

But there's another way to interact with Minecraft—by breaking out of the barriers imposed by the sandbox game and linking it to the physical world. Here you quickly discover that the lines between what is virtual and what is real become blurred, and your gaming experience becomes even more creative and exciting.

In this adventure you find out how to link Minecraft to a small electronic computer called the BBC micro:bit. First you will test that everything works by sensing button presses from your BBC micro:bit and then you create a program that displays an icon of a house on your BBC micro:bit display when you walk into your house. You use the display as a countdown and use a real banana as an input device to trigger a countdown to an explosion (so you'll never have any difficulty clearing space for your building adventures in Minecraft again). Finally you build a ball-rolling game where you tilt your BBC micro:bit to collect objects and avoid holes on a virtual game table. Your friends will marvel at your new magic tricks and ask you to create game controllers with a BBC micro:bit for them too!

What You Need for This Adventure

Here is a list of everything you need to build the projects described in this adventure:

- A BBC micro:bit
- A USB cable for your BBC micro:bit
- Two or more crocodile clip leads
- A banana (optional; an orange works too!)
- Our starter kit from the companion website, or a copy of the 'bitio' package

For Windows users, you may need to connect to the Internet to download and install a small driver program so that you can send and receive data to and from the BBC micro:bit. Full instructions are given later in this adventure.

If you don't have a spare banana to hand, don't worry – you can make the projects in this adventure work by just touching the pins on the BBC micro:bit (but using a banana is much more fun!)

What Is a BBC micro:bit?

The BBC micro:bit is a small codeable computer, designed by the BBC and more than 29 industry partners and released in 2015. A free BBC micro:bit was given to every year 7 school child (11 to 12 year olds) in the UK in 2016 as part of a digital literacy project called Make It Digital, which aims to inspire the next generation of engineers, designers and technologists.

You can buy a BBC micro:bit from any of the official sellers, which are listed on this page: microbit.org/resellers.

In this adventure, you use your BBC micro:bit with some pre-written software that turns the BBC micro:bit into a simple games controller, and you use that controller as both an input and an output device for your Minecraft games. However, the BBC micro:bit is a fully programmable computer that can be programmed in many languages, including **MicroPython**.

MicroPython is a tiny version of the Python language designed specifically for small computers like the BBC micro:bit.

If you would like to find out more about the programmable capabilities of the BBC micro:bit, please visit the Micro:bit Educational Foundation's website at `http://microbit.org` for more information.

Understanding Inputs and Outputs

Any computer system has a range of inputs and outputs, which are used with the on-board processor to build exciting and useful devices. The BBC micro:bit might be a small, hand-held computer half the size of a credit card, but it has many features. Figure 8-1 shows the layout of your BBC micro:bit.

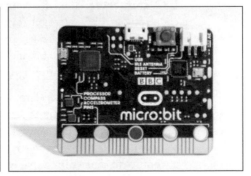

FIGURE 8-1 The BBC micro:bit front (left) and back (right)

The following are the inputs and outputs that are built into your BBC micro:bit and that you will use in this adventure:

- **Buttons A and B:** These two buttons on the front allow you to trigger actions by pressing the buttons. With the right amount of extra program code, you can also measure how long a button is pressed for.

- **Display:** The display is a 5x5 light emitting diode (LED) matrix. An LED is a component that lights up (in this case, red) when current flows through it. The LEDs on the BBC micro:bit can be individually programmed to create icons, animations and even scrolling text. The intensity of these LEDs can also be changed individually to one of 10 different brightness levels.

An **LED (light emitting diode)** is a component that lights up when current flows through it. In the case of the BBC micro:bit, the LED is red.

- **Rings 0, 1 and 2:** These gold rings can be used to connect to crocodile clip leads and allow connection to external circuits. You can also touch the pins with your finger and your BBC micro:bit senses that you have touched them. The rings can be used for a variety of input and output purposes.

- **3V and GND:** These two gold rings can be used to provide a small amount of power to external circuits that you build. The GND (ground) is also used as a return path for the touch-sensing circuit.

- **Battery connector:** The white battery connector on the back of the BBC micro:bit allows you to power it from a battery pack, such as one that holds two AAA batteries.

- **USB connector:** The USB connector is mainly used to transfer new program code to your BBC micro:bit (overwriting any previous program code that you stored on it). You can also use the USB connector to provide a small amount of power to the BBC micro:bit and to send and receive data to another computer while your program is running.

- **Accelerometer:** An accelerometer measures acceleration forces and can be used by the BBC micro:bit to sense various forms of movement, including shaking and tilting. It is the same sort of device that is used inside smartphones to sense which way up the screen is facing. You use the accelerometer later in this adventure to sense tilting that will move a ball inside your Minecraft world.

Using Your BBC micro:bit as a Game Controller

In this adventure, you load a program onto your BBC micro:bit so that you can use it as a game controller with Minecraft. The BBC micro:bit is used as an input and output device that both controls and reacts to the Minecraft games that you code.

It is really easy to write new programs for your BBC micro:bit. If you want to find out more about how to write your own programs for it, please visit `http://microbit.org/code` to learn more.

Setting Up Your Computer to Connect to Your BBC micro:bit

Before you can use your BBC micro:bit as a game controller for your Minecraft games, there is a little bit of setup to do.

Plugging In Your BBC micro:bit

Plug your BBC micro:bit into the USB lead, and plug the other end of the USB lead into your computer in a spare USB port. After a few seconds, you should see a MICROBIT drive appear in the Explorer (PC), File Manager (Raspberry Pi) or in the Finder (Apple Mac). See Figure 8-2 for an example of what you should see.

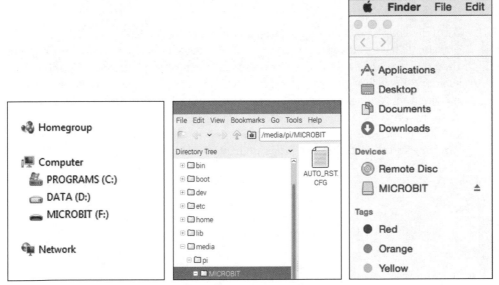

FIGURE 8-2 The MICROBIT drive appears in the Explorer/File Manager/Finder

If you are using Microsoft Windows, you may see a message pop up in the bottom right of your computer screen saying that the mbed serial driver could not be installed. Don't worry, your BBC micro:bit is working fine, but there is an extra step you need to follow. Go to `support.microbit.org` and search for 'windows serial driver', then follow the instructions on that page to install the mbed windows serial driver for your Windows PC.

Loading the Game Controller Code onto Your BBC micro:bit

The final step of the setup is to load some code that helps the BBC micro:bit work as a game controller. I have written a package called `bitio` (pronounced *bitty-o*) that turns your BBC micro:bit into an input/output device for your Minecraft Python games. The package has two parts to it: some code that is loaded onto the BBC micro:bit and some code that you run on your main computer. All of this code is provided in the starter kit that you downloaded as part of Adventure 1.

You can always get the latest version of the `bitio` package (including the `.hex` file that has the code for the BBC micro:bit) from `https://github.com/AdventuresInMinecraft/bitio`. If you want to use this package for other things apart from Minecraft gaming, it is a standalone package so that you can do this independently of the rest of our starter kits.

All of this code is provided in the starter kit that you downloaded as part of Adventure 1; you should have a file called `bitio.hex` inside your `MyAdventures` folder. Drag and drop this file onto the MICROBIT drive to load the program into your BBC micro:bit's memory. The yellow system LED on the back flashes for a few seconds. When the LED has finished flashing, you should see the bitio logo (Io) on the display to let you know that the program has loaded correctly. Don't worry if your computer 'ejects' the MICROBIT drive at the end; this is normal and is just a result of your BBC micro:bit resetting and then starting the program that you just downloaded to it.

You can find help on flashing code to your micro:bit on the official micro:bit website here: `http://microbit.org/guide/quick`.

Your BBC micro:bit is now ready to receive commands from your Python code that you write on your main computer. Figure 8-3 shows what the display on your BBC micro:bit looks like.

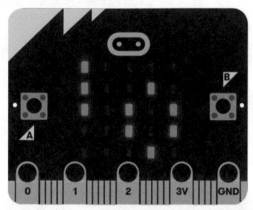

FIGURE 8-3 The bitio logo shows on your BBC micro:bit.

Hello BBC micro:bit

In Adventure 1 you wrote 'Hello Minecraft World' as a way to test that everything was working. In this adventure you're going to create a Hello program to test that your BBC micro:bit game controller is working. Fortunately I have done a lot of the hard work for you, and all you need is a single-line program. Do the following:

1. Start a new program by choosing File ➪ New File and save it as `hellomb.py`. Make sure you save it in your `MyAdventures` folder; otherwise your program won't be able to find the necessary microbit module.

2. Import the microbit module:

   ```
   import microbit
   ```

That's it. That's all there is to it! The microbit Python module that I have provided in the starter kit does all of the hard work of detecting and connecting to your BBC micro:bit for you.

Now run `hellomb.py` and follow the onscreen instructions to locate your BBC micro:bit. Your program automatically remembers your BBC micro:bit for the next time you use it. You should see a screen similar to Figure 8-4:

```
======= RESTART: /Users/davidw/Documents/AIM/MyAdventures/hellomb.py =======
No device has previously been detected
Scanning for serial ports
remove device, then press ENTER
scanning...
found 132 devices
plug in device, then press ENTER
scanning...
found 133 devices
found 1 new device
selected:/dev/tty.usbmodem1412
Do you want this device to be remembered? (Y/N)y
connecting...
Your micro:bit has been detected
Now running your program
>>> |
```

FIGURE 8-4 Scanning for a BBC micro:bit serial port

If you move your BBC micro:bit to a different USB port, your program might not detect it. The `bitio` package remembers the name and number of your BBC micro:bit device in a file called `portscan.cache`. Just delete this file then run your program again to force the microbit Python package to rescan for your BBC micro:bit.

Sensing Button Presses

Now that you know your BBC micro:bit is communicating correctly with Python on your computer, you are going to sense an input by reading a button press from the BBC micro:bit and making something happen on your computer as a result. Use these steps:

1. Start a new program by choosing File ➪ New File and save it as `button.py`.

2. Import the necessary modules:

    ```
    import time
    import microbit
    ```

3. Display a friendly message to the user in the Python console window:

    ```
    print("press button A to test")
    ```

4. Create a game loop that loops round forever; this is so that you can press the button at any time and your program still detects it:

    ```
    while True:
    ```

5. Using an `if` statement, check to see if your BBC micro:bit A button has been pressed. If it has, display a message on the Python console:

```
if microbit.button_a.was_pressed():
    print("Button A pressed")
    time.sleep(0.5)
```

Run the program `button.py`. You should see `press button A to test` on the Python shell window. Now press the A button on your BBC micro:bit, and you should see `Button A pressed` as shown in Figure 8-5.

```
======== RESTART: /Users/davidw/Documents/AIM/MyAdventures/button.py ========
connecting...
Your micro:bit has been detected
Now running your program
press button A to test
Button A pressed
Button A pressed
Button A pressed
```

FIGURE 8-5 The Python shell shows a message when you press the A button.

CHALLENGE

Can you improve the program so that it does something different when you press button B on your BBC micro:bit?

Using Your BBC micro:bit Display

Before you connect your BBC micro:bit with Minecraft, you should check that you can also output something to the BBC micro:bit. You do this by modifying the `button.py` program to write to the display when you press a button.

Modify your `button.py` to look like this (the new lines have been added in **bold**):

```
if microbit.button_a.was_pressed():
    print("Button A pressed")
    microbit.display.show("A")
    time.sleep(0.5)
    microbit.display.clear()
```

Run the program again, and make sure that when you press the A button, the letter A is displayed on the display of your BBC micro:bit.

The Magic Doormat Revisited

Now you have proved that you can use your BBC micro:bit as an input device and an output device, it's time to use Python to link the BBC micro:bit into your Minecraft game world. To do this you're going to revisit the magic doormat program from Adventure 2 and add a bit of a twist to it. This time, you're going to display a house icon on the BBC micro:bit display whenever you're standing on your doormat. This is the first example of linking your Minecraft world to the physical world.

Developing the Magic Doormat Program

1. Start a new program by choosing File ⇨ New File and naming it house.py.

2. Import the necessary modules, which includes both the microbit module and the minecraft modules. (This is the first time that you use both together.) Also create a connection to the Minecraft game:

```
import microbit
import mcpi.minecraft as minecraft
import mcpi.block as block
import time
mc = minecraft.Minecraft.create()
```

3. Set some constants that will be the coordinates of your welcome home mat. You need to decide where you want the mat to appear in your world and choose these constants accordingly. On the Raspberry Pi you can see your coordinates in the top left of the Minecraft window. On the PC or Mac you can press F3 to find out the coordinates of your player.

```
HOME_X = 0
HOME_Y = 0
HOME_Z = 0
```

4. Below these constants, create a block out of wool at the mat home location. This is your doormat—just like the doormat you created in Adventure 2:

```
mc.setBlock(HOME_X, HOME_Y, HOME_Z, block.WOOL.id, 15)
```

5. Write a game loop that looks like the code shown here. Take special care with the indentation. This code repeatedly reads the player position and geo-fences it to see if you are on the doormat. If you are, an image of a house is displayed on your BBC micro:bit. If you're not standing on your doormat, ? is shown on the display:

```
while True:
  time.sleep(1)
  pos = mc.player.getTilePos()
  if pos.x == HOME_X and pos.z == HOME_Z:
    microbit.display.show(microbit.Image.HOUSE)
  else:
    microbit.display.show("?")
```

Run your program and make sure that when you stand on your doormat, a picture of a house is displayed on your BBC micro:bit screen. When you are not standing on the doormat, the screen should display ?.

This is fantastic! You now have all the ingredients you need to break out of the virtual world of the Minecraft sandbox and link the game to real-world objects. You can sense inputs and control outputs, so you are limited only by your imagination and willingness to experiment!

Designing Your Own Icon for the Display

The BBC micro:bit has a number of built-in images. You can find a list of them by creating and running a short program that lists all of their names:

1. Create a new program by choosing File➪New File and save it as `imagelist.py`.

2. Import the microbit module so that you can communicate with your BBC micro:bit:

   ```
   import microbit
   ```

3. Print the value of the STD_IMAGE_NAMES module variable. This variable is a list that has the names of all the supported image names that are loaded onto your BBC micro:bit:

   ```
   print(microbit.Image.STD_IMAGE_NAMES)
   ```

Run your program, and you should see a big list of image names appear, as shown in Figure 8-6.

```
======= RESTART: /Users/davidw/Documents/AIM/MyAdventures/imagelist.py =======
connecting...
Your micro:bit has been detected
Now running your program
['HEART', 'HEART_SMALL', 'HAPPY', 'SMILE', 'SAD', 'CONFUSED', 'ANGRY', 'ASLEEP',
 'SURPRISED', 'SILLY', 'FABULOUS', 'MEH', 'YES', 'NO', 'TRIANGLE', 'TRIANGLE_LEF
T', 'CHESSBOARD', 'DIAMOND', 'DIAMOND_SMALL', 'SQUARE', 'SQUARE_SMALL', 'RABBIT'
, 'COW', 'MUSIC_CROTCHET', 'MUSIC_QUAVER', 'MUSIC_QUAVERS', 'PITCHFORK', 'XMAS',
 'PACMAN', 'TARGET', 'TSHIRT', 'ROLLERSKATE', 'DUCK', 'HOUSE', 'TORTOISE', 'BUTT
ERFLY', 'STICKFIGURE', 'GHOST', 'SWORD', 'GIRAFFE', 'SKULL', 'UMBRELLA', 'SNAKE'
, 'CLOCK12', 'CLOCK11', 'CLOCK10', 'CLOCK9', 'CLOCK8', 'CLOCK7', 'CLOCK6', 'CLOC
K5', 'CLOCK4', 'CLOCK3', 'CLOCK2', 'CLOCK1', 'ARROW_N', 'ARROW_NE', 'ARROW_E', '
ARROW_SE', 'ARROW_S', 'ARROW_SW', 'ARROW_W', 'ARROW_NW']
>>>
```

FIGURE 8-6 The list of standard images that are loaded onto your BBC micro:bit

CHALLENGE

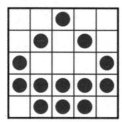

Now that you know the names of all the standard images, modify some of your earlier programs so that they display different images on the display.

Images for the BBC micro:bit are stored as a 5x5 grid of digits. Each digit can be between 0 and 9, and represents the brightness. Figure 8-7 shows an example grid with a design for an image of a house, and below it you see the line of code to create that image.

FIGURE 8-7 A grid design for a house icon

Here is the line of code you need to create a house for the BBC micro:bit display:

```
MYHOUSE = microbit.Image("00900:09090:90009:99999:09990")
```

Note how each row is made up of five digits, with a : character separating them. So in the MYHOUSE example, there are five rows of data, each with five columns. The 0 means the LED is off, and the 9 means the LED is at full brightness. Numbers 0 through 9 create different intensities, and you can set the intensity of each pixel of the display independently of the others.

Now that you know how to design a custom image, you can build a program that displays that image on your BBC micro:bit display:

1. Add this line of code towards the top of your house.py program but after the import line:

```
MYHOUSE = microbit.Image("00900:09090:90009:99999:09990")
```

2. Change the code so that it looks like the following (the changed line is marked in **bold**):

```
if pos.x == HOME_X and pos.z == HOME_Z:
  microbit.display.show(MYHOUSE)
else:
  microbit.display.show("?")
```

Run your program again and stand on your doormat to make sure that your custom house image is displayed.

> ### CHALLENGE
>
> If you display more than one image with a delay in between you can create an animation. See if you can modify your house.py program so that it animates a house rising out of the ground when you stand on the doormat, and it animates a house going back into the ground when you step off of the doormat.

Making a Detonator

In this project, you build a detonator using a banana as an input device. You touch the banana to start a countdown on the BBC micro:bit display to give your player time to run away from the blast, and then a huge crater appears at the point where your player was standing when you touched the banana. This program is a handy addition to your toolbox as a quick way to clear some space as you move around your Minecraft world and build things. This project introduces you to another type of input called a *touch input*, which senses when one of the pins on the BBC micro:bit (or something connected to that pin) is touched. You'll put your BBC micro:bit display to good use too!

Attaching a Banana to Your BBC micro:bit

To add a bit of extra fun to this project, you use a banana as an input device rather than using the buttons of the BBC micro:bit. Touch inputs on the BBC micro:bit sense when you complete a circuit between one of the pins (P0, P1 or P2) and the GND pin.

If you don't have a banana, you can get the same effect by touching P0 with your left finger and thumb and GND with your right finger and thumb.

Using two crocodile clip leads, clip the first lead into the hole of P0, and connect the other end to part of the skin of the banana. Use the second crocodile clip lead to connect to the GND pin of the BBC micro:bit. Figure 8-8 shows this circuit.

FIGURE 8-8 A banana connected to the BBC micro:bit
Photo courtesy of Gemma May Latham

Sensing Touch Inputs

Now that you have wired up your banana, the next step is to write a Python program that senses when you touch the banana. Later you extend this to make something happen inside Minecraft.

1. Create a new program by choosing File ➪ New File and save it as `banana.py`.

2. Import the necessary modules:

   ```
   import microbit
   import time
   ```

3. Create a custom image of a banana:

   ```
   BANANA = microbit.Image("00090:00090:00990:09900:99000")
   ```

4. Create a game loop with a short delay. This delay is so that the display doesn't flicker too much if you are not very accurate in touching the banana:

```
while True:
    time.sleep(0.25)
```

5. Use `is_touched()` to sense whether the P0 pin is touched. If it is touched, display your custom banana image; if it is not touched, display a ?:

```
if microbit.pin0.is_touched():
    microbit.display.show(BANANA)
else:
    microbit.display.show('?')
```

Run your code and make sure that when you touch your banana, your custom banana image is displayed on your BBC micro:bit display.

Remember that you have to hold the GND pin (or the crocodile lead attached to the ground pin) at the same time you touch the banana, so that you complete the circuit. If you don't have a banana, you can use most other types of fruit, or you can just touch your fingers and thumbs on both the P0 and GND pads.

Writing the Detonator Program

Now that you have your banana input working, this next program builds on these ideas but links them up to your Minecraft game world. When you touch the banana, you see the display of your BBC micro:bit count from five down to zero and then blow a massive crater in the Minecraft world!

1. Start a new program by choosing File ⇨ New File and save it as `detonator.py`.

2. Import the necessary modules:

```
import microbit
import mcpi.minecraft as minecraft
import mcpi.block as block
import time
```

3. Create a new custom banana image for the display:

```
BANANA = microbit.Image("00090:00090:00990:09900:99000")
```

4. Connect to the Minecraft game:

```
mc = minecraft.Minecraft.create()
```

5. Write a function that drops a block of TNT to mark where the bomb will go off, counts down to zero, then blows a big crater where the TNT block was. The following code builds the TNT block slightly to the side of the player so it doesn't land on top of him! Note that the crater is 20 blocks in size (10 to the left and 10 to the right of your player) and this size is set by the calculations done in `setBlocks()` here:

```python
def bomb(x, y, z):
    mc.setBlock(x+1, y, z+1, block.TNT.id)

    for t in range(6):
        microbit.display.show(str(5-t))
        time.sleep(1)

    mc.postToChat("BANG!")
    mc.setBlocks(x-10, y-5, z-10, x+10, y+10, z+10,
        block.AIR.id)
```

6. Write the main game loop so that it waits for a banana touch and then sets off a bomb:

```python
while True:
    time.sleep(0.1)
    if microbit.pin0.is_touched():
        microbit.display.show(BANANA)
        pos = mc.player.getTilePos()
        bomb(pos.x, pos.y, pos.z)
    else:
        microbit.display.show("?")
```

Save your program and run it. Remember that you must also hold the GND connection to complete the circuit.

The crocodile clips can be quite sharp, so don't try to clip them on your fingers because it could hurt! All you need to do is to touch the metal part of the crocodile clip that is wired to the GND terminal to complete the circuit.

Run to somewhere in the Minecraft world and touch the banana, and then run for your life! Figure 8-9 shows the aftermath of the explosion—a massive crater.

FIGURE 8-9 A crater blown into the Minecraft World

The size of the crater is set by the numbers inside the `setBlocks()` statement. Do you think this is a good way of setting the size of the crater? What if you wanted to make your crater twice the size? How much of the program would you have to change to make this work? Don't you think I'm being a little lazy here?! Why don't you try and improve on my program, so that it is very easy to change the size of your crater?

CHALLENGE

To make the detonator more exciting, try adding some geo-fencing code like what is used in Adventure 2 to detect when your player is still in the blast zone. When the bomb goes off, if you are in the blast radius, use a `mc.player.setTilePos()` to catapult your player into the sky.

Writing a Ball-Rolling Game

In the final project of this adventure you put together all the things from this and previous adventures to build a complete mini-game. This mini-game consists of a table in the Minecraft world with treasure dotted around it at random locations. You use your BBC micro:bit with its accelerometer to sense tilt movements so that the ball will roll around the table and collect treasure. The display on your BBC micro:bit tells you how many more items there are to collect. Figure 8-10 shows you the game mid-play.

FIGURE 8-10 Playing the ball-rolling game

This is a game of great skill, because once you have collected an item of treasure there will be a hole in the table that you have to avoid, and you'll get a time penalty if you fall into a hole. The objective of the game is to complete it in the fastest time possible.

There is quite a bit of code in this program, but you can learn a lot about coding by typing it in and testing it piece by piece. Be careful of the indentation though! If you get stuck, remember that you can download a pre-written version of the program from the companion website to consult that as a reference to check the indentation!

Building the Structure of the Program

This is quite a large program, so the best approach is to write the code in small steps, testing each step as you go. That way you don't have to write and test the whole program in one go, but you can come back to it every so often and add more to it. Just like a real software engineer, you're building a large program as a series of small parts. The first thing to do is to get the basic structure of the program written and tested. You can then add new parts to this program gradually as you add and test new features. Use these steps for the first part:

1. Start a new program by choosing File ⇨ New File and save it as `ballgame.py`.

2. Import the necessary modules. You also use the random module so that the treasure is placed at random coordinates, which makes the game more challenging to play:

```
import microbit
import mcpi.minecraft as minecraft
import mcpi.block as block
import time
import random
```

3. Add a comment. In a later step you replace this with some constant numbers that configure the game:

```
# CONSTANTS
```

4. Connect to the Minecraft game, and post a message saying that the BBC micro:bit has joined the game:

```
mc = minecraft.Minecraft.create()
mc.postToChat("BBC micro:bit joined the game")
```

5. Add a comment. In a later step you replace this with some variables that maintain the state of the running game:

```
# VARIABLES
remaining = 1
```

6. Create skeleton functions for all the major parts of the program. You fill each of these gradually as you work through the later steps of this adventure:

```
def build_table(x, y, z):
  print("build table")

def place_treasure():
  print("place treasure")

def move_ball():
  print("move ball")

def move_ball_to(x, y, z):
  print("move ball")

def new_speed(speed, tilt):
  return 0

def check_tilt():
  print("check tilt")

def is_on_table(x, z):
  return True

def check_below():
  print("check below")

def wait_for_start():
  print("wait for start")

def build_game():
  print("build game")
```

7. Write the play_game() function. This function contains the main game loop, as well as some Python code to time how long the game takes to play. Remember that this is a time-trial game, so the player must be told at the end how long it took them, so they can challenge their friends to beat their time! See the 'Digging into the Code' section later to learn about how you can measure time in Python.

```
def play_game():
    start_time = time.time()
    while remaining > 0:
        time.sleep(0.1)
        check_tilt()
        move_ball()
        check_below()
    end_time = time.time()
    mc.postToChat("game time=" + str(int(end_time-
        start_time)))
```

8. Create an infinite loop that keeps playing the game over and over again:

```
while True:
    wait_for_start()
    build_game()
    play_game()
```

Save the program and run it to see whether you have made any typing errors. When the program runs—if there are no errors—it should loop round and round telling you what it is doing. If you have any errors in your program, look back carefully, fix them and run it again until all the errors are corrected. Figure 8-11 shows what the output of this program looks like on the Python shell.

```
======= RESTART: /Users/davidw/Documents/AIM/MyAdventures/ballgame.py =======
connecting...
Your micro:bit has been detected
Now running your program
wait for start
build game
wait for start
build game
wait for start
build game
wait for start
build game
wait for start
build game
wait for start
build game
```

FIGURE 8-11 The output generated by running the skeleton program

This type of program is called a *skeleton program* because it provides just the bare bones of the program structure, with no 'meat' on the bones. It is a really good starting point for a bigger program, and it is then much easier to write and test each function one by one, because it will be easier to always move forwards from a working program when adding new features.

DAVID SAYS...

Measuring how much time has elapsed in computer programs is a very important skill to learn, and it is something you will do over and over again. In the skeleton program, you imported the time module, which has a function called `time.time()`. This function returns the amount of time that has passed since a fixed point in time in the past (usually 1/1/1970) in seconds and milliseconds. It will be quite a big number.

By measuring the time when the game starts and storing it in the `start_time` variable and then measuring the time again when the game stops and storing it in the `end_time` variable, you have two numbers. The exact values of these two numbers is not that important or interesting, but the difference between them is very interesting. This is because it tells you precisely in seconds and milliseconds how long the game lasted.

Finally the program uses `int()` to remove the fractional part of the number, as our player is probably not interested in how many milliseconds they took.

Measuring elapsed time is a common coding pattern you use over and over again. It is important to realise that because `time.time()` is based on a hardware clock inside the computer, it is very accurate.

Another method of measuring time would be to set your game loop to delay in one-second increments, and then add one to a counter each time round the loop. However, this is a very inaccurate method of measuring elapsed time because it does not account for small delays in the running of other code inside the loop. Errors in the calculations add up, and your elapsed time measurement will be inaccurate. So, you should always use some method of measuring time that is independent of how long it takes for individual program statements to run. Most computer programming languages provide a function that you can use that returns to you the number of seconds since some reference time.

Adding a Button and a Countdown

At the moment, your skeleton program doesn't do much, but it is a really good start. It's now time to add some inputs and outputs to make things a bit more interactive. You use a button press to start the game, and before the game starts a countdown displays on your BBC micro:bit to give your player time to prepare and get excited about playing the game.

1. Modify the existing `wait_for_start()` function in your `ballgame.py` program so that it looks like the following code. The `time.sleep()` function is required inside the `while` loop because the rules of the Python language state that all conditionals must have at least one statement in them. The `while` loop spins round and round doing nothing until you press the B button on your BBC micro:bit.

```
def wait_for_start():
    mc.postToChat("press B to start")
    microbit.display.show("?")
    while not microbit.button_b.was_pressed():
        time.sleep(0.1)

    for t in range(6):
        microbit.display.show(str(5-t))
        time.sleep(0.5)
```

Save your program and run it again. It should now ask you to press B to start. When you press the B button, you should see a countdown from 5 to 0 on the display of your BBC micro:bit. Because the rest of the game is not written yet, the program loops round and waits for another button press, but this is enough testing to make sure that you can start your game properly.

Building the Game

Any good game most likely needs some constants that set the parameters of the game, and some variables that manage the state of the game while it is being played. Python programmers use a convention where any name that is in uppercase is used to show that the item is a constant and you should not really change it while the program is running. It is normal to put all the program constants at the top of the program where another programmer could change them easily to change how your game works, without requiring the other programmer to read the rest of the Python code.

First you add some constants and variables and build the table that the ball will roll around:

1. Find the # CONSTANTS section in ballgame.py and replace it with the items shown here. Later you might want to change these values to make the game different and more interesting to play. The table has a certain width and depth; there are always a fixed number of treasure blocks created and the block types of various blocks are set here so that you can easily change them later:

```
TABLE_WIDTH    = 20
TABLE_DEPTH    = 20
TREASURE_COUNT = 25
TABLE          = block.STONE.id
BALL           = block.CACTUS.id
TREASURE       = block.GOLD_BLOCK.id
```

2. Find the # VARIABLES section in ballgame.py and replace it with the items shown here. These are global variables, so we initialise most of them to None just so that the variables are created and can be used later in the program. None just means that no value is stored in the variable, but the variable is still defined correctly. The ball has zero speed, and there are currently no remaining

items of treasure to collect. All of these variables now completely define everything that your game needs to know while the game is being played.

```
table_x = None
table_y = None
table_z = None
ball_x = None
ball_y = None
ball_z = None
speed_x = 0
speed_z = 0
remaining = 1
```

3. Next build the game table so that you can see some visible progress inside the Minecraft world when you next run the program. The table is built as a rectangular layer of blocks, but because you might be standing near a mountain or a tree when you run the game, a GAP of 10 blocks around the table is created so that you can see the table regardless of where you build it. Replace the build_table() function in your skeleton ballgame.py with the following code:

```
def build_table(x, y, z):
  global table_x, table_y, table_z
  GAP = 10
  mc.setBlocks(x-GAP, y, z-GAP, x+TABLE_WIDTH+GAP,
               y+GAP, z+TABLE_DEPTH+GAP, block.AIR.id)
  mc.setBlocks(x-1, y, z-1,
               x+TABLE_WIDTH+1, y+1,
               z+TABLE_DEPTH+1, TABLE)
  mc.setBlocks(x, y+1, z,
               x+TABLE_WIDTH, y+1, z+TABLE_DEPTH,
               block.AIR.id)
  table_x = x
  table_y = y
  table_z = z
```

4. Change the build_game() function so it looks like this:

```
def build_game():
  pos = mc.player.getTilePos()
  build_table(pos.x, pos.y-2, pos.z)
```

Save and run your program. After you have fixed any typing errors, you should see a table appear on the screen, and your player should be standing on the table. Move around a bit and explore the table to make sure it is the right size and to confirm there is a gap of air all around it to make it easy to see. Figure 8-12 shows an example of what my world looked like when I ran this program.

FIGURE 8-12 The table is now built inside the Minecraft world.

When you play the game later, if you find it a bit too hard to play, you can change the `TREASURE_COUNT` constant to a smaller number and you'll get fewer blocks built onto the table.

Sensing Tilt Movements with Your BBC micro:bit

Now that you have a table, the next step is to use your BBC micro:bit to sense tilt. It is this movement that rolls the ball up, down, left and right on the table. Your BBC micro:bit has a special device on it called an accelerometer, which can be used to sense which way you are tilting the device.

An accelerometer senses forces due to gravity, so as you tilt your BBC micro:bit left and right, an x reading value changes between about –1024 and +1024 to indicate how far the device has tilted. When you tilt forwards and backwards, a y reading changes between about –1024 and +1024.

Be careful with the x, y and z axes here. The accelerometer uses x to mean left and right, y to mean forwards and backwards and z to mean up and down. Compare this to the Minecraft world, where x is used to indicate East and West, z is used to indicate North and South and y is used to indicate up and down.

Now add in tilt-sensing features to your game:

1. Update the function called `new_speed()` that works out by how much the speed of the rolling ball adjusts for a given amount of tilt. The speed of the ball is designed to be 'laggy' to make the game more interesting to play. Because you can tilt your BBC micro:bit in both the x and y axes, it's better to write a function that does all this maths once and then use it for each of the two axes. (Read about how this maths works in the 'Digging into the Code' section later.) Change the existing `new_speed()` function to look like this:

```python
def new_speed(speed, tilt):
    if abs(tilt) < 300:
        tilt = 0
    tilt = tilt / 300
    if tilt < speed:
        speed = speed - 1
    elif tilt > speed:
        speed = speed + 1
    return speed
```

2. Each time around the main game loop, your game reads the x and y accelerometer values and adjusts the `speed_x` and `speed_z` variables. Don't be confused by the use of x,y and x,z in that sentence though. Remember that the accelerometer labels the axes differently to the Minecraft game, and here you use the Minecraft labelling convention for the speeds. Change the `check_tilt()` function so it looks like this:

```python
def check_tilt():
    global speed_x, speed_z
    speed_x = new_speed(speed_x, microbit.accelerometer. ↵
      get_x())
    speed_z = new_speed(speed_z, microbit.accelerometer. ↵
      get_y())
    print(speed_x, speed_z)
```

DAVID SAYS...

I have added a `print()` to the bottom of the `check_tilt()` function. This is here only whilst you are testing that the tilt function works; later, when the full game is finished, you can take this out.

Save and run your program. Tilt your BBC micro:bit left and right, forwards and backwards, and make sure that you see numbers scrolling on the Python shell that change as you tilt your device. Figure 8-13 shows what my screen looked like when I tested this program.

```
move ball
check below
-3 -2
move ball
check below
-2 -1
move ball
check below
-3 -2
move ball
check below
-2 -1
```

FIGURE 8-13 The accelerometer x and y values scrolling up the Python shell screen

CHALLENGE

Can you work out how long you have to hold your BBC micro:bit flat before the numbers go to zero again? What part of the program that you have just written creates this 'lag' in the readings?

DIGGING INTO THE CODE

There was a bit of maths going on in the `new_speed()` function that is worth explaining. This function is written with two special features that improve the realism of the movement. Let's dig into what they are, and how they work:

1. Accelerometer values between −299 and +299 are ignored and assumed to be 0 (flat). This creates a dead-spot in the readings as you tilt your BBC micro:bit, which makes the tilting slightly less sensitive and a bit easier to play the game without the ball rolling all over the place.

   This line in the program creates that dead-spot:

   ```
   if abs(tilt) < 300: tilt = 0
   ```

   `abs()` is the absolute value of a number, so if it is negative it becomes positive, and if it is positive it stays positive. All this line of code is saying is 'if the tilt is between −299 and +299, set it to zero'.

   continued

continued

2. The speed value is designed to be laggy, so that if you tilt your BBC micro:bit all the way in one direction, it takes a bit of time for the ball to speed up, and if you tilt it in the other direction it takes a bit of time for the ball to slow down, change direction, and speed up again. This makes the movement of the ball a bit more realistic. Let's look at the whole function again:

```python
def new_speed(speed, tilt):
    if abs(tilt) < 300: tilt = 0
    tilt = tilt / 300
    if tilt < speed:
        speed = speed - 1
    elif tilt > speed:
        speed = speed + 1
    return speed
```

The tilt value read from either the x or the y reading is passed to this function as a parameter called tilt. After the dead-spot is optionally added, dividing a reading from a range of –1024 to +1024 by 300 turns it into a range of about –3 to +3. Finally, because this `new_speed()` function is called each time round the game loop and there is a small delay in the game loop, the speed can become only one smaller or one bigger (or stay the same) each time round the loop. So, the speed variable changes in a laggy way, creating a more realistic movement of the ball.

Moving the Ball When You Tilt Your BBC micro:bit

Now that you can sense tilt of your BBC micro:bit and adjust the `speed_x` and `speed_z` variables, it's time to use this new magic power to actually move the ball on the table!

1. You need to make sure that the ball does not fall off of the table, so write a function called `is_on_table()` that works out where the ball is. This is just geofencing, like the code that you wrote in earlier adventures. Replace the `is_on_table()` function with the following Python code:

```python
def is_on_table(x, z):
    if x < table_x or x > table_x + TABLE_WIDTH:
        return False
    if z < table_z or z > table_z + TABLE_DEPTH:
        return False
    return True
```

2. Update the function `move_ball_to()` that places the ball at a specific location. There are already three global variables that you set up in the variables section earlier—`ball_x`, `ball_y` and `ball_z`—and when the game first starts these are set to `None`. The `if` statement checks to see whether the ball block has been previously built. If it has the program clears the block to `AIR` for its old position, before then changing the ball global variables to the new position and building a `BALL` block. Change the `move_ball_to()` function to look like this:

```python
def move_ball_to(x, y, z):
    global ball_x, ball_y, ball_z
    if ball_x is not None:
        mc.setBlock(ball_x, ball_y, ball_z, block.AIR.id)
    ball_x = x
    ball_y = y
    ball_z = z
    mc.setBlock(ball_x, ball_y, ball_z, BALL)
```

3. The `move_ball()` function is called each time round the game loop, so this has to work out which way the ball is moving and move it. The ball moves based on the `speed_x` and `speed_z` variables calculated earlier. If the ball has not moved (for example, because the speed is zero) it is not redrawn. This is a game programmer's trick, where you update the screen only if something has changed, which prevents unnecessary flickering due to repeated screen redrawing. Then, as long as the ball would not fall off of the table, it is moved. So, change the `move_ball()` function to look like this:

```python
def move_ball():
    new_x = ball_x - speed_x
    new_z = ball_z - speed_z
    if ball_x != new_x or ball_z != new_z:
        if is_on_table(new_x, new_z):
            move_ball_to(new_x, ball_y, new_z)
```

4. Finally, the ball has to be placed on the table somewhere, and the game is more exciting if you make that random. Add the line that is in **bold** to the `build_game()` function:

```python
def build_game():
    pos = mc.player.getTilePos()
    build_table(pos.x, pos.y-2, pos.z)
    move_ball_to(table_x + random.randint(0, TABLE_WIDTH),
                 table_y+1,
                 table_z + random.randint(0, TABLE_DEPTH))
```

Save and run your program. Remember that if you have any typing errors, try to fix those first. You can always look up the final program listing on the companion website if you want to see the whole program in one listing.

Now you should be able to almost play the game! Tilt your BBC micro:bit left and right and forwards and backwards, and the ball rolls around the table! If it reaches the edge of the table it doesn't fall off. Figure 8-14 shows what my screen looked like at this point in the game.

FIGURE 8-14 Rolling a ball around the table

Collecting Items from the Table

Rolling a ball around a table is quite fun, but so far there is nothing in the game that makes it addictive and competitive—two essential ingredients that can lead to a great game. In this next step, you write some Python that places treasure at random locations and also add a feature that collects the treasure when the ball rolls over it.

1. First develop the `place_treasure()` function. This function has to build treasure blocks at random locations all over the table. Fortunately the random module provides a way to create random numbers, and those random numbers can be generated in a range that is compatible with the size of the game table. The blocks are created in the table, so that later when blocks are collected it leaves a hole behind for the ball to fall down. Modify the `place_treasure()` function so it looks like this:

```
def place_treasure():
  y = table_y
  for i in range(TREASURE_COUNT):
    x = random.randint(0, TABLE_WIDTH) + table_x
    z = random.randint(0, TABLE_DEPTH) + table_z
    mc.setBlock(x, y, z, TREASURE)
```

2. Now develop the check_below() function, which monitors the block type that is directly below the ball (at y–1). If it is a TREASURE block, the block is collected. If it is an AIR block, the ball falls down the hole and then pops out and lands at a random location near the hole. Collecting the treasure is easy; all you have to do is set the TREASURE block to AIR, and it disappears. Change the check_below() function so it looks like this:

```
def check_below():
  global remaining
  block_below = mc.getBlock(ball_x, ball_y-1, ball_z)
  if block_below == TREASURE:
    mc.setBlock(ball_x, ball_y-1, ball_z, block.AIR.id)
    remaining = remaining - 1
    microbit.display.show(remaining)

  elif block_below == block.AIR.id:
    move_ball_to(ball_x, ball_y-1, ball_z)
    time.sleep(0.5)
    move_ball_to(table_x + random.randint(0, TABLE_WIDTH),
                 table_y+1,
                 table_z + random.randint(0, TABLE_DEPTH))
```

Save your program and run it again.

Did it work? Well, not quite! A common programming error is to write a new function that does something, but then forget to modify the rest of your program so that it actually calls that function, which is the problem you have here!

Finishing the Game Play

There is one other small modification to make so that the treasure is placed correctly:

Add the lines in **bold** to the build_game() function to finish it off:

```
def build_game():
  global speed_x, speed_z, remaining

  pos = mc.player.getTilePos()
  build_table(pos.x, pos.y-2, pos.z)
  move_ball_to(table_x + random.randint(0, TABLE_WIDTH),
               table_y+1,
               table_z + random.randint(0, TABLE_DEPTH))
  place_treasure()
  mc.player.setTilePos(table_x + TABLE_WIDTH/2, table_y+1,
    table_z)
  remaining = TREASURE_COUNT
  speed_x = 0
  speed_z = 0
```

Save your program and run it again. This time your `build_game()` function calls the `place_treasure()` function, so you should now have treasure randomly dotted all over the table. Also the `check_below()` function should already be called from within `play_game()`, so every time round the game loop it checks for treasure and holes. Figure 8-15 shows what my game table looked like when I ran the program at this point.

FIGURE 8-15 The table with treasure on it

Adding a Time Penalty for Falling into a Hole

There is a small time penalty for falling down a hole, but it is only a fraction of a second. A good way to add an exciting penalty to a game is to make the user do something different, which means your player has to coordinate multiple movements correctly (tilting left and right, tilting forwards and backwards, and pressing a button) and that makes the game harder but more exciting to play.

Add the lines marked in **bold** to the `check_below()` function, so that when the ball falls down a hole, the user has to press the B button to bounce the ball out of the hole again.

```
elif block_below == block.AIR.id:
  move_ball_to(ball_x, ball_y-1, ball_z)
  while not microbit.button_b.was_pressed():
    time.sleep(0.1)
```

Save your program and run it again to try out the new time penalty feature. It should be slightly harder to play now, but a bit more interesting as a result, because you have to coordinate your hands to tilt your BBC micro:bit and also press the button when you fall down a hole. As you collect more treasure, there are more holes, so the game gets harder. Figure 8-16 shows what my game table looked like after I collected some treasure and fell down a hole.

FIGURE 8-16 The table with treasure and holes in it, and the ball stuck in a hole

CHALLENGE

Think of other penalties that you could add if the ball falls down a hole. The trick here is to make the game just hard enough that it is on the verge of being impossible, but is actually achievable with enough skill. The way to get this right is to test your game with lots of different people and make it easier or harder based on their feedback

CHALLENGE

Try different block types for the treasure, ball, and table. The SAND, WATER_FLOWING and LAVA blocks are all interesting because they have their own gravity and they fall down if there is nothing underneath them.

When your user quits the game by pressing CTRL-C, it leaves the game table in your Minecraft world, and the next time you run the program you get another table. Use the Internet to research how you can detect a CTRL-C within Python and automatically clear the game table when the program exits. Hint: Remember that in your detonator program you used a technique to clear a lot of space very quickly.

Further Adventures with Your BBC micro:bit Game Controller

In this adventure you have linked the Minecraft world to the physical world and expanded your horizons into the fascinating world of physical computing by sensing and controlling things in the real world. You have used this new knowledge to sense buttons, display icons on the BBC micro:bit display, sense when a banana is touched and also sense when you tilt your BBC micro:bit. But most importantly, you have escaped the confines of the Minecraft sandbox world. With this newfound knowledge you can make your own amazing game controllers and display devices!

- The BBC micro:bit display has 25 LEDs on it, called pixels. One of the children in my computer club had a fantastic idea of building a Minecraft game with an adventure map. You could use your BBC micro:bit as a kind of electronic navigator, turning on and off different LEDs to indicate treasure nearby, and scrolling the screen as you move around in the game. This way, your BBC micro:bit display could help you locate hidden treasure and other challenges within your game.

- The BBC micro:bit accelerometer measures acceleration forces, which means that instead of tilting it, if you shake it in any direction, the value that comes back will be much higher—that is, larger than 1024—in the x, y or z directions. Build a game in Minecraft where you sense shaking the BBC micro:bit in different directions to create AIR blocks in that direction, and use the tilt to move your player. This allows you to really go mining inside Minecraft to dig and navigate your own maze of underground tunnels! (Hint: Because it is dark underground, you could make a shake to the left clear some space to the left and also place a torch nearby, so you can see where you are heading.)

DAVID SAYS:

The microbit Python module that you have been using in this adventure is documented at https://github.com/whaleygeek/bitio.

Quick Reference Table

Command	Description

```import microbit```
 	
```microbit.display.show(```
 	
``` microbit.Image.HOUSE)```
	Display standard images

```import microbit```
 	
```microbit.display.show('?')```
	Display single letters or symbols

```import microbit```
 	
```microbit.display.scroll(str(2367))```
	Display numbers

```import microbit```
 	
```while True:```
 	
``` if microbit.button_a.was_pressed():```
 	
```   print('pressed button A')```
	Sense button presses

```import microbit```
 	
```import time```
 	
```while True:```
 	
``` x = microbit.accelerometer.get_x()```
 	
``` if abs(x) > 300:```
 	
```   print('tilted sideways')```
 	
```   time.sleep(1)```
	Sense tilt

```import microbit```
 	
```BANANA = microbit.Image(```
 	
``` "00090:00090:00990:09900:99000")```
 	
```microbit.display.show(BANANA)```
	Display custom images

```import microbit```
 	
```microbit.display.scroll('hello')```
	Display messages

```import microbit```
 	
```# int uses custom font```
 	
```microbit.display.show(22)```
	Display two-digit numbers

```import microbit```
 	
```import time```
 	
```while True:```
 	
``` if microbit.pin0.is_touched():```
 	
```   print('pin 0 touched')```
 	
```   time.sleep(1)```
	Sense touch

Achievement Unlocked: You have escaped the confines of the Minecraft virtual world into the real world! You're a pioneer in the fascinating new industry of Minecraft physical computing. The boundaries of your gaming experiences are now limitless!

In the Next Adventure. . .

In the next adventure, you use all the skills you have learnt throughout your adventures so far to create a game in which you race against the clock to collect diamonds. But watch out—there are obstacles in the way and they are determined to stop you!

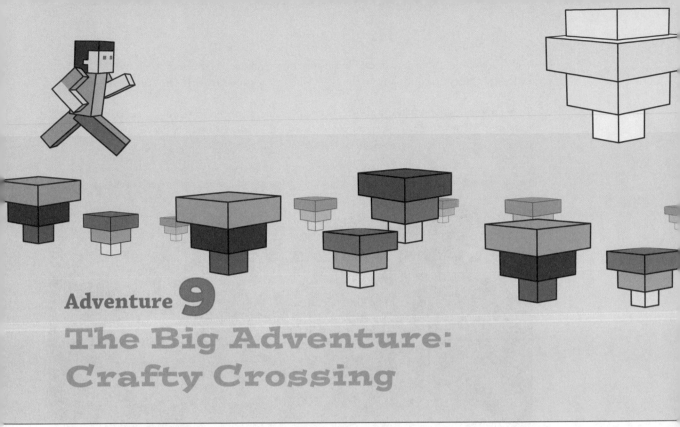

The Big Adventure: Crafty Crossing

YOU HAVE ARRIVED at your last big adventure! You use all the skills you have learned on your journey to create your own fully functional platform game in Minecraft. You will realise just how versatile the Minecraft world is, as well as how you can achieve remarkable things just by using simple commands to get and set a block, and get and set the player's position.

You will also learn a new programming skill and use *threading* to make your program do more than one thing at the same time.

This project can be extended in many ways, and once you've finished, it doesn't mean you're at the end of your adventure. Instead, you will have arrived at the starting point for creating even more creative, sophisticated and challenging games.

A Game within a Game

The game you're going to create here is called Crafty Crossing. The objective of the game is to collect diamonds and get to the other side of the arena before the timer runs out, all the time navigating past a series of pesky obstacles that are designed to slow you down.

You score points for each diamond block you collect, and your points are then multiplied by the number of seconds left on the clock when your player reaches the other side.

To get across the arena in the shortest time possible, your player needs to jump onto a moving platform over a river, get under a wall that moves up and down, and avoid holes that randomly appear in the arena floor (see Figure 9-1).

FIGURE 9-1 Create the Crafty Crossing game.

VIDEO

There is a video of the complete Crafty Crossing game on the companion website at www.wiley.com/go/adventuresinminecraft2e.

Creating a computer game is a major mission. You need to build, test and finally put together a lot of components before your challenging game is ready to go. To make this project easier to follow, I have broken down the instructions into four parts, so you can develop and test the program in sections:

- Part 1: Create the main structure and framework of the program and build the game arena where all the action takes place.

- Part 2: Program the obstacles that get in the player's way and try to slow him down.

- Part 3: Introduce the 'game play' to the program, creating levels of difficulty, scoring and, of course, the inevitable 'Game Over'.

- Part 4: Use the skills you learned in Adventure 8 and re-use your BBC micro:bit to add a start button, a diamond counter and a countdown clock to alert the player that time is running out.

Once your game is complete, you can take it in whatever direction you want, introduce your own creativity and make it your own.

Suggested challenges are included in each part of the adventure. You should not take up these challenges or change the program until you have completed the whole adventure, otherwise you may find yourself tangled up in a whole lot of complications! Come back to them after you've finished the adventure.

Part 1: Building the Arena

The game arena for Crafty Crossing is where all the action is going to take place. The player starts at one end and tries to get to the other—but there are obstacles littering the arena to slow him down.

Before there are any obstacles in it, the arena is a rectangle of GRASS blocks that makes up the floor, and GLASS walls that go all the way round (see Figure 9-2). Constants are used to define the width, height and length (or the x, y and z) of the arena. By modifying the constants, you are able to change the size and shape of the arena and the obstacles automatically resize to fill the space. The arena floor needs to be three blocks deep as the river obstacle goes down two blocks.

FIGURE 9-2 Your game arena will look like this.

Remember the `setBlocks()` function you used to build a house in Adventure 3? You are now going to use it to build your arena.

Start Minecraft, IDLE, and if you are working on a PC or a Mac, start the Minecraft server, too. You should have had a bit of practice with starting everything up by now, but refer to Adventure 1 if you need any reminders.

Create a new program for the Crafty Crossing game. The first step is to set up the initial structure of the game:

1. Open IDLE, create a new file and save the file as `CraftyCrossing.py` in the `MyAdventures` folder.

2. Import the modules you need. You use a new module `threading`, which is described in Part 2 when you create the obstacles:

   ```
   import mcpi.minecraft as minecraft
   import mcpi.block as block
   import mcpi.minecraftstuff as minecraftstuff
   import time
   import random
   import threading
   ```

3. Create three constants for the game arena's width (x), height (y) and length (z):

   ```
   ARENAX = 10
   ARENAZ = 20
   ARENAY = 3
   ```

4. Now insert the functions for the program. You build these through the adventure, until you have a complete game:

   ```
   def createArena(pos):
     pass
   def theWall(arenaPos, wallZPos):
     pass
   def theRiver(arenaPos, riverZPos):
     pass
   def theHoles(arenaPos, holesZPos):
     pass
   def createDiamonds(arenaPos, number):
     pass
   ```

   The statement `pass` doesn't do anything, but it's useful as a placeholder to mark where code will be created in the future.

5. Create a connection to Minecraft:

```
mc = minecraft.Minecraft.create()
```

6. Create a Boolean variable, which will be set to `True` when the game is over, but at the start of the game is set to `False`:

```
gameOver = False
```

As you continue, you either add more code to the main program or complete the functions you have just created.

You can run the program at this point. Nothing happens! But it's still a good idea to run the program as it is because if no errors are displayed in the Python Shell you know that everything is set up correctly.

The next step is to update the `createArena` function, which builds the arena in Minecraft:

1. Start by finding the `createArena` function in the code you have just written, by looking for the following code:

```
def createArena(pos):
  pass
```

Delete the `pass` statement that is indented under the function.

2. Indented under the `def  createArena(pos):` line, create a connection to Minecraft:

```
mc = minecraft.Minecraft.create()
```

3. Now you can create the arena using `setBlocks` by taking the position `(pos)` passed to the function and adding the constants ARENAX, ARENAY and ARENAZ (Figure 9-3 shows how the constants are added to the position to create the arena):

```
mc.setBlocks(pos.x - 1 , pos.y, pos.z - 1,
             pos.x + ARENAX + 1, pos.y - 3,
             pos.z + ARENAZ + 1,
             block.GRASS.id)
```

4. Next, create the glass walls by creating a cube of GLASS blocks and then clearing the area in the middle by creating a cube of AIR inside the GLASS:

```
mc.setBlocks(pos.x - 1, pos.y + 1, pos.z - 1,
             pos.x + ARENAX + 1, pos.y + ARENAY,
             pos.z + ARENAZ + 1,
             block.GLASS.id)
mc.setBlocks(pos.x, pos.y + 1, pos.z,
             pos.x + ARENAX, pos.y + ARENAY,
             pos.z + ARENAZ,
             block.AIR.id)
```

5. The createArena() function is now complete, but it still needs to be called from the main program. Add the following to the bottom of the program to get the player's position and pass it as a variable to the createArena() function:

```
arenaPos = mc.player.getTilePos()
createArena(arenaPos)
```

6. It's time to run the program! You should see the arena built next to the player, as in Figure 9-3.

FIGURE 9-3 Create the game arena

Part 2: Creating the Obstacles

Making a game challenging is one of the aspects of good game play—an easy game very quickly becomes a dull game. In the next part of this adventure, you create some obstacles to slow down the player and make it more difficult for him to get to the other side of the arena.

The Wall

The first obstacle you are going to create is a brick wall that not only goes all the way across the arena but also moves up and down. When it's down it blocks the way, meaning the player has to wait until it goes up before he can pass through (see Figure 9-4).

FIGURE 9-4 The wall you build can slow down the player.

The wall is a simple but very effective way of slowing down the player, but if he gets his timing right he can duck straight under it and move on to the next challenge.

You create the wall using `MinecraftShape` in the `minecraftstuff` module, which you learned about when you created the Alien Invasion in Adventure 7.

Update the `theWall()` function to create the wall obstacle by following these steps:

1. Find the function in the code you wrote earlier by looking for the following code:

   ```
   def theWall(arenaPos, wallZPos):
     pass
   ```

   Delete the `pass` statement that is indented under the function.

2. Indented under the `def theWall(arenaPos, wallZPos):` line, create a connection to Minecraft:

   ```
   mc = minecraft.Minecraft.create()
   ```

3. The `theWall()` function expects two parameters to be passed to it: `arenaPos` (the position of the arena) and `wallZPos` (the Z position along the arena where the wall will be placed). Using these two parameters, create the position for the wall (see Figure 9-5):

   ```
   wallPos = minecraft.Vec3(arenaPos.x,
                            arenaPos.y + 1,
                            arenaPos.z + wallZPos)
   ```

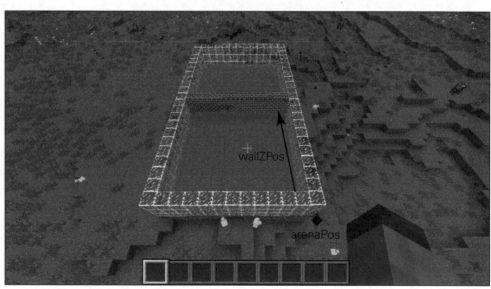

FIGURE 9-5 Create the position of the wall.

4. Create the shape of the wall by passing in the `mc` and `wallPos` variables that you created in steps 2 and 3:

   ```
   wallShape = minecraftstuff.MinecraftShape(mc, wallPos)
   ```

5. Now create the wall shape by using `setBlocks` to create blocks across the arena (x) and upwards (y):

```
wallShape.setBlocks(
    0, 1, 0,
    ARENAX, ARENAY - 1, 0,
    block.BRICK_BLOCK.id)
```

6. Your wall is now finished—but wait, it's still static! To move the wall up and down, you use the `MinecraftShape.moveBy()` function, putting a small delay in between:

```
while not gameOver:
    wallShape.moveBy(0,1,0)
    time.sleep(1)
    wallShape.moveBy(0,-1,0)
    time.sleep(1)
```

The code inside the `while` loop runs until the variable `gameOver` is set to `True` (or `not gameOver`). This is set to `True` at the end of the game when the player either completes the game or loses.

7. The `theWall()` function is now complete. All that is left for you to do is call the function in the main program and add the following to the bottom of the program:

```
WALLZ = 10
theWall(arenaPos, WALLZ)
```

The constant `WALLZ` holds the Z position, which is where you want the wall to be built in the arena.

8. Run the program. You should see the wall going up and down in the middle of the arena.

You haven't written the code that sets the `gameOver` variable to `True` yet, so when you run the program it continues forever! You need to stop the program by clicking Shell⇨Restart Shell or holding Ctrl+C in the Python Shell.

DIGGING INTO THE CODE

The position of `theWall` shape is created using `minecraft.Vec3(x, y, z)`. The `minecraft.Vec3()` is the Minecraft API's way of holding a set of coordinates (x, y, z) together. Vec3 is short for 3D vector.

RUNNING MORE THAN ONE OBSTACLE

You now have a problem! The program you created is stuck. It loops around, moving the wall up and down forever and is never going to do anything else. This is because the program you have written is **sequential**, meaning that each command in your program is run in turn, and the next command waits for the previous one to finish before running. Your program is stuck because it never gets to the next command after the `while` loop.

Sequential means to follow a sequence or order, usually one thing after the other.

How can you create more obstacles and run the rest of the game if the program is stuck and won't do anything other than move the wall up and down?

There is a solution. Meet multi-threading! Until now, all the programs you have written in these adventures have been single-threaded; in other words, they have been sequential, with one command running after the other.

If you imagine your program as a piece of string laid out flat and your commands as knots in that string, you can see how your program runs from one end of the string to the other, running a command whenever it gets to a knot. If you include a loop, it makes your program go back to a previous knot, and if you include an `if` statement it might make the program miss a knot—but it can still run only one command at a time.

When you use multi-threading, you are telling your program to create a new thread (or piece of string), which has its own commands (knots). This runs at the same time as your original program, which keeps on running too. Your program is now doing two things at once, rather than just one (see Figure 9-6).

To make all the obstacles in the game run at the same time, you need to create a new thread each time an obstacle is run, meaning that the programs that make the obstacles work are all running at the same time.

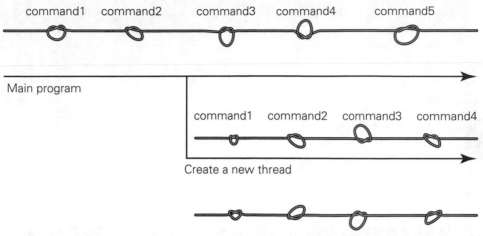

Main program

Create a new thread

FIGURE 9-6 When you create multiple threads, your program can do more than one thing at a time.

Multi-threading is incredibly useful in computer programming, but it is very advanced and it can get complicated very quickly. If you want to know more about multi-threading in Python, visit `www.tutorialspoint.com/ python/python_multithreading.htm`.

Let's return to your wall. To get it running in its own thread, you have to change the line of the program that calls the `theWall()` function, and use the `threading` module you imported at the start of the program:

1. Delete the last line of the program that runs the `theWall()` function, which looks like this:

   ```
   theWall(arenaPos, WALLZ)
   ```

2. Insert the following line at the end of the program to create a new thread, `wall_t`, which calls the `theWall()` function:

   ```
   wall_t = threading.Thread(
       target = theWall,
       args = (arenaPos, WALLZ))
   ```

3. The wall thread now needs to be started:

   ```
   wall_t.start()
   ```

4. Run the program.

You should see the same result as before, with the wall moving up and down in the arena. The difference is that, this time, it is running in its own thread. Now you can continue programming the rest of the game.

DIGGING INTO THE CODE

To run the `theWall()` function in its own thread, you use this code:

```
wall_t = threading.Thread(
    target = theWall,
    args = (arenaPos, WALLZ))
wall_t.start()
```

The `target` parameter is set to the name of the function, which is `theWall`. The second parameter, `args`, provides the variables the function expects to be passed: `arena, WALLZ`.

The variables (parameters) the function expects are passed in brackets `(arena, WALLZ)` because `args` expects them to be passed as a **tuple**.

Any Python function can be called in this way. If you had written the following function to print a message to the screen

```
def printMessage(message)
  print message
```

you could run it in its own thread, using:

```
print_t = threading.Thread(
    target = printMessage,
    args = ("Hello Minecraft World",))
print_t.start()
```

The comma after `"Hello Minecraft World"` tells Python that this is a tuple, but it's a tuple with only one item in it.

If you want your main program to wait until the thread has finished then you can use the `join()` function, which when called waits to continue until all the code in the thread has run:

```
print_t.join()
```

Tuples are similar to lists that you have used in previous adventures—the key difference is that once a tuple has been created it can't be changed, unlike a list where you can change it such as adding or removing items. In programming terms things that can't be changed are known as immutable, whereas those that can be changed are known as mutable. If you want to know more about Python tuples visit www.tutorialspoint.com/python/python_tuples.htm.

Building the River

Your next task is to build a river that runs the width of the arena—in other words, a river that's too wide for the player to jump! Luckily, there is a bridge over it. Not so luckily, the bridge moves backwards and forwards along the river, so the player needs to use careful timing to jump onto the bridge and off again on the other side (see Figure 9-7)

If the player falls into the river he will be taken back to the start of the arena. You write the code to move the player back to the start in Part 3; for now, this section is about building the river and the moving bridge.

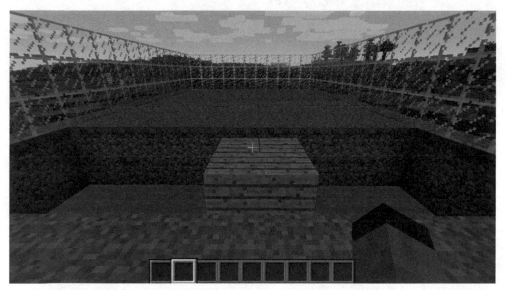

FIGURE 9-7 The player must cross the river.

First you need to create the river itself by clearing away part of the arena floor and putting a layer of water blocks at the bottom. You create the bridge by using MinecraftShape and make it move from side to side using a similar method to the one you used to make the wall move up and down.

Update the `theRiver()` function to create the river obstacle by following these steps:

1. Find the `theRiver()` function by looking for the following code in the code you wrote earlier:

   ```
   def theRiver(arenaPos, riverZPos):
     pass
   ```

   Delete the `pass` statement that is indented under the function.

2. Indented under the `def theRiver(arenaPos, riverZPos):` line, create a connection to Minecraft:

   ```
   mc = minecraft.Minecraft.create()
   ```

3. Create two constants, which are the width of the river (`RIVERWIDTH`) and the width of the bridge (`BRIDGEWIDTH`):

   ```
   RIVERWIDTH = 4
   BRIDGEWIDTH = 2
   ```

4. Now create the river across the arena position using the parameters passed in, `arenaPos` and `riverZPos` (the z position along the arena where the river should be placed):

   ```
   mc.setBlocks(arenaPos.x,
                arenaPos.y - 2,
                arenaPos.z + riverZPos,
                arenaPos.x + ARENAX,
                arenaPos.y,
                arenaPos.z + riverZPos + RIVERWIDTH - 1,
                block.AIR.id)
   mc.setBlocks(arenaPos.x,
                arenaPos.y - 2,
                arenaPos.z + riverZPos,
                arenaPos.x + ARENAX,
                arenaPos.y - 2,
                arenaPos.z + riverZPos + RIVERWIDTH - 1,
                block.WATER.id)
   ```

   You create the river by using `setBlocks()` to create an area of `AIR` in the arena floor and a layer of `WATER` at the bottom.

5. Create the position where the bridge will be placed. You want it in the middle of the river so that the player can't just step onto it but has to jump from the bank onto the bridge:

   ```
   bridgePos = minecraft.Vec3(arenaPos.x,
                              arenaPos.y,
                              arenaPos.z + riverZPos + 1)
   ```

6. Create the shape of the bridge by passing in the `mc` and `bridgePos` variables you created in steps 2 and 5:

```
bridgeShape = minecraftstuff.MinecraftShape(mc, bridgePos)
```

7. Create the shape that will be the bridge. You do this in a similar way to how you made the wall using `setBlocks`, with the bridge (x) and river width (z):

```
bridgeShape.setBlocks(
    0, 0, 0,
    BRIDGEWIDTH - 1, 0, RIVERWIDTH - 3,
    block.WOOD_PLANKS.id)
```

When creating the bridge, 3 is subtracted from `RIVERWIDTH` to create a gap of one block between the river bank and the bridge, meaning the player has to jump on and off the bridge (see Figure 9-8).

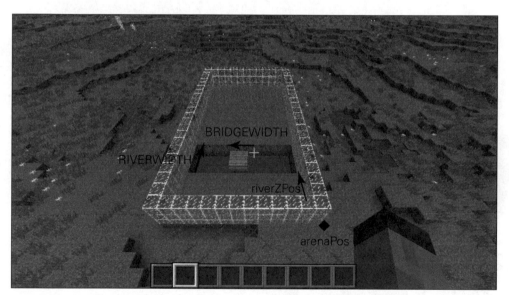

FIGURE 9-8 Because the bridge does not completely span the river, your player has to jump.

8. To move the bridge across the arena one block at a time, you need to calculate the number of steps the bridge would have to go through in order to get from one side to the other; this is the width of the arena minus the width of the bridge:

```
steps = ARENAX - BRIDGEWIDTH + 1
```

9. Move the bridge from side to side by using two `for` loops (one to go left and one to go right) and by using the `MinecraftShape.moveBy()` function to move the bridge one block to the side for each step, adding a small delay between steps:

```
while not gameOver:

    for left in range(0, steps):
        bridgeShape.moveBy(1,0,0)
        time.sleep(1)

    for right in range(0, steps):
        bridgeShape.moveBy(-1,0,0)
        time.sleep(1)
```

10. Your river function is now complete. It needs to be called from the main program in a new thread, so add the following code to the bottom of the program:

```
RIVERZ = 4
river_t = threading.Thread(
    target = theRiver,
    args = (arenaPos, RIVERZ))
river_t.start()
```

The `RIVERZ` constant is the z position down the arena where the river obstacle will be created.

11. Time to run the program! You should now see the arena with the wall in the middle, the river towards the start of the arena and the bridge going back and forth.

MARTIN SAYS:

Enter the arena and try to get across the bridge. If you're good with the controls you might find this pretty easy—but wait until you are under pressure to collect the diamonds at the same time *and* do it as quickly as possible! Chances are you will miss the jump a lot more.

Creating the Holes

The final obstacles you need to create in Crafty Crossing are the holes. These are random holes in the arena floor that close up every few seconds and open again in different positions (see Figure 9-9).

You use the `randint()` function to find random positions for the holes. BLACK WOOL blocks appear briefly in the floor before the holes open, giving the player some warning and a chance to get out of the way. You create the holes by turning blocks in the arena floor to AIR. They stay that way for a few seconds before being turned back to GRASS, and new holes are created elsewhere.

FIGURE 9-9 Holes appear, and your player must be careful not to fall into one!

As with the river, if the player falls into a hole they are returned to the start of the arena, but you don't introduce the code to do that until Part 3 of this adventure.

Now, you're going to update the `theHoles` function to create the holes obstacle:

1. Find the `theHoles` function by looking for the following code in the code you wrote earlier:

   ```
   def theHoles(arenaPos, holesZPos):
     pass
   ```

   Delete the `pass` statement that is indented under the function.

2. Indented under the `def theHoles(arenaPos, holesZPos):` line, create a connection to Minecraft:

   ```
   mc = minecraft.Minecraft.create()
   ```

3. Create two constants, which are the number of holes that will be created (`HOLES`) and the width of the holes obstacle (see Figure 9-10):

   ```
   HOLES = 15
   HOLESWIDTH = 3
   ```

4. Create the holes `while` loop, which continues until the game is over:

   ```
   while not gameOver:
   ```

   The rest of the code in the `theHoles` function is indented under this `while` loop.

FIGURE 9-10 Create the position and width of the holes.

5. Create random positions for the holes by using the `random.randint()` function to create x and z coordinates, (the y position is the position of the arena) and append them to a Python list:

```
holes = []
for count in range(0,HOLES):
  x = random.randint(
    arenaPos.x,
    arenaPos.x + ARENAX)

  z = random.randint(
    arenaPos.z + holesZPos,
    arenaPos.z + holesZPos + HOLESWIDTH)

  holes.append(minecraft.Vec3(x, arenaPos.y, z))
```

6. Loop through all the positions in the holes list and turn the blocks to BLACK WOOL, the next 3 for loops should all be indented under `while not gameOver`:

```
for hole in holes:
  mc.setBlock(hole.x, hole.y, hole.z,
              block.WOOL.id, 15)
time.sleep(0.25)
```

By turning the holes in the arena floor black, you give the player a warning that a new hole is about to appear and they have the chance to get out of the way.

7. Open the holes by setting the blocks below the hole position to be AIR using `setBlocks()`:

```
for hole in holes:
  mc.setBlocks(hole.x, hole.y, hole.z,
               hole.x, hole.y - 2, hole.z,
               block.AIR.id)
time.sleep(2)
```

You include a delay after the holes are created so the holes stay there for two seconds.

8. Close the holes by using the same loop you used to open them, but this time set the blocks back to GRASS:

```
for hole in holes:
  mc.setBlocks(hole.x, hole.y, hole.z,
               hole.x, hole.y - 2, hole.z,
               block.GRASS.id)
time.sleep(2)
```

The program now returns to the top of the `while` loop and creates a new set of holes.

9. Your `holes` function is now complete. Add the following code to the bottom of the program:

```
HOLESZ = 15
holes_t = threading.Thread(
    target = theHoles,
    args = (arenaPos, HOLESZ))
holes_t.start()
```

The `HOLESZ` constant is the z position down the arena where the holes obstacle will be created.

10. Run the program. As before, you should see the arena created with the wall and river obstacles, but now you should also see the holes continually opening and closing in random locations towards the end of the arena.

Try out the arena. See if you can get backwards and forwards over and through the obstacles without falling down or getting stuck.

> You can adjust the constants in the game to make it your own. Perhaps make the arena longer or wider, put the obstacles in different positions or make it more difficult by making them faster or harder to get across.

The functions that create the obstacles are like mini-programs, and because they use multi-threading they all run independently. Because of this, if you want to have more than one type of obstacle in the arena, it's really easy to create a new one. Perhaps you'd like to have two walls? If you call the `theWall` function again but give it a different z position to the first wall, a second wall appears and goes up and down just like the first one:

```
WALL2Z = 13
wall_t2 = threading.Thread(
    target = theWall,
    args = (arenaPos, WALL2Z))
wall_t2.start()
```

CHALLENGE

You don't have to stop there. Using the same methods you used to create the wall, river and holes, can you create a new type of obstacle? Perhaps you can conjure a cage that randomly appears and traps the player, or a series of platforms the player has to jump to reach the end of the arena.

If you find the obstacles too easy or too difficult you can change their difficulty by setting the constants to different values. For example, you can increase or decrease the delays to make the obstacles move slower or faster. To speed up the bridge, change the `time.sleep(1)` code in the move left and move right `for` loops to `time.sleep(0.5)`.

Part 3: Game Play

The next part of your big adventure is to add game play to your program. Your aim is to turn the arena from an obstacle course into a game where the player wants to play again and again, and get to the next level.

To achieve this, the game needs to be exciting and challenging, and it should include risk, a reward and a goal.

The challenge is for the player to collect all the diamonds that are randomly placed around the arena while he also tries to get through the obstacles in a set time limit.

Points are given to the player as a reward for collecting diamonds and for getting to the end of the level. The faster the player completes the level, the more points he will get. The goal is to complete all the levels and get as many points as possible.

Your game is going to have three levels, and you are going to make each level more difficult than the last by adding more diamonds and shortening the time limit.

Starting the Game

In this section you set up the game and create constants that establish how many diamonds and the amount of time available in each level.

The program has two main loops:

- **The `game` loop:** This loop continues until the game is over (`while not gameOver`). This is where each level is set up and started. Points are calculated at the end of each level.

- **The `level` loop:** This loop continues until the end of each level—so, either when the level is complete or the game is over (`while not gameOver and not levelComplete`). This loop also returns a player to the start if he falls into the river or a hole, clears diamonds if the player hits them, and checks to see if the time has run out.

The instructions for this part of the adventure refer to indenting code under either the game loop or the `level` loop. It is important that you put the code in the right place; otherwise the game doesn't work properly.

First, add the structure of the game and create the two main loops by following these steps to add the necessary code to the bottom of the program:

1. Create three constants for the number of levels in the game, the number of diamonds that will be created and the amount of time (in seconds) the player will be given to complete each level:

```
LEVELS = 3
DIAMONDS = [3,5,9]
TIMEOUTS = [30,25,20]
```

The DIAMONDS and TIMEOUTS constants are Python lists. Both have three items, which are the values for each level; for example, in the first level, the player has to collect three diamonds and has 30 seconds to do it and get to the other side.

2. Create two variables to hold the points the player has scored and the level they are currently on:

```
level = 0
points = 0
```

3. Create the game loop. Place a comment over it to remind you where it is, as further instructions in this adventure refer to indenting code under the game loop:

```
#game loop
while not gameOver:
```

The variable gameOver is set to False at the start of the program; it is set to True when the player runs out of time or completes the game. This variable is also used in the obstacles functions, and when it is set to True it results in all the obstacles stopping.

4. Indented under the game loop, change the position of the player so that he is at the start of the arena and ready to begin:

```
mc.player.setPos(arenaPos.x + 1,
                 arenaPos.y + 1,
                 arenaPos.z + 1)
```

5. Start the clock for the level by getting the current time and putting it into a variable:

```
start = time.time()
```

6. Set the level complete flag to False and create the level loop. As you did with the game loop, create a comment here to remind you where the level loop is, as further instructions refer to indenting code under the level loop:

```
levelComplete = False
#level loop
while not gameOver and not levelComplete:
```

7. Indented under the level loop, put in a small delay. You need this because the program loops all the time while the game is playing and, without it, the program would use all of the computer's processing power:

```
time.sleep(0.1)
```

8. Run the program. The only change you see is that the player is automatically put at the start of the arena, but it gives you the chance to check that everything is working properly and no errors have occurred.

When the player is put at the start of the arena, he starts the level in the right corner. Would it be better if he started in the middle? Change the code so that the player is put in the middle of the arena rather than the corner at the start of each level.

Collecting Diamonds

The main objective of the game is to collect diamonds. You are now going to program these to appear in random positions in the arena (see Figure 9-11); the player collects the diamonds by "hitting" them (or rather, right-clicking the block while holding a sword).

FIGURE 9-11 Diamonds appear in random positions.

The diamonds disappear as soon as they have been hit, and, once he has collected all the diamonds, the player can go on to complete the level by getting to the other side of the arena.

Update the `createDiamonds()` function and call it from the `game` loop by following these steps:

1. Find the `createDiamonds()` function by looking for the following in the code you wrote earlier:

```
def createDiamonds(arenaPos, number):
    pass
```

Delete the pass statement that is indented under the function.

2. Indented under the def createDiamonds(arenaPos, number): line, create a connection to Minecraft:

```
mc = minecraft.Minecraft.create()
```

3. Create the number of diamonds you require by finding random x and z positions in the arena and setting the block to a DIAMOND_BLOCK:

```
for diamond in range(0, number):
  x = random.randint(arenaPos.x, arenaPos.x + ARENAX)
  z = random.randint(arenaPos.z, arenaPos.z + ARENAZ)
  mc.setBlock(x, arenaPos.y + 1, z,
              block.DIAMOND_BLOCK.id)
```

4. The createDiamonds() function now needs to be called at the start of the game loop; every time a new level starts, a new set of diamonds is created. Indented under the game loop, directly under the while loop, add the following code:

```
#game loop
while not gameOver:
  createDiamonds(arenaPos, DIAMONDS[level])
  diamondsLeft = DIAMONDS[level]
```

The variable diamondsLeft is also created; this holds the number of diamonds remaining for the player to collect.

5. Run the program. Because you are on the first level, you should see three diamonds created at random locations in the arena.

After you have created the diamonds, you can add the code to monitor the player's hit events using the pollBlockHits function (which you learned in Adventure 4) and, when the player hits a DIAMOND block, turn it to AIR.

Add the following code under the level loop to turn the DIAMOND_BLOCK to AIR if the player hits it:

1. Indented under the level loop, call the pollBlockHits function to get any block hit events:

```
#level loop
while not gameOver and not levelComplete:
  hits = mc.events.pollBlockHits()
```

2. Loop through the block hit events and get the type of block that was hit:

```
for hit in hits:
  blockHitType = mc.getBlock(hit.pos.x,
                             hit.pos.y,
                             hit.pos.z)
```

3. Check to see if the type of block hit was DIAMOND_BLOCK. If it was, turn it to AIR and subtract 1 from the diamondsLeft variable:

```
if blockHitType == block.DIAMOND_BLOCK.id:
    mc.setBlock(hit.pos.x, hit.pos.y, hit.pos.z,
                block.AIR.id)
    diamondsLeft = diamondsLeft - 1
```

The diamondsLeft variable is used to check that all the diamonds have been collected when the player gets to the end of the arena.

4. Run the program; when you hit the DIAMOND blocks, they should turn to AIR and disappear.

Remember that, in order to hit a block, you must be holding a sword and using the right-click button on the mouse.

CHALLENGE

Can you make the diamonds harder to hit? Perhaps you can make them rise up and down and allow the player to hit them only when they are in the air.

Out of Time

If your player was given an infinite amount of time, the game would be really easy (and boring). By introducing a time limit, you make the game challenging; and by making the player get all the diamonds and get to the other side before the time runs out, you give him a goal.

If the time runs out, it's game over. Your next task is to add the code to the level loop that checks to see whether the time has run out and, if it has, sets the gameOver flag to True:

1. Indented under the level loop, tell the program to calculate the number of seconds left in this level:

```
#level loop
while not gameOver and not levelComplete:
    secondsLeft = TIMEOUTS[level] - (time.time() - start)
```

2. If there are less than zero seconds left, set the `gameOver` flag to `True` and post a message to the chat:

```
if secondsLeft < 0:
  gameOver = True
  mc.postToChat("Out of time...")
```

3. Run the program. After 30 seconds (as this is level 1), the program should end and the message 'Out of time. . .' should appear (see Figure 9-12).

FIGURE 9-12 Let your players know when they run out of time.

DIGGING INTO THE CODE

The number of seconds that are left for the level is calculated using the following code:

```
secondsLeft = TIMEOUTS[level] - (time.time() - start)
```

The variable `secondsLeft` is set by taking the number of seconds that are allowed for this level from the `TIMEOUTS` constant:

```
TIMEOUTS[level]
```

Then you subtract how many seconds the player has been playing the level. This is the time now, minus the time when the level started:

```
(time.time() - start)
```

Tracking the Player

When the player has collected all the diamonds and reached the end of the arena, he has completed the level. If he falls into the river or a hole, he is returned to the start of the arena. To make these things happen, your program needs to know where the player is.

After checking where the player is, the program can either set the `levelComplete` flag to `True` if he has collected all the diamonds or set his position back at the start of the arena.

When you have completed this section, the game is going to be playable, albeit only on one level—the first and easiest one. It might be wise for you to practice your moves now, because in the next section the difficulty is going to be cranked up!

Your next task is to add the code to the `level` loop to track the player and either put him back to the start or complete the level:

1. Indented under the `level` loop, get the player's position:

   ```
   #level loop
   while not gameOver and not levelComplete:
     pos = mc.player.getTilePos()
   ```

2. Check to see if the player's height, y, is lower than the height of the arena. If it is, he must have fallen into the river or a hole, so put him back to the start:

   ```
   if pos.y < arenaPos.y:
     mc.player.setPos(arenaPos.x + 1,
                      arenaPos.y + 1,
                      arenaPos.z + 1)
   ```

3. Check to see if the player has reached the end of the arena and has collected all the diamonds. You do this by checking whether the player's z position is the same as the end of the arena and, if it is, setting the `levelComplete` flag to `True`:

   ```
   if pos.z == arenaPos.z + ARENAZ and diamondsLeft == 0:
     levelComplete = True
   ```

   When the `levelComplete` flag is set to `True`, the `level` loop ends, the diamonds are re-created and the game starts again.

4. Run the program. The game should reset when all the diamonds have been collected and the player reaches the end of the arena; and, if the player falls into the river or a hole, he should be returned to the start of the arena.

Setting the Level as Complete and Calculating Points

When the player completes a level, the program needs to calculate how many points he has scored and put the game on to the next level. The player scores points if he completes the level. He receives one point for every diamond he has collected, multiplied by the number of seconds left on the clock.

To do that, you need to include the following code. The new code needs to be indented under the game loop, but it has to come after the level loop has finished:

1. Indented under the game loop, but after the level loop, check to see whether the level was completed:

```
#game loop
while not gameOver:
  [your code]

  #level loop
  while not gameOver and not levelComplete:
    [your code]

  if levelComplete:
```

2. If the level was completed, calculate the points scored and add them to the points variable, before posting the results to the chat:

```
    points = points + (DIAMONDS[level] * int(secondsLeft))
    mc.postToChat("Level Complete - Points = " + ↵
      str(points))
```

3. Set the game to the next level by adding 1 to the level variable:

```
    level = level + 1
```

4. If this is the last level, set the gameOver flag to True and post a message of congratulations to the chat:

```
    if level == LEVELS:
      gameOver = True
      mc.postToChat("Congratulations - All levels complete")
```

The LEVELS constant holds the total number of levels in the game.

5. Run the program.

Your game is very nearly complete! When the player has collected all the diamonds and battled his way to the end of the arena before the time runs out, the game restarts on the next level. Here it gets a little bit harder, with more diamonds and less time. If the player manages to complete all the levels, it's game over, and congratulations!

Adding the Game Over Message

The very last thing you need to do to complete the game play is to add a message right at the end of the program, telling the player the game is over and giving him his final score (see Figure 9-13). Simply add the following code to the very bottom of the program:

```
mc.postToChat("Game Over - Points = " + str(points))
```

FIGURE 9-13 Tell the player when the game is over and then display the score.

All levels complete—156 points. Beat that!

You can download the complete Crafty Crossing program on the companion website at `www.wiley.com/go/adventuresinminecraft2e`.

It doesn't really have to be game over! The program is made so you can extend it, play around with the settings, introduce new obstacles or create a magnificent arena. It's up to you.

Part 4: Adding a Button and Display

There are a couple of problems with the Crafty Crossing program. The game starts automatically, whether the player is ready or not, and there is no display of useful information such as how many diamonds are left to collect and whether the time is running out.

In the last part of this adventure, you are going to re-use the BBC micro:bit introduced in Adventure 8 to add a button for you to press when you want the game to start and using the LED display to show how many diamonds are left to collect and countdown when there are only five seconds left to complete the level.

Set Up the BBC micro:bit

You need the BBC micro:bit you used in Adventure 8, connected in the same way with the USB cable. Look back at Adventure 8 if you need a reminder of how to set up the BBC micro:bit.

Modify your Craft Crossing program to import the `microbit` library and wait for button A to be pressed before starting the game:

1. Import the microbit module under the existing `import` statements at the top of the program:

   ```
   import microbit
   ```

2. Just before the `game` loop, add the code to wait for button A to be pressed:

```
mc.postToChat("Press button A to start")
microbit.display.scroll("A to start")
while not microbit.button_a.was_pressed():
    time.sleep(0.1)

#game loop
while not gameOver:
```

You have also made a message scroll along the screen on the micro:bit telling the player to press 'A to start'.

3. Run the program and test the new start button.

When you run your program, a message may appear in the Python Shell telling you to scan for your BBC micro:bit. Follow the instructions and refer to Adventure 8 if you need more information.

CHALLENGE

Can you change the program so that you can press a button at the end of the game to start a new game rather than having to rerun the program?

Countdown Clock

When the time is running out, the display is going to show a simple clock that counts from 5 to 0 as the game ends, giving the player a visual indicator that they need to hurry up.

To do this, you need to modify the Crafty Crossing program to update the display, using the `microbit.display.show` function, when the number of seconds left in the game is less than 6:

1. After the `secondsLeft` variable has been calculated in the game loop, add an `if` statement to check whether the `secondsLeft` is less than 6:

```
secondsLeft = TIMEOUTS[level] - (time.time() - start)
if int(secondsLeft) < 6:
```

2. Indented under the `if` statement, add the code to display a clock image on the BBC micro:bit's display:

```
microbit.display.show(
    microbit.Image.ALL_CLOCKS[int(secondsLeft)])
```

The `ALL_CLOCKS` image is different than those used in Adventure 8, as it is a list of 12 images, one for each of the hourly positions on a clock face.

3. Run the program. When the time is running out, you see a clock counting down on the BBC micro:bit.

Diamonds to Collect

Your very last task in this adventure is to update the display to show the number of diamonds left to collect.

To do this, you need to modify the Crafty Crossing program to update the display when there are more than 5 seconds left to run:

1. Add an `else` to the `if` statement that displays the countdown clock. Also add the code to show the `diamondsLeft` on the display:

```
if int(secondsLeft) < 6:
    microbit.display.show(
        microbit.Image.ALL_CLOCKS[int(secondsLeft)])
else:
    microbit.display.show(diamondsLeft)
```

2. Run the program. The number of diamonds should be displayed and should decrease each time the player hits one, until it reaches 0, or the time starts to run out and the countdown clock appears.

CHALLENGE

When a new level starts, use the display to flash the level number before showing the number of diamonds to be collected.

Quick Reference Table	
Command	**Description**
`import threading`	Imports the Python threading module

`t = threading.Thread(`
 	
`    target = function,`
 	
`    args = (variable1, variable2))`
	Calls a function in its own thread

`t.start()`	Start the thread and call the function.
`t.join()`	Wait for the thread to finish.
`import time`	Imports the Python time module
`timeNow = time.time()`	Gets the current time

Further Adventures in Your Continuing Journey with Minecraft

Minecraft gives you a fantastic canvas for creativity and adventure. Add to this the power of being able to control the game through code and the only limitation is your imagination. What will you do next?

Here are some ideas and resources that will hopefully give you inspiration:

- Creating games is a great way to stretch your programming skills. Check out `www.classicgamesarcade.com` for some ideas.

- Minecraft is multiplayer game. Why not take advantage of that and create programs that many people can use and enjoy?

- Interacting with electronics brings Minecraft into the real world. Take your skills further with Adventures in Arduino `eu.wiley.com/WileyCDA/WileyTitle/productCd-1118948475.html`.

- There are many open data sources on the Internet. How about integrating Minecraft with websites such as Twitter (`dev.twitter.com`) or weather forecasts from the Met Office (`www.metoffice.gov.uk/datapoint`)?

Achievement Unlocked: **Your big Minecraft project!**

Appendix A

Where to Go from Here

WE HOPE THE adventures in this book have given you a whole range of ideas, code snippets and skills, and inspired you to take your Minecraft programming adventures further. Where you go from here is up to you and your imagination! If you're not sure what you want to do yet, or have an idea for your next project but don't know where to start, here are some interesting resources you can investigate to get those ideas flowing!

Websites

The Internet has a wealth of useful websites with information about Minecraft, almost too much to sort through, but here are some sites that Martin and David have found useful when learning, playing and programming Minecraft:

Minecraft

- `www.wiley.com/go/adventuresinminecraft2e`—This is the companion website for this book. It includes downloadable quick-reference sheets, badges, complete program listings, and videos for each of the projects in this book.

- `http://adventuresinminecraft.github.io`—Here you can find all the code resources for *Adventures in Minecraft*. It includes code repositories for the starter kits, RaspberryJuice plug-in and Python modules, useful links and downloads.

- `www.stuffaboutcode.com`—This is Martin's very successful blog. It has a whole section about Minecraft with lots of project ideas and experiments that you can try out yourself. Martin also hosts the *Adventures in Minecraft* forum where you can get help, advice and the best Minecraft API reference that you will find anywhere on the Internet!

- `http://arghbox.wordpress.com`—Craig Richardson regularly develops exciting Minecraft programming projects to help support the teaching of the new computing curriculum. Be sure to have a look at his open source Minecraft programming book and his Minecraft controller built from real fruit!

- `http://jimchristian.net`—Jim Christian's website is packed with a wealth of coding resources. Jim regularly runs Minecraft training courses via Fire Tech Camp and other providers, and he also wrote the highly successful *How to Code in Minecraft* MagBook that you can buy directly from the shelf in most newsagents. He's done some amazing builds using MCEdit and other Minecraft design tools; you should definitely check out his site.

- `https://codekingdoms.com`—Code Kingdoms provides an online Minecraft coding platform where you host your own server online and invite others to join in. You code mods in Java that change how the games work, and they offer a wide range of challenge-led educational resources around their online platform.

- `www.minecraftforum.net`—This is the official Minecraft Forum where you can get help on any topic related to Minecraft, such as new features, setting up servers, and tips for creative and survival mode.

- `http://minecraft.gamepedia.com/Minecraft_Wiki`—The Minecraft Wiki is a community-managed collection of information about Minecraft. And because it is community managed, this means you can contribute to it, too!

- `www.spigotmc.org`—Here you can find Minecraft server resources, including tools that enable you to build your own server and a huge library of plug-ins.

- `www.scarabcoder.com`—This is the blog of a young coder named Nicholas Harris, who started programming by using Minecraft on the Raspberry Pi. He posts updates on his adventures in coding and technology. Be sure to look at his series on Bukkit plugins.

- `www.minecraftmaps.com`—Minecraft allows you to load and save adventure maps, which are complete snapshots of a Minecraft world. This site has a huge repository of community-developed maps that you can load into your Minecraft world so that you can then build on top of them.

- `https://minecraft.curseforge.com`—This is an open-source exchange hosting site (a bit like sourceforge, but for Minecraft), where projects are hosted so you can download them.

- `https://minecraft-seeds.net`—Minecraft worlds are generated by a computer algorithm built inside Minecraft. Random numbers are "seeded" from a start number. If you enter a known seed, you re-create that world. This site lists seeds you can type to create specific Minecraft worlds.

- `www.mcedit.net` and `www.worldpainter.net`—These are free downloadable tools that you can use to design and paint your own custom world maps using onscreen editing tools.

- `http://mcreator.pylo.si`—MCreator is a mod maker for Minecraft that uses a simple point-and-click interface with no programming. With it, you can create fantastic Minecraft mods such as new block types, mobs, armour, commands and many other items.

- `www.firetechcamp.com`—Fire Tech Camp runs coding camps for teenagers during every school holiday all around the UK and in many other countries. They have some great courses teaching video games design, Minecraft construction, Python programming, Arduino and many other tech courses tailored for teens interested in tech.

- `www.immersiveminds.com`—Stephen from Immersive Minds is well known all over the world for his educational workshops using Minecraft as an immersive platform. He's worked with many organisations and individuals to develop some of the most impressive Minecraft builds of real-world places. Some of his collaborative historic building projects in Minecraft are well worth seeking out!

Python

- `www.python.org` and `https://docs.python.org/3`—These pages are where you go for the official download and documentation for the Python programming language.

- `www.codecademy.com/tracks/python`—Codecademy provides a free online course on this page. You can follow the lessons yourself to gradually learn the Python programming language.

- `http://inventwithpython.com/chapters`—This is a free online book with many great Python projects to teach you how to program in Python.

- `https://docs.python.org/3/library/idle.html`—This is the official guide for using the IDLE integrated development environment. As a guide, it's quite precisely written, but there are no pictures. We prefer to use these tutorials from Dr Anne Dawson: `www.annedawson.net/Python_Editor_IDLE.htm`.

- `http://thonny.org`—IDLE is a very small and simple programming environment. After a while, you'll probably want something a bit more full-featured. Try Thonny; it's a much nicer environment to use.

- `http://blog.whaleygeek.co.uk`—This is David's blog. It has a number of Python and Raspberry Pi projects, hints and tips, and some downloadable flashcards to remind you of the important syntax of Python and Minecraft. Print these out and keep them in your top pocket for when you need a reminder!

Others

- `www.microbit.org`—The BBC micro:bit formed part of the physical computing adventure in Adventures 8 and 9, but it is a complete programmable computer in its own right. You can code the BBC micro:bit directly in a number of different languages including MicroPython, JavaScript Blocks and C++. You will find a wealth of ideas and resources on the micro:bit website.

- `http://www.maplin.co.uk`—Maplin Electronics are a good high-street retailer, and it's great to be able to have an idea on a Sunday afternoon and just walk into a shop and buy the necessary components while you still have the idea fresh in your mind! You can even buy a boxed BBC micro:bit off-the-shelf in any Maplin store, for completing Adventure 8 and 9 with your journey into physical computing!

Other Ways to Make Things Happen Automatically

Programming Minecraft in Python is not the only way to automate tasks—Minecraft already has three built-in control methods called redstone, command blocks, and tags. Each of these can be combined with the other to make parts of your Minecraft world do different things automatically.

- `http://minecraft.gamepedia.com/Tutorials/Command_Block`—Command blocks can be triggered to automate tasks for you. You can wire them up to a redstone signal that triggers the command to run. There are many things you can build; just take a look at the booby traps and teleporters on this tutorial page.

- `www.minecraft101.net/redstone/redstone101.html`—Redstone is the Minecraft equivalent of electricity. It is deceptively simple, but out of lots of very simple circuits you can build very complex devices.

- `www.spigotmc.org/wiki/spigot-plugin-development`—Take your Minecraft coding to the next level, learn Java and create your own server plug-ins.

Projects and Tutorials

Sometimes it's fun to come up with your own project ideas, but sometimes you need that little extra inspiration to get going. The websites listed here have a very nice collection of example projects, many of which are contributed by hobbyists and developers in the community.

- `https://minecraft.gamepedia.com/Tutorials/Advanced_redstone_circuits`—This tutorial shows how redstone can be used to piece together lots and lots of small redstone circuits to make a really large automated structure, and it walks you through how to build a complete computer out of redstone, step by step!

- `https://learn.adafruit.com/search?q=minecraft`—Adafruit has a really nice collection of tutorials with instructions written by Adafruit staff and other people in the community. The site includes an area for Minecraft projects that link to electronics, and it looks like they are adding more to it.

- `www.stuffaboutcode.com/2013/04/raspberry-pi-minecraft-cannon.html`—One of Martin's first Minecraft projects was to create a Minecraft cannon. This isn't a typical TNT cannon; you can rotate, tilt and fire it.

- `http://hackaday.com/2013/01/30/controlling-minecraft-with-a-raspberry-pi`—Here's another way to control real hardware from Minecraft, using redstone. A server plug-in communicates with the Raspberry Pi, making levers and signs inside Minecraft control and monitor real-world electronics.

- `www.instructables.com/howto/minecraft`—The instructables website has a huge collection of really well-written, step-by-step instructions on how to build projects, and they now have a Minecraft project area, too.

- `www.gemmamaylatham.co.uk/portfolio-item/patterncraft/`—Gemma May Latham is a well-known participatory artist/maker who is working tirelessly to get more children into coding. Her highly successful PatternCraft project spun out of a chance meet-up on Twitter as a result of purchasing the first edition of this book.

- `http://warksjammy.blogspot.co.uk/?view=snapshot`—This is a fantastic blog from a computing teacher in Warwickshire, UK, which includes a wealth of Minecraft, Raspberry Pi, BBC micro:bit and physical computing resources. Look out especially for the series of Minecraft HackPacks, which contain a compendium of very well-presented teaching resources centred around using Minecraft in the classroom.

Videos

Minecraft, like many modern games, is very visual, and one of the best ways to get ideas and inspiration is to watch what others are doing. Many of these videos are from bloggers and hobbyists that have become famous through their videos alone, and many of them post videos weekly or even daily.

- `www.youtube.com/user/sethbling`—Seth Bling has a huge and very active YouTube channel with lots of Minecraft projects and ideas. Be sure to check out his TNT Olympics!

- `www.youtube.com/user/stampylonghead`—Stampy releases at least one new Minecraft video per day on his YouTube channel and has a lot of fun building awesome structures.

- `www.youtube.com/user/scarabcoder`—Nicholas Harris has a good YouTube channel with lots of interesting projects. He has also written an e-book, available on Amazon, about how to write Minecraft programs.

- `www.youtube.com/user/SimplySarc`—Take a look at SimplySarc, especially his well-described Vanilla Camera (`www.youtube.com/watch?v=NyMHCabq_rs`) that uses command blocks to make a camera that takes a photo with no mods at all!

- `www.youtube.com/watch?v=7t4bH7Z-Yt4`—Our very own Martin O'Hanlon shows a Python program that turns any block you hit into a bomb that goes off after a few seconds.

- `www.youtube.com/user/ThatMumboJumbo`—MumboJumbo has a regular YouTube series about building with redstone, pistons and levers. Take a look at his version of a Minecraft lift made from pistons: `www.youtube.com/watch?v=jQulvbivtYI`.

- `www.youtube.com/user/HiFolksImAdam`—Adam creates some interesting visual illusions with command blocks and builds a TARDIS (`www.youtube.com/watch?v=3QpqUCaz8fk`) that really is bigger on the inside than it is on the outside!

- `www.youtube.com/user/AsdjkeAndBro`—Asdjke and Bro have built a number of mini-games inside Minecraft. One of our personal favourites is the battleship game: `www.youtube.com/watch?v=6AbPlT-cAm8`.

Books

There's still something nice about having a printed book by your side—propped open with personalised sticky notes or pencil marks or turned-over page corners—when working through your Minecraft adventures. We both have learnt a lot from these other authors and think that you'll find many additional projects and ideas that will complement your learning and fun gained from this book.

- ***How to Code in Minecraft*** by Jim Christian (PC Pro, 2016)
- ***Minecraft for Dummies (portable edition)*** by Jacob Corderio (Wiley, 2013)
- ***Minecraft for Dummies*** by Jesse Stay (Wiley, 2015)
- ***Minecraft Modding for Kids for Dummies*** by Sarah Guthals, Stephen Foster and Lindsey Handley (Wiley 2015)
- ***Minecraft: The Official Beginners' Handbook, Updated Edition*** (Egmont, 2015)
- ***Minecraft: The Official Redstone Handbook*** (Egmont, 2015)
- ***Minecraft: Blockopedia: An Official Minecraft Book from Mojang*** (Egmont, 2014)
- ***Learn to Program with Minecraft Plugins*** by Andy Hunt (Pragmatic Bookshelf, 2014)
- ***Adventures in Raspberry Pi, 3rd Ed.*** by Carrie Anne Philbin (Wiley, 2017)
- ***Adventures in Arduino*** by Becky Stewart (Wiley, 2014)
- ***Adventures in Python*** by Craig Richardson (Wiley, 2014)
- ***Python for Kids*** by Jason R. Briggs (No Starch Press, 2012)

Appendix B
Quick Reference

Table 1 Python input, output, variables	
Leaving reminders by using comments	**Using constants**

`# whole-line comment`
 	
`print("hello") # end-of-line comment`
	`SIZE = 100 # upper case name`

Printing to the screen	**Reading from the keyboard (Python V3)**

`print(10)       # print a number`
`print("hello") # print a string`
`print(a)        # print a variable`
	`name = input("your name?")`
	
	`age  = int(input("how old?"))`

Storing values in variables	**Using Boolean variables**

`a = 10   # an integer (whole) number`
`b = 20.2 # a decimal number`
`message = "hello" # a string`
`finished = True   # a Boolean`
`high_score = None # no value`
	`anotherGo = True`
	`while anotherGo:`
	`   choice = int(input("choice?"))`
	`   if choice == 8:`
	`      anotherGo = False`

Converting strings to (integer) numbers	**Converting numbers to strings**
`size = int(size)` `size = size + 1`	`age = str(age)` `print("Your age is " + age)`
Calculating with number variables	**Calculating absolute values and differences**

`b = a + 1 # addition`
`c = a - 1 # subtraction`
`d = a * 2 # multiplication`
`e = a / 2 # division`
`f = a % 2 # remainder after division`
	`absolute   = abs(-1) # absolute is 1`
	`difference = abs(x1-x2)`
	`smallest   = min(x1, x2)`
	`largest    = max(x1, x2)`

Table 2 Python loops

Looping	Using counted loops
```a = 0\nwhile a<100:\n print(a)\n a = a + 1```	```for a in range(10):\n print(a) # 0..9\nfor a in range(5, 50, 5):\n print(a) # 5..45 in steps of 5```
Looping through all characters in a string	**Splitting comma-separated strings**
```name = "Charlotte"\nfor ch in name:\n print(ch)```	```line = "one,two,three"\ndata = line.split(",")\nfor d in data:\n print(d)```

Table 3 Python conditions

Using if statements	Using if/else statements
```if a==42:\n print("the ultimate answer")```	```if a==5:\n print("correct")\nelse:\n print("wrong")```
Using elif/else for multiple choices	**Checking multiple conditions with** *and, or*
```if a==1:\n print("option A")\nelif a==2:\n print("option B")\nelse:\n print("anything else")```	```if choice>0 and choice<=8:\n print("in range")\nif choice<1 or choice>8:\n print("out of range")```
Checking for *different* **or** *same* **with** *if*	**Checking for** *less* **with** *if*
```if a!=1:\n print("not equal")\nif a==1:\n print("equal")```	```if a<1:\n print("less than")\nif a<=1:\n print("less than or equal")```
Checking opposites with *not*	**Checking for** *greater* **with if**
```playing = True\nif not playing:\n print("finished")```	```if a>1:\n print("greater than")\nif a>=1:\n print("greater than or equal")```

Table 4   Python functions

Defining and calling functions	Passing parameters to functions
| ```python
def myname():
  print("my name is Laura")
myname()
myname()
``` | ```python
def hello(name):
  print("hello " + name)
hello("Andrew")
hello("Geraldine")
``` |
| **Returning values from functions** | **Writing to global variables inside functions** |
| ```python
def smallest(a, b):
  if a<b:
    return a
  return b
print(smallest(10, 20))
``` | ```python
treasure_x = 0


def build():
  global treasure_x
  treasure_x = 10
``` |

Table 5   Python lists

Creating lists	Adding to the end of a list
| ```python
a = [] # an empty list
a = [1, 2, 3]# a populated list
``` | ```python
a.append("hello")
``` |
| **Printing the contents of a list** | **Working out the size of a list** |
| ```python
print(a)
``` | ```python
print(len(a))
``` |
| **Accessing items in a list by their index** | **Accessing the last item in a list** |
| ```python
print(a[0]) # 0=first item, 1=second
``` | ```python
print(a[-1])
``` |
| **Removing the last item from a list** | **Looping through all items in a list** |
| ```python
word = a.pop() # remove last item
print(word)    # item just removed
``` | ```python
for name in ["David","Gail","Janet"]:
  print(name)
``` |

Table 6   Other Python modules

Delaying for a short amount of time	Generating random numbers
| ```python
import time
time.sleep(1) # wait 1 second
``` | ```python
import random
print(random.randint(1,100))
``` |
| **Getting the current date/time** | **Using maths functions** |
| ```python
import datetime
dateNow = datetime.datetime.now()
import time
timeNow = time.time()
``` | ```python
import math
radians    = math.radians(angle)
sin        = math.sin(radians)
cos        = math.cos(radians)
squareRoot = math.sqrt(number)
``` |

Table 7 File processing

Reading lines from a file	Writing lines to a file

``
f = open("data.txt", "r")
tips = f.readlines()
f.close()
for t in tips:
  print(t)
``
	``
	f = open("scores.txt", "w")
	f.write("Victoria:26000\n")
	f.write("Amanda:10000\n")
	f.write("Ria:32768\n")
	f.close()
	``

Getting a list of matching filenames	**Stripping unwanted white space from strings**

``
import glob
names = glob.glob("*.csv")
for n in names:
  print(n)
``
	``
	a = "\n\n hello \n\n"
	a = a.strip()
	print(a)
	``

Table 8 shows the key functions of the bitio API. For a complete list of functions, visit `github.com/whaleygeek/bitio`.

For full documentation about the BBC micro:bit, visit: `www.microbit.org`.

Remember to flash the `bitio.hex` file onto your BBC micro:bit first, before using the microbit module in your Python programs.

Table 8 Using the BBC micro:bit with the bitio library

Connecting to the BBC micro:bit	Scrolling text
`import microbit`	`microbit.display.scroll("hello")`
Displaying a single character	**Displaying numbers**
`microbit.display.show("A")`	`microbit.display.scroll(str(1234))`
Displaying two-digit numbers	**Printing a list of standard images**
`microbit.display.show(12)`	`print(microbit.Image.STD_IMAGE_NAMES)`
Displaying a standard image	**Spinning a clock**

``
microbit.display.show(
    microbit.Image.HAPPY)
``
	``
	for c in microbit.Image.ALL_CLOCKS:
	    microbit.display.show(c)
	    microbit.sleep(250)
	``

Displaying a custom image	**Clearing the display**
``` B = microbit.Image("99999:90009:90009:90009:90009:99999") microbit.display.show(B) ```	`microbit.display.clear()`

Sensing a button press	Sensing a touched pin
```if microbit.button_a.was_pressed(): print("pressed")```	```if microbit.pin0.is_touched(): print("pin touched")```
Reading accelerometer values	**Sensing tilt in the X plane**
```print(microbit.accelerometer .get_values())```	```x = microbit.accelerometer.get_x() if abs(x) > 200: print("tilt")```

Table 9 shows the key functions of the Minecraft Python API. For a complete list of functions, visit `www.stuffaboutcode.com/p/minecraft-api-reference.html`.

Table 9   Minecraft API

Importing the Minecraft API	Importing and using the block name constants
```import mcpi.minecraft as minecraft```	```import mcpi.block as block b = block.DIRT.id```
Creating a connection to Minecraft	**Posting a message to the Minecraft chat**
```mc = minecraft.Minecraft.create()```	```mc.postToChat("Hello Minecraft")```
Getting the player's tile position	**Setting the player's tile position**
```# what are the coordinates of tile # that player is standing on? pos = mc.player.getTilePos() x = pos.x y = pos.y z = pos.z```	```x = 5 y = 3 z = 7 mc.player.setTilePos(x, y, z)```
Getting the player's position	**Setting the player's position**
```# get precise position of player # in the world (e.g. x=2.33) pos = mc.player.getPos() x = pos.x y = pos.y z = pos.z```	```# set precise position of player x = 2.33 y = 3.95 z = 1.23 mc.setPos(x, y, z)```

continued

Table 9 continued

Getting the height of the world	Getting the block type at a position

`# y position of first non-AIR block`
 	
`height = mc.getHeight(5, 10)`
	`# id of block (e.g. block.DIRT.id)`
	
	`blockId = mc.getBlock(10, 5, 2)`

Setting/changing a block at a position	**Setting/changing lots of blocks in one go**
`mc.setBlock(5, 3, 2, block.DIRT.id)`	`mc.setBlocks(0,0,0, 5,5,5, block.` `AIR.id)`
Finding out which blocks have been hit	**Clearing any block hits**

`# which blocks hit since last time?`
 	
`events = mc.events.pollBlockHits()`
 	
`for e in events:`
`  pos = e.pos`
`  print(pos.x)`
	`# clear(ignore) hits since last time`
	
	`mc.events.clearAll()`

Table 10 shows the sample of the block types available in Minecraft. Where appropriate, the data values that can be used are included, and the Pi and PC/Mac columns show whether this block can be used on those platforms. For a complete list of block IDs and block data values, visit `www.stuffaboutcode.com/p/minecraft-api-reference.html`.

Table 10   Minecraft API block types

ID	Constant	Data ID	Subtype	Pi	PC/MAC
0	AIR	–	–	Y	Y
1	STONE	–	–	Y	Y
2	GRASS	–	–	Y	Y
3	DIRT	–	–	Y	Y
4	COBBLESTONE	–	–	Y	Y
5	WOOD_PLANKS	0	Oak	Y	Y
		1	Spruce	N	Y
		2	Birch	N	Y
		3	Jungle	N	Y
7	BEDROCK	–	–	Y	Y
8	WATER	–	–	Y	Y
9	WATER_STATIONARY	0	High	Y	Y
		..7	Low	Y	Y
10	LAVA	–	–	Y	Y
11	LAVA_STATIONARY	0	High	Y	Y

ID	Constant	Data ID	Subtype	Pi	PC/MAC
		..7	Low	Y	Y
12	SAND	-	-	Y	Y
13	GRAVEL	-	-	Y	Y
14	GOLD_ORE	-	-	Y	Y
15	IRON_ORE	-	-	Y	Y
16	COAL_ORE	-	-	Y	Y
17	WOOD	0	Oak (up/down)	Y	Y
		1	Spruce (up/down)	Y	Y
		2	Birch (up/down)	Y	Y
		3	Jungle (up/down)	N	Y
		4	Oak (east/west)	N	Y
		5	Spruce (east/west)	N	Y
		6	Birch (east/west)	N	Y
		7	Jungle (east/west)	N	Y
		8	Oak (north/south)	N	Y
		9	Spruce (north/south)	N	Y
		10	Birch (north/south)	N	Y
		11	Jungle (north/south)	N	Y
		12	Oak (only bark)	N	Y
		13	Spruce (only bark)	N	Y
		14	Birch (only bark)	N	Y
		15	Jungle (only bark)	N	Y
18	LEAVES	1	Oak leaves	Y	Y
		2	Spruce leaves	Y	Y
		3	Birch leaves	Y	Y
20	GLASS	-	-	Y	Y
24	SANDSTONE	0	Sandstone	Y	Y
		1	Chiselled Sandstone	Y	Y
		2	Smooth Sandstone	Y	Y
35	WOOL	0	White	Y	Y
		1	Orange	Y	Y
		2	Magenta	Y	Y
		3	Light Blue	Y	Y
		4	Yellow	Y	Y
		5	Lime	Y	Y
		6	Pink	Y	Y
		7	Grey	Y	Y
		8	Light grey	Y	Y

continued

Table 10 continued

ID	Constant	Data ID	Subtype	Pi	PC/MAC
		9	Cyan	Y	Y
		10	Purple	Y	Y
		11	Blue	Y	Y
		12	Brown	Y	Y
		13	Green	Y	Y
		14	Red	Y	Y
		15	Black	Y	Y
37	FLOWER_YELLOW	-	-	Y	Y
38	FLOWER_CYAN	-	-	Y	Y
41	GOLD_BLOCK	-	-	Y	Y
42	IRON_BLOCK	-	-	Y	Y
45	BRICK_BLOCK	-	-	Y	Y
46	TNT	0	Inactive	Y	Y
		1	Ready to explode	Y	Y
49	OBSIDIAN	-	-	Y	Y
50	TORCH	0	Standing on the floor	Y	Y
		1	Pointing east	Y	Y
		2	Pointing west	Y	Y
		3	Pointing south	Y	Y
		4	Pointing north	Y	Y
53	STAIRS_WOOD	0	Ascending east	Y	Y
		1	Ascending west	Y	Y
		2	Ascending south	Y	Y
		3	Ascending north	Y	Y
		4	Ascending east (upside down)	Y	Y
		5	Ascending west (upside down)	Y	Y
		6	Ascending south (upside down)	Y	Y
		7	Ascending north (upside down)	Y	Y
57	DIAMOND_BLOCK	-	-	Y	Y
80	SNOW_BLOCK	-	-	Y	Y
89	GLOWSTONE_BLOCK	-	-	Y	Y
246	GLOWING_OBSIDIAN	-	-	Y	N
247	NETHER_REACTOR	0	Unused	Y	N
		1	Active	Y	N
		2	Stopped/used up	Y	N

Table 11 MinecraftStuff API (MinecraftDrawing)	
Importing the MinecraftStuff API	**Creating the MinecraftDrawing object**
``import mcpi.minecraftstuff as ↵
minecraftstuff```	```mc = minecraft.Minecraft.create()
mcdrawing =
minecraftstuff.MinecraftDrawing(mc)```
Drawing a line between two points	**Getting all the block positions of a line, as a list**
``mcdrawing.drawLine(0, 0, 0,
10, 10, 10, block.DIRT.id)```	```line = mcdrawing.getLine(
0,0,0,10,10,10)
pos1 = line[0]
print(pos1.x)```
Drawing a sphere	**Drawing a circle**
``mcdrawing.drawSphere(0, 0, 0,
radius, block.DIRT.id)```	```mcdrawing.drawCircle(0, 0, 0,
radius, block.DIRT.id)```
Drawing a flat polygon (e.g. a triangle)	
``tri = Points()
filled = True
tri.add(0,0,0)
tri.add(10,0,0)
tri.add(5,10,0)
mcdrawing.drawFace(tri, filled,
block.DIRT.id)```	

Table 12 MinecraftStuff API (MinecraftShape)

Creating a MinecraftShape	Drawing and clearing a shape
| ```
mc = minecraft.Minecraft.create()
pos = mc.player.getTilePos()
shape =
  minecraftstuff.MinecraftShape(mc,
    pos)
shape.setBlock(0,0,0,block.DIRT.id)
shape.setBlock(1,0,0,block.DIRT.id)
``` | ```
shape.draw()
shape.clear()
``` |
| **Moving a shape to a position** | **Moving a shape by a number of blocks** |
| ```
shape.move(10, 10, 10)
``` | ```
ymove = 1
shape.moveBy(0, ymove, 0)
``` |

Glossary

absolute coordinates (Adv.3) A set of coordinates that uses numbers at a fixed location to represent the location of a point (or in the case of Minecraft, a block).

API (Application Programming Interface; Adv. 2) A way to safely access parts of an application program from within your programs. It is the Minecraft API that gives you access to the Minecraft game from within your Python programs.

boolean (Adv.5) A variable that holds one of two values—either `True` or `False`.

call (Adv.4) When you call a function, Python remembers where it has gotten to in your program and temporarily jumps into the function at the point you defined with `def`. When the end of the function is reached, Python jumps back to just after where it was when it jumped into that function.

case-sensitive (Adv.1) When characters in a programming language must be entered using the correct case (in upper- or lowercase).

constant (Adv.2) A name for a part of the computer's memory (just like a variable) where you can store values that normally don't change while the program is running.

coordinate (Adv.2) A set of numbers that uniquely represents a position. In Minecraft, 3D coordinates are used to represent the exact position within the three-dimensional Minecraft world, and each coordinate consists of three numbers.

counted loop (Adv.3) A loop that counts a fixed number of times. The `for` loop is a counted loop or a count controlled loop.

CSV (Adv.5) (also called Comma Separated Values)—A type of text file where values are stored separated by commas.

face (Adv. 6) A single flat surface that is part of a larger object; for example, one side of a cube or the top of a drum.

Function (Adv.3) A way to group together related Python program statements and give them a name. Whenever you want to run those program statements as a group, you just use the name of the function with brackets after it. Functions can return values to the calling program or not.

Geo-fencing (Adv.2)—A general technique that builds a virtual fence around coordinates on any map.

Global (Adv.3)—A variable that can be used anywhere in the program.

IDLE (Adv.1) A Python runtime environment, code editor and debugger.

indentation (Adv.2; also called indents) The space at the left edge of each line of a program. Indents are used to show the structure of the program and to group together program statements under loops and other statements. In Python, the indents are important as they also change the meaning of the program. Indents are created by using the Tab key.

index (Adv.4) A number that identifies which item in a list of items to access. You specify the index in square brackets like `a[0]` for the first item and `a[1]` for the second item. Indexes in Python are always numbered from 0, so 0 is always the first item in a list.

infinite loop (Adv.2) A type of loop that never ends. It goes on and on to infinity. The only way to break out of an infinite loop is to stop the Python program.

interface (Adv.2) A set of rules that explain how, as a programmer, you can access some other part of a computer system.

LED (Adv.8) An LED is a component that lights up when current flows through it. In the case of the BBC micro:bit, the LED is red.

list (Adv.4) A type of variable in a programming language that can store any number of items of data. You can add new items to the list, count the length of the list, access items at particular positions, remove items from anywhere in the list and do many other things.

metadata (Adv.5) Data about data. If data in your file represents a Minecraft object, then the metadata (data about data) might describe how big the object is, what it is called and who designed it.

MicroPython (Adv.8) is a tiny version of the Python language designed specifically for small computers like the BBC micro:bit.

nested Loop (Adv.5) A loop inside another loop. The first loop is called the *outer loop*, and the second loop is called the *inner loop*. Loops are nested in Python by indenting the second loop another level. You can nest loops inside loops inside loops any number of times.

newline (Adv.5) A special invisible character that the computer uses to mark the end of a line of text created by inserting \n into text.

parameter (Adv.6) When a function needs information in order to run—such as setBlock(), which needs an x, y, z and a block type—these values are known as parameters. When a program uses that function it is said to call it and pass parameters.

plugin (Adv.1) A program that runs inside the Minecraft server to modify the game.

pop (Adv.4) Removing the last item from a list.

predictable (Adv.7) When you are able to foresee what is going to happen before it happens.

probability (Adv. 7) The measurement of how likely it is that something will happen, i.e. when flipping a coin there is a 50% (or 1 in 2) chance that it will land on heads.

Program (Adv.2) A series of instructions or *statements* that you type in a particular programming language, which the computer then follows automatically.

Python (Adv.1) The programming language used in *Adventures in Minecraft*.

random number (Adv.3) A number that is usually generated from a random number sequence—a list of numbers designed not to have any obvious pattern or repeating sequence.

relative coordinates (Adv.3) A set of coordinates such that their position is relative to some other point (or in Minecraft, your player).

return (Adv.5) A way of passing back a value from a function, when it jumps back to the program that called the function in the first place.

sequential (Adv 9.) Sequential means to follow a sequence or order, usually one thing after the other.

square root (Adv.7) The square root of a number is the value that can be multiplied by itself to give the original number. For example, the square root of 9 is 3, because 3 x 3 = 9.

statement (Adv.2) A general computing term that usually means one complete instruction that you give to the computer—for example, one line of a computer program, such as `print("Hello Steve")`.

string (Adv.2) A type of variable that can store a sequence of letters, numbers, and symbols. It is called a string because you can imagine a long piece of string with beads that you slide on it like a necklace or a wrist band. Each of the beads could have a different number, letter, or symbol printed on it. The string then keeps them all in the same order for you.

syntax (Adv.2) The rules of a language (in this case, the Python language); mainly related to the order in which you type.

thread (Adv.9) A single set of commands that a computer runs in order. Single-threaded programs can only do one thing at a time, whereas multi-threaded programs can seem to do many.

trigonometry (Adv.6) A form of mathematics that helps you understand triangles, their angles and their lengths.

variable (Adv.2) A name for a location in the computer's memory. You can store new values in variables at any time in your program, and you can read back the values and display them or use them in calculations.

wildcard (Adv.5) A special character or series of characters (e.g. *.*) that can be used to select lots of similar names or words. It's like a joker or a "wild card" in a pack of playing cards; it can represent anything you want it to be.

Index